Contents

Preface

This book is a collaborative effort of five authors who have collectively been teaching sport management courses in universities for more than 55 years. Our desire to write this book was borne out of frustration with the lack of an appropriate introductory text in sport management we could prescribe to our students that provided a balance between management theory and contextual sport industry information. Our intention with this book is not to replace the numerous introductory texts on management theory, or to ignore the many books describing the nature of the international sport industry. Rather, our aim is to provide in a single text sufficient conceptual detail for students to grasp the essentials of management, while also highlighting the unique aspects of management in a sporting context.

The book provides a comprehensive introduction to the principles of management and their practical application to sport organizations operating at the community, state/provincial, national and international levels. The book is primarily written for first and second year university students studying sport management courses and students who wish to research the commercial dimensions of sport. It is especially suitable for students studying sport management within business focused courses, as well as students studying human movement or physical education courses seeking an overview of sport management principles.

The book is divided into three parts. Part one provides a concise analysis of the evolution of sport, the unique features of sport and sport management, the current drivers of change in the sport industry, and the role of the state, nonprofit and professional sectors of sport. Part two covers core management principles and their application in sport, highlighting the unique features of how sport is managed compared to other industrial sectors. This part includes chapters that examine strategic management, organizational structure, human resource management, leadership, organizational culture, governance, and performance management. Part three comprises a single chapter that focuses on international sport management and the future challenges that managers will face in the sport industry.

To assist lecturers and instructors, all chapters include a set of objectives, a summary of core principles, a set of review questions, suggestions for further reading, and a list of relevant websites for further information. In addition, Chapters 2 through 11 each contain three substantial cases that help illustrate concepts and accepted practice at the community, state/provincial, national, and international levels of sport. A total of 30 cases from around the world are used to illuminate the special nature of managing sport organizations.

We would like to thank Sally North, Commissioning Editor at Elsevier Butterworth-Heinemann, for her support for the book and Fran Ford for steering the book through the production process. We would also like to thank our colleagues and students who have directly and indirectly assisted in developing the teaching material that appears in the book. Finally, we would like to acknowledge the support and understanding provided by our respective partners and families for the time they gave us to produce the final manuscript.

Russell Hoye
Aaron Smith
Hans Westerbeek
Bob Stewart
Matthew Nicholson

List of cases

Part One
The Sport Management Environment

Chapter 1
Sport management

Overview

This chapter reviews the development of sport into a major sector of economic and social activity and outlines the importance of sport management as a field of study. It discusses the unique nature of sport and the drivers of change that affect how sport is produced and consumed. A three sector model of public, nonprofit and professional sport is presented, along with a brief description of the salient aspects of the management context for sport organizations. The chapter serves as an introduction to the remaining sections of the book, highlighting the importance of each of the topics.

After completing this chapter the reader should be able to:

- Describe the unique features of sport;
- Understand the environment in which sport organizations operate;
- Describe the three sectors of the sport industry; and
- Explain how sport management is different to other fields of management study.

What is sport management?

Sport employs many millions of people around the globe, is played or watched by the majority of the world's population, and at the elite level, has moved from being an amateur pastime to a significant industry. The growth and professionalization of sport has driven changes in the consumption, production and management of sporting events and organizations at all levels.

Managing sport organizations at the start of the 21st century involves the application of techniques and strategies evident in the majority of modern business, government and nonprofit organizations. Sport managers engage in strategic planning, manage large numbers of human resources, deal with broadcasting contracts worth billions of dollars, manage the welfare of elite athletes who sometimes earn 100 times the average working wage, and work within highly integrated global networks of international sports federations, national sport organizations, government agencies, media corporations, sponsors and community organizations.

Students of sport management therefore need to develop an understanding of the special features of sport and its allied industries, the environment in which sport organizations operate, and the types of sport organizations that operate in the public, nonprofit and professional sectors of the sport industry. The remainder of the chapter is devoted to a discussion of these points and highlights the unique aspects of sport organization management.

Unique features of sport

Stewart and Smith (1999) provide a list of ten unique features of sport which can assist us to understand why the management of sport organizations requires the application of specific management techniques. A unique feature of sport is the phenomenon of people developing irrational passions for sporting teams, competitions, or athletes. Sport has a symbolic significance in relation to performance outcomes, success and celebrating achievement that does not occur in other areas of economic and social activity. Sport managers must learn to harness these passions by appealing to people's desire to buy tickets for events, become a member of a club, donate time to help run a voluntary association, or purchase sporting merchandise. They must also learn to apply clear business logic and management techniques to the maintenance of traditions and connections to the nostalgic aspects of sport consumption and engagement.

There are also marked differences between sport organizations and other businesses in how they evaluate performance. Private or publicly listed companies exist to make profits and increase wealth of shareholders or owners, whereas in sport, other imperatives such as winning premierships, providing services to stakeholders and members, or meeting community service obligations may take precedence over financial outcomes. Sport managers need to be cognizant of these multiple organizational outcomes, while at the same time be responsible financial managers.

Competitive balance is also a unique feature of the interdependent nature of relationships between sporting organizations that compete on the field but cooperate off the field to ensure the long term viability of both clubs and their league. In most business environments the aim is to secure the largest market share, defeat all competitors and secure a monopoly. In sport, clubs and teams need the opposition to remain in business, so they must cooperate to share revenues and playing talent, and regulate themselves to ensure the uncertainty in the outcome of games between them, so that fans' interest will be maintained. In some ways such behaviour could be construed as anti-competitive.

The sport product, when it takes the form of a game or contest, is also of variable quality. While game outcomes are generally uncertain, one team might dominate, which will diminish the attractiveness of the game. The perception of those watching the game might be that the quality has also diminished as a result, particularly if it is your team that loses! The variable quality of sport therefore makes it hard to guarantee quality in the marketplace relative to providers of other consumer products.

Sport also enjoys a high degree of product or brand loyalty, with fans unlikely to switch sporting codes because of a poor match result, or the standard of officiating. Consumers of household products have a huge range to choose from and will readily switch brands for reasons of price or quality, whereas sporting competitions are hard to substitute. This advantage is also a negative, as sporting codes that wish to expand market share find it difficult to attract new fans from other codes due to their familiarity with the customs and traditions of their existing sport affiliation.

Sport engenders unique behaviours in people, such as emulating their sporting heroes in play, wearing the uniform of their favourite player, or purchasing the products that celebrity sports people endorse. This vicarious identification with the skills, abilities, and lifestyles of sports people can be used by sport managers and allied industries to influence the purchasing decisions of individuals who follow sport.

Sport fans also exhibit a high degree of optimism, at times insisting that their team, despite a string of bad losses, is only a week, game or lucky break away from winning the next championship. It could also be argued that the owners or managers of sport franchises exhibit a high degree of optimism by toting their star recruits or new coach as the path to delivering them on-field success.

Sporting organizations, argue Stewart and Smith (1999), are relatively reluctant to adopt new technologies unless they are related to sports science, where on-field performance improvements are possible. In this regard sport organizations can be considered conservative, and tied to traditions and behaviours more than other organizations.

The final unique aspect of sport is its limited availability. In other industries, organizations can increase production to meet demand, but in sport, clubs are limited by season length and the number of scheduled games. This constrains their ability to maximize revenue through ticket sales and associated income. The implication for sport managers is that they must understand the nature of their business, the level of demand for their product and services (whatever form that may take) and the appropriate time to deliver them.

Sport management environment

Globalization has been a major force in driving change in the ways sport is produced and consumed. The enhanced integration of the world's economies have enabled communication to occur between producers and consumers at greater speed and variety, and sport has been one sector to reap the benefits. Consumers of elite sport events and competitions such as the Olympic Games, World Cups for rugby, cricket and football, English Premier League Football, the National Basketball Association (NBA), and Grand Slam tournaments for tennis and golf enjoy unprecedented coverage. Aside from actually attending the events live at a stadium, fans can view these events through free to air and pay or cable television; listen to them on radio and the internet; read about game analyses, their favourite players and teams through newspapers and magazines; receive progress scores, commentary or vision on their mobile phones; and sign up for special deals and information through online subscriptions using their email address. The global sport marketplace has become very crowded, and sport managers seeking to carve out a niche need to understand the global environment in which they must operate. Thus, one of the themes of this book is the impact of globalization on the ways sport is produced, consumed and managed.

Most governments view sport as a vehicle for nationalism, economic development, or social development. As such, they see it as within their purview to enact policies and legislation to support, control or regulate the activities of sport organizations. Most governments support elite training institutes to assist in developing athletes for national and international competition, provide funding to national sporting organizations, support sport organizations to bid for major events, and facilitate the building of major stadiums. In return for this support, governments can influence sports to recruit more mass participants, provide services to discrete sectors of the community, or have sports enact policies on alcohol and drug use, gambling, and general health promotion messages. Governments also regulate the activities of sport organizations through legislation or licensing in areas such as industrial relations, anti-discrimination, taxation and corporate governance. A further theme in the book is the impact that governments can have on the way sport is produced, consumed and managed.

The management of sport organizations has undergone a relatively rapid period of professionalization over the last 30 years. The general expansion of the global sports industry and commercialization of sport events and competitions, combined with the introduction of paid staff into voluntary governance structures and the growing number of people who now earn a living managing sport organizations or playing sport, has forced sport organizations and their managers to become more professional. This is reflected in the increased number of university sport management courses, the requirement to have business skills as well as industry specific knowledge or experience to be successful in sport management, the growth of professional and academic associations devoted to sport management, and the variety of professionals and specialists that sport managers must deal with in the course of their careers. Sport managers will work with accountants, lawyers, taxation specialists, government policy advisors, project management personnel, architects, market researchers, and media specialists, not to mention sports agents, sports scientists, coaches, officials, and volunteers. The ensuing chapters of the book will highlight the ongoing professionalization of sport management as an academic discipline and a career.

The final theme of the book is the notion that changes in sport management frequently result from developments in technology. Changes in telecommunications have already been highlighted, but further changes in technology are evident in areas such as performance enhancing drugs, information technology, coaching and high performance techniques, sports venues, and sporting equipment. These changes have forced sport managers to develop policies about their use, to protect intellectual property with a marketable value, and generally adapt their operations to incorporate their use for achieving organizational objectives. Sport managers need to understand the potential of technological development but also the likely impact on future operations. These changes are further examined in the final chapter of the book where we introduce the notion of a DreamSport Society. The Dream-Sport Society conceptualizes a range of different markets for sport, all created by the continuing changes to sport as a result of globalization, government policy, professionalization, and technology.

Three sectors of sport

In order to make sense of the many organizations that are involved in sport management, and how these organizations may form partnerships, influence each others' operations and conduct business, it is useful to see sport as comprising three distinct sectors. The first is the State or public sector, which includes national, state/provincial, regional and local governments, and specialist agencies that develop sport policy, provide funding to other sectors, and support specialist roles such as elite athlete development or drug control. The second is the nonprofit or voluntary sector, made up of community based clubs, governing associations and international sport organizations that provide competition and participation opportunities, regulate and manage sporting codes, and organize major championship events. The third sector is professional or commercial sport organizations, comprising professional leagues and their member teams, as well as allied organizations such as sporting apparel and equipment manufacturers, media companies, major stadia operators and event managers.

These three sectors do not operate in isolation, and in many cases there is significant overlap. For example, the State is intimately involved in providing funding to nonprofit sport organizations for sport development and elite athlete programmes, and in return nonprofit sport organizations provide the general community with sporting opportunities and as well as developing athletes, coaches, officials and administrators to sustain sporting participation. The State is also involved in commercial sport, supporting the building of major stadia and other sporting venues to provide spaces for professional sport to be played, providing a regulatory and legal framework for professional sport to take place and supporting manufacturing and event organizations to do business. The nonprofit sport sector supports

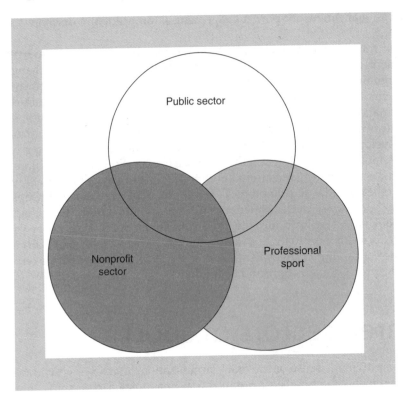

Figure 1.1 Three sector model of sport

professional sport by providing playing talent for leagues, as well as developing the coaches, officials and administrators to facilitate elite competitions. Indeed, in some cases the sport league itself will consist of member teams which are technically nonprofit entities, even though they support a pool of professional managers and players. In return, the professional sport sector markets sport for spectators and participants and in some cases provides substantial funds from TV broadcast rights revenue. Figure 1.1 illustrates the three sectors and the intersections where these relationships take place.

What is different about sport management?

Sport managers utilize management techniques and theories that are similar to managers of other organizations, such as hospitals, government departments, banks, mining companies, car manufacturers, and welfare agencies. However, there are some aspects of strategic management, organizational structure, human resource management, leadership, organizational culture, governance and performance management that are unique to the management of sport organizations.

Strategic management

Strategic management involves the analysis of an organization's position in the competitive environment, the determination of its direction and goals, the selection of an appropriate strategy and the leveraging of its distinctive assets. The success of any sport organization may largely depend on the quality of their strategic decisions. It could be argued that nonprofit sport organizations have been slow to embrace the concepts associated with strategic management because sport is inherently turbulent, with on-field performance and tactics tending to dominate and distract sport managers from the choices they need to make in the office and boardroom. In a competitive market, sport managers must drive their own futures by undertaking meaningful market analyses, establishing a clear direction and crafting strategy that matches opportunities. An understanding of strategic management principles and how these can be applied in the specific industry context of sport are essential for future sport managers.

Organizational structure

An organization's structure is important because it defines where staff and volunteers 'fit in' with each other in terms of work tasks, decision-making procedures, the need for collaboration, levels of responsibility and reporting mechanisms. Finding the right structure for a sport organization involves balancing the need to formalize procedures while fostering innovation and creativity, and ensuring adequate control of employee and volunteer activities without unduly affecting people's motivation and attitudes to work. In the complex world of sport, clarifying reporting and communication lines between multiple groups of internal and external stakeholders while trying to reduce unnecessary and costly layers of management, is also an important aspect of managing an organization's structure. The relatively unique mix of paid staff and volunteers in the sport industry adds a layer of complexity to managing the structure of many sport organizations.

Human resource management

Human resource management, in mainstream business or sport organizations, is essentially about ensuring an effective and satisfied workforce. However, the sheer size of some sport organizations, as well as the difficulties in managing a mix of volunteers and paid staff in the sport industry, make human resource management a complex issue for sport managers. Successful sport leagues, clubs, associations, retailers and venues rely on good human resources, both on and off the field. Human resource management cannot be divorced from other key management tools, such as strategic planning or managing organizational culture and structure, and is a further element that students of sport management need to understand to be effective practitioners.

Leadership

Managers at the helm of sport organizations need to be able to influence others to follow their visions, empower individuals to feel part of a team working for a common goal, and be adept at working with leaders of other sport organizations to forge alliances, deal with conflicts or coordinate common business or development projects. The sport industry thrives on organizations having leaders who are able to collaborate effectively with other organizations to run a professional league, work with governing bodies of sport, and coordinate the efforts of government agencies, international and national sport organizations, and other groups to deliver large scale sport events. Sport management students wishing to work in leadership roles need to understand the ways in which leadership skills can be developed and how these principles can be applied.

Organizational culture

Organizational culture consists of the assumptions, norms and values held by individuals and groups within an organization, which impact upon the activities and goals in the workplace and in many ways influence how employees work. Organizational culture is related to organizational performance, excellence, employee commitment, cooperation, efficiency, job performance and decision-making. However, how organizational culture can be defined, diagnosed, and changed is subject to much debate in the business and academic world. Due to the strong traditions of sporting endeavour and behaviour, managers of sport organizations, particularly those such as professional sport franchises or traditional sports, must be cognizant of the power of organizational culture as both an inhibitor and driver of performance. Understanding how to identify, describe, analyse and ultimately influence the culture of a sport organization is an important element in the education of sport managers.

Governance

Organizational governance involves the exercise of decision-making power within organizations and provides the system by which the elements of organizations are controlled and directed. Governance is a particularly important element of managing sport organizations, many of whom are controlled by elected groups of volunteers, as it deals with issues of policy and direction for the enhancement of organizational performance rather than day-to-day operational management decision-making. Appropriate governance systems help ensure that elected decision-makers and paid staff seek to deliver outcomes for the benefit of the organization and its members and that the means used to attain these outcomes are effectively monitored. As many sport managers work in an environment where they must report to a governing board, it is important that they understand the principles of good governance and how these are applied in sport organizations.

Performance management

Sport organizations over the last 30 years have undergone an evolution to become more professionally structured and managed. Sport organizations have applied business principles to marketing their products, planning their operations, managing their human resource and other aspects of organizational activity. The unique nature of sport organizations and the variation in missions and purposes has led to the development of a variety of criteria with which to assess the performance of sport organizations. Sport management students need to understand the ways in which organizational performance can be conceptualized, analysed and reported and how these principles can be applied in the sport industry.

Summary

Sport has a number of unique features:

- people develop irrational passions;
- differences in judging performance;
- the interdependent nature of relationships between sporting organizations;
- anti-competitive behaviour;
- sport product (a game or contest) is of variable quality;
- it enjoys a high degree of product or brand loyalty;
- it engenders vicarious identification;
- sport fans exhibit a high degree of optimism;
- sport organizations are relatively reluctant to adopt new technology; and
- sport often has a limited supply.

Several environmental factors influence the way sport organizations operate, namely globalization, government policy, professionalization, and technological developments.

The sport industry can be defined as comprising three distinct but inter-related industries: the State or public sector, the nonprofit or voluntary sector, and the professional or commercial sector. These sectors do not operate in isolation and often engage in a range of collaborative projects, funding arrangements, joint commercial ventures and other business relationships.

There are some aspects of strategic management, organizational structure, human resource management, leadership, organizational culture, governance and performance management that are unique to the management of sport organizations. The remainder of the book explores the three sectors of the sport industry and examines each of these core management issues in more detail.

Review questions

1. Define sport management.
2. What are the unique features of sport?
3. Describe the main elements of the environment that affect sport organizations.
4. What sort of relationships might develop between sport organizations in the public and nonprofit sectors?
5. What sort of relationships might develop between sport organizations in the public and professional sport sectors?
6. What sort of relationships might develop between sport organizations in the professional and nonprofit sectors?
7. Explain the major differences between managing a sport organization and a commercial manufacturing firm.
8. Explain why the sport industry needs specialist managers with tertiary sport management qualifications.
9. Identify one organization from each of the public, nonprofit and professional sport sectors. Compare how the environmental factors discussed in this chapter can affect their operation.
10. Discuss whether the special features of sport discussed in this chapter apply to all levels of sport by comparing the operation of a professional sports league with a community sporting competition.

Further reading

Beech, J. & Chadwick, S. (2004). *The Business of Sport Management*. London: Pearson Education.

Masteralexis, L.P., Barr, C.A. & Hums, M.A. (1998). *Principles and Practice of Sport Management*. Maryland: Aspen.

Parkhouse, B.L. (2001). *The management of sport: Its foundation and application.* 3rd ed. NY: McGraw-Hill.

Parks, J.B. & Quarterman, J. (2003). *Contemporary sport management*, 2nd ed. Champaign, IL: Human Kinetics.

Shilbury, D. & Deane, J. (2001). *Sport management in Australia: An organisational overview*, 2nd ed. Melbourne: Strategic sport management.

Slack, T. (1997). *Understanding Sport Organizations: The Application of Organization Theory*. Champaign, IL: Human Kinetics.

Smith, A. & Stewart, B. (1999). *Sports Management: A Guide to Professional Practice*. Sydney: Allen and Unwin.

Trenberth, L. & Collins, C. (eds) (1999). *Sport Business Management in New Zealand*. Palmerston North, N.Z.: Dunmore.

Westerbeek, H. & Smith, A. (2003). *Sport Business in the Global Marketplace*. London: Palgrave MacMillan.

Relevant websites

The following websites are useful starting points for general information on the management of sport:

* European Association for Sport Management at http://www.easm.org
* North American Society for Sport Management at http://www.nassm.com
* Sport Management Association of Australia and New Zealand at http://www.griffith.edu.au/school/gbs/tlhs/smaanz/home.html

Chapter 2

The role of the State in sport development

Overview

This chapter examines the different ways in which the State can influence the development of sport systems and practices. Particular attention is paid to the reasons why the State should want to intervene in the building of sport infrastructure and its operation, and the different forms the intervention can take. A clear distinction will be made between interventions that assist and promote sport, and interventions that control and regulate sport. A distinction will also be made between State initiatives that increase levels of participation, and State initiatives that improve levels of elite athlete performance. Throughout the chapter incidents and cases will be used to illustrate both the concepts and theories that underpin State intervention in sport, and the outcomes that arise from this intervention.

After completing this chapter the reader should be able to:

- Explain the role and purpose of the State;
- Explain how and why the State intervenes in a nation's economic, social and cultural landscape;
- Identify the different forms the intervention can take;
- List the different ways the State can influence the development of sport structures and practices;
- Distinguish between socialist, reformist, neo-liberal and conservative ideologies, and how they influence the way the State goes about assisting and regulating sport; and
- Explain how each of the above ideologies shapes the values, structure and operation of sport.

Defining the State

The State, by which we mean the structures that govern and rule societies, has always played an important role in the provision of sport experiences to people. The ancient Olympic Games and other sport festivals were funded and organized by the various city states that made up ancient Greece, and ruling monarchs in Europe during the Middle Ages organized an array of tournaments and combat games to hone the skills of their warrior classes (Mechikoff & Estes, 1993). As the world became industrialized and modernized the State expanded its provision of sport activities. In the USA for example, many government funded schools and colleges established sport facilities ranging from manicured playing fields and small indoor arenas to large stadiums seating anywhere from 10 000 to 50 000 spectators.

Today, the State, through its government institutions, provides a complex array of sport facilities and services. Many sport stadiums throughout the world were initially financed by government funds, and while subsequently controlled and operated by independent operators, are subject to government legislation and policy guidelines (John & Sheard, 1997). In most Western nations the central government has funded both the establishment of training centres for elite athletes, and their ongoing operation. As a result many thousands of coaches, sport scientists, and sport facility managers are on the government payroll.

State and society

The first thing to be said about the State is that it is just one component of society. In some societies the State may play a dominant role, but in other societies its role may be far more circumspect and contained. A useful way of understanding the relationship between the State and society is to distinguish between three distinct but interdependent 'social orders' (Ibsen & Jorgensen, 2002). The first social order is the *State and its apparatus*. The role of the State is to govern members of society by establishing a bureaucracy that enforces an array of rules and regulations. It will also mobilize resources through its taxing powers, and use them to establish an economic and cultural infrastructure that allows commerce and the arts to flourish. The second social order is *the market*, which is the focal point for business activity. This is the home of the private sector, which is driven primarily by the desire for market expansion and profits. The third social order is *civil society* which comprises a complex web of informal, non-market relationships that are mainly situated around households, neighbourhoods and local communities. Civil society is most visible in the spontaneous and unstructured networks that characterize the dynamics of small social and friendship groups.

The intersections of these three social orders create four different sectors and organizational forms. They are the nonprofit public sector, which is driven by the State, the profit-based commercial sector, which is driven by

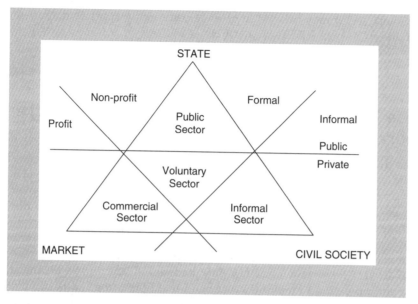

Figure 2.1 A sector model of society
Adapted from Ibsen and Jorgensen (2002)

the market, the informal sector, which is driven by civil society, and finally, the voluntary sector which is driven by aspects of all three social orders. The organization of society between the State, the market and civil society is illustrated in Figure 2.1.

Sport can fit into any of the four sectors depending on first, the traditions and values that underpin the sport experience, and second, the scale of resources that each sector can command. In Australia, for example, sport has traditionally taken place in the voluntary and informal sectors, but over recent years there has been a growing interest in the sport by the commercial sector. Together with greater direct involvement by the State and public sector, this has resulted in a significant allocation of sport resources into these areas of society.

The above model provides a useful context within which to discuss the role of the State in sport. It indicates that while the State may have enormous influence over the structure and practice of sport in one set of political conditions, it can just as easily have minimal influence over sport in some other situation. The model also suggests that even where the State is passive with respect to sport development, there may be a flourishing sport system in one or more of the other sectors, depending on how highly sport is valued in each sector. The model also implies that there is no single or best way for society to organize its sport systems and practices. It all depends upon which sector is seen to be the appropriate provider of sport facilities and activities, and what types of sport outcomes are intended. For example, the State may be seen as the most effective provider of elite athlete training facilities, while the voluntary sector may be used to provide community sport, and sport-for-all activities (DaCosta & Miragaya, 2002).

Case 2.1   The role of the State in establishing elite sport training institutes

Over the last two decades the world has changed dramatically. Large slabs of the Communist world fell apart with the fragmentation of the Soviet Union, the United States asserted both its economic and cultural power over the rest of the world, and international trade expanded in response to the dismantling of many trade barriers. This was accompanied by a revolution in the telecommunication industry, culminating in the mass consumption of mobile phone and internet services. In short, the world has become globalized. Globalization has not only had significant impact on the structure and operation of major resource and manufacturing industries like oil, iron ore, coal, motor vehicles, electronics, telecommunications, and pharmaceutical supplies, but also on less tangible industries like international finance, tourism, the arts, and sport. In fact sport is an exemplar of how the forces of globalization create an international market in which global brands are traded around the world, and customers regularly shift between the parochial and the international. As a result, local leagues and competitions thrive while mega-sport events like the Olympic Games and World Soccer Cup saturate the global sports landscape.

The globalization of sport has also created a hyper-competitive international environment where hundreds of nations seek their moment of glory on the world sport stage (Miller et al., 2001). In reality only a few nations share the limelight, and most of them got there by being wealthy or powerful enough to allocate significant resources to sport development. During the last 30 years of international sport competition a number of nations have decided that investing in elite sport is an effective means of gaining international credibility and respectability. The Soviet Union (USSR) and GDR mobilized the State apparatus in the 1970s and 1980s to establish a successful sport factory system that regularly produced world champions in a wide array of sport activities (Riordan, 1977). Their success, and those of other communist countries like Cuba, demonstrated that a State managed system of Olympic sport development produced superior elite athlete outcomes to a system that depended upon an energetic but relatively uncoordinated combination of the commercial and volunteer sectors. During the 1970s and early 1980s the German Democratic Republic, with a population of less than 20 million, amazed the world sporting community as it accumulated a swag of Olympic Games medals. At the 1976 Montreal Games it came third on the medal count with ninety, which was only bettered by the USSR and the USA. In fact its gold medal haul of forty exceeded the USA count of thirty-four. While it was later established that a significant number of medals were won with the aid of performance enhancing drugs, there was no doubt that the GDR had put in place a very effective system for developing talented athletes in a variety of sports (Brohm, 1978).

More recently China, another Communist nation, has mobilized its State apparatus to achieve impressive performances on the international sporting stage. Since 1949, when the People's Republic of China was founded, sport has played a significant role in shaping Chinese society. Not only was sport seen to be a means of making its citizens physically and mentally tough, it was also used to demonstrate the superiority of Communism over the various forms of Western style capitalism (Riordan, 1978). One of the key features of Chinese Communism is its bureaucratic structure with power and funds flowing from the Communist Party Central Committee to tightly controlled administrative bodies in the cities and provinces. Sport was slotted into this model and as a result the Chinese sport development system has for the most part been centrally planned and managed by the Chinese Sport Ministry. Notwithstanding the economic reforms that occurred during the rule of Deng Xiaoping in the 1980s, the State still controls most sport programmes, although there is now more authority in the hands of city and provincial councils (Fan Hong, 1997). This centralized sport development system has enabled the Chinese to identify talented young athletes at an early age and provide them with specialist training and coaching. The Chinese sport bureaucracy has also been effective in targeting sports in which it already has a competitive advantage, like table tennis, gymnastics, diving, and women's weight-lifting, and allocated the resources to ensure a smooth pathway to international success. China's haul of 32 Gold, 17 Silver and 14 Bronze medals at the 2004 Athens Olympic Games (which gave it second place behind the USA) was testament to the effectiveness of its elite sport system.

So what was it that gave the State sponsored systems of sport development such a competitive edge in international sporting competitions? The fundamental advantage that centrally planned and coordinated systems had over systems entrusted to the voluntary sector (with varying degrees of State support) was their capacity to target young athletes with potential, and provide them with a highly structured pathway to elite competition. While this approach was seen by critics to be mechanistic, and taking the fun out of sport, it was efficient in that it would not waste resources on athletes who did not have the potential to succeed. A State controlled system of sport development also enables athletes to train and compete on a full-time basis, which allows them to hone their skills and improve performance. In contrast, a voluntary sector system was frequently underpinned by a romanticized notion of amateurism, which meant that not only were athletes not allowed to obtain material benefits from their international success, but were also expected to earn a living in an occupation outside of sport. This clearly disadvantaged athletes from many non-Communist nations throughout the 1970s and 1980s (Bloomfield, 2003).

This centralized and highly rationalized model of sport development has been copied by many Western nations that would have normally left sport development to the commercial and volunteer sectors. France was an early adopter of the Communist model of sport development when it designed a Sport Charter in 1975, which included provision for State support of elite training institutes, sport facility construction, and funding of amateur athletes (Chalip et al., 1996). This was followed by the establishment of a National Sport Development Fund in 1979, which increased the funding to elite athletes. The funding base was further expanded in 1985 when a Sports Lottery was set up. Canada followed a similar path, and in the mid-1970s began to fund national sporting bodies so they could improve their levels of international sport performance. In 1979 an Athletic Assistance Program was introduced in which athletes (who were nominally amateur) were handsomely rewarded for doing well in international sport competitions. During the 1980s and 1990s countries as disparate as Australia, Brazil and Japan adopted the Communist sport development model and set up training institutes, elite coach education programmes, sport science support systems, and generally increased the level of financial support to elite athletes (Henry & Uchium, 2001). For the most part there was a subsequent improvement in their international sports standing. More recently Great Britain has established elite sport training institutes. Using Australia as a template, Great Britain has jettisoned the old amateur/volunteer/club-centred sport development model and embraced the sport academy/talent nurturing model in a variety of sports including highly traditional ones like rowing and cricket (Houlihan & White, 2002).

Reasons for State intervention

The State has always intervened in the affairs of its society for the fundamental reason that it enables it to set the nation's economic and political direction. More specifically, the State believes that by its various interventions it can improve the well-being of society. For example, by providing rail and road infrastructure it can improve transport systems and thereby increase the levels of overall efficiency in industry and commerce. Similarly, by funding the establishment of schools, universities and hospitals it can go a long way to not only improve the educational abilities of its citizens, but also enhance their capacity to work more productively, and more vigorously participate in the cultural and commercial affairs of the nation. The same sort of logic underpins the State's goal of having a fit and healthy people that can defend the nation's sovereignty in times of war, and generate international kudos and prestige through the success of its elite athletes.

At the same time the State may wish to more directly control the behaviour if its citizens by establishing laws that prohibit things like anti-competitive behaviour by businesses, and various forms of discrimination and anti-social behaviour of individuals. In this context the State has a history of regulating sport to ensure the safety of it participants. One of the best examples is boxing, where the risk of injury is very high, and rules are essential to ensure a lower chance of sustaining acute injury and long-term brain damage.

Because of sport's potential to deliver significant social benefits, there are a number of sound reasons for the State wanting to invest in it. However, government resources and taxpayer funds are always scarce, and sport is one of many institutions that wants to claim part of the government budget. As a result, sport assistance cannot always be guaranteed, and it must compete with defence, health, policing, social welfare and education. And, in capitalist economies at least, sport has also traditionally been seen as outside the scope of government responsibility on the grounds that it is far removed from commerce, and more in the territory of volunteer amateurs. However, it is not that difficult to mount a case for State intervention in sport. For example, a case can be made to support the view that not only will society be better off with more sport facilities and services, but that without State support, the resources invested in sport will be far less than optimal.

Market failure and the supply of sport services

In capitalist nations like Australia, Canada, Great Britain, New Zealand and the USA, resources are in the main allocated in markets through the interaction of demand, supply, and prices. However, there are often cases where markets do not operate in the best interests of the community or nation. This is known as market failure. Market failure can occur when the full benefits of markets are not realized because of an under-supply of socially desirable products, or alternatively, an over-supply of less desirable products. Market failure and under-supply arises in situations where there are significant external or social benefits in addition to private benefits. Private benefits are the value consumers obtain from the immediate purchase of a good or service and are measured by the prices people are prepared to pay for the experience. In sport, private benefits arise from a number of activities and practices. They include attending a major sport event, working out at a gymnasium, playing indoor cricket or spending time at a snow resort. Social benefits, on the other hand, comprise the additional value communities obtain from the production of a good or service. These social benefits are over and above the private benefits. In those cases where social benefits can be identified, society would be better served by allocating additional resources into those activities. However, private investors will not usually do this because of a lack of profit incentive. Consequently, it will be left to government to fill the breach, and use taxpayers' money to fund additional sporting infrastructure and services.

In other words, since sport provides significant social benefits, it deserves State support to ensure that the welfare of the whole community is maximized. According to the proponents of sport assistance, social benefits can arise from both active participation and spectator sport. In the case of active participation, the benefits include improved community health, a fall in medical costs, a reduction in the crime rate, the inculcation of discipline and character, the development of ethical standards through the emulation of sporting heroes, greater civic engagement, and the building of social capital. Research into social capital building suggests that sport not only expands social networks, but also produces safer neighbourhoods and

Table 2.1 Social benefits of sport development

Arising from active participation	Arising from elite athlete successes
Improvement in community health and productivity	Tribal identification and belonging
Fall in medical costs	Social cohesion
Reduction in juvenile crime rate	Civic and national pride
Development of 'character' and sense of 'fair play'	International recognition and prestige
Building of social capital, social cohesion, and civic engagement	Economic development and tourism
Adapted from Stewart et al. (2004)	

stronger communities (Productivity Commission, 2003). Moreover, the social benefits linked to social capital are extended when sport groups and clubs look outward and encompass people across diverse social cleavages. This bridging or inclusive social capital can be contrasted with bonding social capital, which characterizes sport groups and clubs with a narrow ethnic, social, or occupational base (Putnam, 2000, p. 22). Either way, sport is seen to be a great builder of social capital.

In the case of elite and spectator sports, the social benefits include tribal identification with a team or club, social cohesion, a sense of civic and national pride, international recognition and prestige, economic development, and the attraction of out-of-town visitors and tourist dollars (Gratton & Taylor, 1991). When these social benefits are aggregated the results are quite extensive, as can be seen in Table 2.1. At the same time, they are often difficult to quantify, and in some cases the evidence to support the claimed benefit is soft and flimsy.

Sport as a public good

A case can also be made for the State's involvement in sport on the grounds that sport is often a public or collective good (Sandy et al., 2004). Public goods are those goods where one person's consumption does not prevent another person's consumption of the same good. For example, a decision to visit a beach, or identify with a winning team or athlete, will not prevent others from doing the same. Indeed, the experience may be enhanced by others being in proximity. This is the non-rival feature of the good. Public goods are also goods where, in their purest form, no one can be prevented from consuming the good. Again, a visit to the beach, and identifying with a winning team meet this criterion. This is the non-excludable feature of the good. Public goods can provide substantial benefits throughout the whole of society, and are usually not rationed through high prices. However, they are not attractive to private investors since there is no assurance that all users will pay the cost of providing the benefit. As the number of so-called free-riders increase there is a shrinking incentive for private operators to enter the public good market. In this instance it is argued that the State should provide for this higher demand by increasing its funding to ensure an appropriate infrastructure and level of service.

Sport equity and inclusiveness

Finally, it can be argued that the State should be funding sport on equity grounds. For example, it might be argued that the whole community benefits from being fit and healthy, and therefore no one should be excluded because of low income or lack of facilities. In these cases, the optimal community benefit can only be realized if everyone has access to appropriate sport and recreation services help them to improve their health and fitness, enhance their self-image, and build the community's social capital. In order to improve accessibility, and ensure equality of opportunity, the State can establish its own low-cost sport facilities, subsidize existing sport activity providers, and design targeted programmes for disadvantaged groups (Tribe, 2005).

Regulation and control

There are also many situations where the State may want to regulate and control the provision of sport activities, and limit the resources devoted to some activities (Baldwin & Cave, 1999). For example it may be necessary to enact laws and rules that safeguard public order when a large number of people are spectators of, or are playing in a sport event. In most countries there are laws that clearly define the parameters within which sport grounds are to be constructed. These laws will cover things like design specifications, the provision for seating, the number of entry and exit points, and fire prevention facilities (Frosdick & Walley, 1997). There may also be rules that govern the behaviour of spectators. Most commonly these laws will relate to the consumption of alcohol and disorderly and violent behaviour.

There are also rules and regulations that govern the conduct of a specific sport activity. As mentioned above, one of the most highly regulated sports is boxing. Many countries have legislation which effectively sets up government controlled agencies that both issue licences to promoters and participants, and monitor the conduct of the sport. In fact, in Norway, professional boxing is banned, and any Norwegian boxer who wants to enter the professional ranks must relocate to another country. Another highly regulated activity is horse-racing. It is not just a case of ensuring the animals are treated humanely, but of also making sure the gaming and gambling practices that surround the sport are tightly controlled.

Case 2.2   State assistance to sport: The Australian experience

Australia has always seen itself as a sports-loving nation, and has used sport as a means of generating civic pride, national identity, and international recognition (Stewart et al., 2004). Between 1945 (the end of the Second World War) and 1972 (the election of a Labor reformist government for the first time in twenty-three years) Australians were very successful on the world sporting stage, producing a proliferation of world champions in swimming, tennis, cricket, rugby league and cycling (Cashman, 1995). However, this was achieved with a minimum of government support. While local government provided many excellent playing fields and indoor sport facilities, the national government provided nothing to most national sport governing bodies, and neither did it fund the construction of many sport venues. All it did was contribute to Olympic and Commonwealth Games teams every two years, provide small annual grants to help life saving clubs to patrol beaches, and provide financial assistance to State government run fitness councils. In short, sport was left to run its own affairs.

However, this all changed in the 1970s in response to two significant forces. First, a reformist Labor national government was elected which had a mandate to change the social conditions in Australia. It replaced the stable but conservative Menzies Government that had increased the nation's prosperity, but had done next to nothing for sport. One of the first things the Whitlam Government did was to establish a Ministry of Sport, and start funding a programme that both increased the number of community leisure centres around Australia, and assisted national sporting bodies to improve their operations. Second, the failure of the Olympic Games team to win a gold medal at Montreal in 1976 traumatized the nation to such an extent that the national government resolved to directly intervene in the sport development process. Although the Fraser Liberal Government (which replaced the Whitlam Government in 1975) was for the most part highly conservative, it decided to establish a training academy for talented young athletes in response to growing community agitation that Australia was no longer a world leader in sport. The Australian Institute of Sport (AIS) was opened for business in 1981 and quickly became internationally recognized as a successful training centre for elite athletes (Bloomfield, 2003). In 1984 the Australian Sports Commission was established in order to better manage the national government's sport funding initiatives, and generally implement government sport policy in a systematic and orderly manner. The rest, as they say, is history, and in the space of 25 years the national government's annual sports budget increased from around $A5 million to just over $A150 million (Stewart et al., 2004). These funds have been used to both increase Australia's sporting infrastructure, and expand the operations of the national governing bodies for sport. At the same time, there has been a change in the values and culture of Australian sport as sport became more commercialized in response to a growing involvement from the market sector. When combined with the ever-increasing national government support for sport, the whole sport system became more professionalized, and created many career opportunities for players, administrators and coaches.

Current government sport assistance is multi-dimensional, but it fundamentally wants to strike the elusive balance between elite sport development and community sport participation (Stewart et al., 2004). It can be conveniently divided into four strategic, but interconnected outcomes.

First, it aims to develop an effective national sports infrastructure by enhancing the management capabilities of national sporting bodies. Programmes are directed at improving coaching standards, the management skills of officials, the day-to-day operation of national sporting bodies, and the capacity of Australian sport to export its expertise. Second, it aims to improve participation in sport activities by encouraging more people to engage in club-based sport through its junior sport activities, and assisting marginalized groups in securing places in sport clubs and associations. These groups include aboriginals, people with disabilities, women, children and older adults. Third, it aims to provide for continuous improvement in the performances of Australians in international sport. In this case, programmes are directed at assisting national sporting bodies to nurture talented athletes, enhancing the Australian Institute of Sport scholarship programme, providing sport science support, and assisting athletes in managing their future careers. Finally, it aims to provide a climate and culture of fair play. The focus here is not only on drug control, but also eliminating discrimination and harassment, assisting indigenous communities, and dismantling barriers to disabled athlete participation. The breadth of the current government sport-assistance arrangements is revealed in Table 2.2.

Table 2.2 Australian national government interventions in sport: 1980–2005

Focus of intervention	Examples
High performance	Australian Institute of Sport (AIS), athlete scholarships/grants, elite coach education
Management improvement	Australian Sports Commission (ASC) training programmes, grants for management improvement and staff training
Economic benefit	Government agencies to secure significant sport festivals and championships. Subsidies to ensure viability of mega-sport events
Drug education and enforcement	Australian Sports Drug Agency (ASDA), drug education programmes, testing and sanctions
Community participation	Programmes and funding to encourage greater participation at grass-roots level. Working with national sport bodies to develop modified games, and implement junior development programmes
Social capital	Volunteer training programmes, and grants to local sport bodies to improve sport facilities
Diversity and equity	Women's sport programmes, anti-harassment and anti-discrimination programmes including design of member protection policies (MPP), funding to assist indigenous and disabled sport

Adapted from Stewart et al. (2004)

All of these programmes beg the question as to whether or not Australia's sport system has been improved by State intervention, or whether Australia's sport development should have been left in the hands of the commercial and voluntary sectors. If Olympic and Commonwealth Games medal tallies are any indication, then State intervention is the best thing that has ever happened to Australian sport. Whereas Australian athletes won only 9 medals at the 1980 Moscow Olympic Games, the tally increased to 14 at the 1988 Seoul Games, 27 at Barcelona in 1992 and 41 at Atlanta in 1996. Even better results were achieved at Sydney in 2000 when 58 medals were snared, while in Athens in 2004, Australia (with a population of only 20 million) placed fourth in the medal tally when its athletes collected 49 medals. However, sport development is about much more than just winning medals at international sport events. The State also has a responsibility to provide the community with rewarding sport experiences, and to make sure disadvantaged groups have open and easy access to facilities (Houlihan, 1997). In the past decade the Australian government has made some good progress to increase the general level of participation, but at the moment it has plateaued. Australia is now one of the most obese nations in the world, second only to the United States. This is another challenge the Australian government will be facing over the next few years. It will be interesting to see if more State funding of sport participation will solve this serious public health problem.

Extent and form of State intervention

As indicated above, the State can intervene in sport in all sorts of ways. The extent of the intervention, and the form it takes, is strongly influenced by the ideology, values and overall philosophy of the State and its governing institutions.

The first ideology is *conservatism*. A conservative ideology values tradition, and customary ways of doing things. Conservative governments have a tendency to regulate the social lives of people, and therefore want to censor works of art and literature they find offensive. They also want to control the distribution of legal drugs like alcohol, and generally act to protect people from themselves. On the other hand, they believe that business should be left to its own devices, where the combination of individual self-interest, the profit motive, and market forces, will ensure a favourable outcome. However, because conservative governments believe a strong private sector is the key to progress, they are prepared to assist and protect industry when the need arises. While on one hand they recognize sport as an integral part of the social life of most people, they do not want to assist or protect it since it is not part of the world of business. Indeed, for many conservatives, it is another world altogether that should be best kept at a distance from business. This sport-world is underpinned by the belief that sport ful-fils its function best when it is done for its own sake, played by amateurs, managed by volunteers, and generally left to look after its own affairs.

The second ideology is *reformism*, or as it is also known, *welfare statism*, or *social democracy*. Reformism is primarily concerned with social justice and equity. While reformists recognize the necessity of a strong private sector they believe it cannot be trusted to deliver fair and equitable outcomes. It there-fore needs to be strictly managed. This could take the form of additional state owned enterprises, or tight regulations on business behaviour. Reformists share the conservative view that assistance and protection may be neces-sary in the public interest. Unlike conservatives, though, reformists believe primarily in social development, which not only means legislating for social freedom, but also for social justice. Income redistribution to disadvantaged groups is important, and is done by ensuring that wealthy individuals and cor-porations are taxed most heavily. State spending is also crucial to reformists, since it is used to stimulate the economy when demand and spending is low. Reformist governments tend to be more centralist, and aim to use this centralized power to engineer positive social outcomes. Reformists conse-quently see sport as a tool for social development, and aim to make sport more accessible to the whole community. In these cases programmes are established to cater for the needs of minority groups like the disabled, migrants who speak another language, and women. In short, reformist government policy focuses more on community, and less on elite sport development.

The third ideology is *neo-liberalism*. Neo-liberals believe that society is at its most healthy when people can run their daily lives without the chronic intrusion of the State. The rule of law is important, but beyond that, people should be free to choose how they organize their social lives, and business should be free to organize their commercial lives as they see fit. Neo-liberals see little value in State owned enterprises, and argue that the privatization of government services produces greater efficiency and higher quality out-comes. Moreover, deregulated industries are seen to run better than tightly controlled ones. In short, neo-liberals believe government should not engage directly in most economic activity, but rather provide only base level infra-structure, and legislative guidelines within which private business can thrive. Sport is valued as an important social institution, but should not be strictly controlled. However, neo-liberals also believe sport can be used as a vehicle for nation building and economic development, and should be supported in these instances. This produces a sport policy that tends to focus on elite sport at the expense of community sport.

The final ideology is *socialism*. Socialists believe that a combination of privately owned and unregulated markets will produce severe levels of inequality and alienation. As a result, capitalist modes of production and distribution need to be replaced by a strong State where resource alloca-tion is centrally controlled. Like neo-liberals, socialists agree that sport is an important social institution, but unlike neo-liberals, go on to assert that sport should be controlled from the centre to ensure a fair spread of clubs and facilities throughout society. To this end, a socialist system of sport devel-opment will be driven by a central bureaucracy that sets the sport agenda.

Table 2.3 Links between political ideology and sport development

Ideological type	Features	Implications for sport development
Conservatism	Private ownership of business Regulation of social practices	Arms-length association with sport. Sport is seen as a private activity that grows out of the community, and is managed by the volunteer sector
Reformism	Mixed economy Regulation of both social and economic affairs	Direct involvement in sport facility construction and community sport participation
Neo-liberalism	Emphasis on the market De-regulation of industry	Most resources go to the elite end of sport development and its commercial outcomes
Socialism	Limited scope for the market Central planning Bureaucratic control over resource allocation	Direct involvement in all aspects of sport development. Often tightly regulated. Both community and elite sport are resourced.

The State also provides most of the funds and resources by which to develop sport at both the community and elite levels.

Each ideology not only contains quite different assumptions about the proper role of the State, but also different ideas about what sport can do to improve the welfare of society. As a result each ideology will produce different sport development outcomes, and the ideology often overrides the claims of interest groups like sport scientists, coaches, and officials. The four ideologies described provide a simplified typology, and in practice, the State will often take bits and pieces of each ideology when forming its position on a particular sport issue or problem. At the same time, most States will be characterized by more of one, and less of another, ideology. Table 2.3 outlines the different ideologies and indicates how they can shape the State's views on sport development.

As a result there are a broad array of arrangements by which the State can fund, develop, and deliver sport facilities and programmes. At one extreme, the State can distance itself from sport development by claiming that sport is a private matter for individuals and communities, and is therefore best left to the market and voluntary sectors to run. This arrangement was the primary feature of Australian sport until the 1970s when the national government resolved to fund sport facilities and programmes (Stewart et al., 2004). In the USA the national government has also adopted an arms-length approach to sport, and has left the funding and development of sport to the market, and the school and university sectors (Chalip et al., 1996). At the other extreme the State sets the sport agenda by both establishing sport facilities across the nation, and funding the management of their operations. This approach was exemplified in the sport development programmes of most communist nations during the 1970s and 1980s. In the Soviet Union (USSR) and the German Democratic Republic (GDR), a national sport programme was integrated into the school curricula, and sport schools were used to identify and nurture talented young athletes. In addition, sports that had a strong civil defence and para-military flavour were conducted in factory and trade union facilities. Cuba had a similar sport development model in which the State through its government bureaucracy managed the whole sport experience for both the sport-for-all participant and the Olympic athlete. While Cuba banned professionalism in sport, it handsomely rewarded its national sporting heroes by giving them government jobs or enrolling them in college and university courses that they could complete at their convenience. In Cuba, like the USSR and GDR, sport success was not just a sporting victory but a 'psychological, patriotic and revolutionary' one as well (Riordan, 1978, p. 147).

Case 2.3   The regulation of sport in England

In early 2005 the English Parliament passed legislation that made fox hunting with hounds and horses illegal. While there was a groundswell of support for the legislation, there was also strong resistance from many residents of regional England who argued it would destroy an archetypal English custom. However it is not uncommon for English sport followers to be subject to laws that basically curtail their behaviour at sport events (Greenfield & Osborn, 2001).

England is the birthplace of modern sport, having been largely responsible for the invention and global spread of sports as varied as boxing, tennis, cricket, rugby, and of course, association football, or soccer as it is more colloquially known in some English speaking countries apart from Britain. English sport has also become quite highly regulated in response to a number of social problems associated with the development of football over the last 40 years. The first problem arose from chronic displays of football hooliganism during the 1970s and 1980s, while the second problem arose from a fire at the Bradford City ground in 1985, and the Hillsborough (Sheffield) disaster of 1989 when 95 fans were crushed to death (Perryman, 2001). Each of these crisis events produced an enormous amount of public consternation, and as a result legislation was passed in order to first, regulate fan behaviour and punish disorderly conduct in public, and second, to ensure minimum levels of safety at all football stadiums (Greenfield & Osborn, 2001).

One of the first things the ruling Thatcher Government did was to introduce controls over the consumption of alcohol. The *Sporting Events Act 1985* made it illegal to possess intoxicating liquor on public transport vehicles carrying passengers to and from a sporting event. The legislation also made it illegal for ground management to sell alcohol to fans unless a special exemption was granted. Even when permission was given, the bar was not to provide direct viewing of the game. A number of so-called public order acts were also introduced in the 1980s, culminating in the *Football (Offences) Act 1990*, and the *Football (Offences and Disorders) Act 1999*. Under this legislation it was illegal for fans to throw anything to either the playing arena or other fans, to chant in an indecent or racist nature, or to go to the playing arena at any time.

The ground safety problem was addressed through the introduction of the *Fire Safety and Safety of Sport Grounds Act 1987*. Under this legislation any sport venue which had a stand that would cover at least 500 people was required to seek a safety certificate from the appropriate local government authority. In issuing the certificate the local authority would consider things like entry and exit points, seat quality, fire protection, and spectator and player safety.

These regulations are clearly intended to provide minimum levels of public safety. But the price to be paid is a loss of individual and commercial freedom. In the case of English sport, there has been an appreciable improvement in venue quality, and unruly fan behaviour has been reduced to manageable proportions. However, in getting to this point the ability of venue managers to raise more revenue from liquor sales has been thwarted, and many fans have had to radically curtail their exuberant behaviour.

Summary

The first point to be made here is that the State is just one of three social orders or supports that underpin the operation of society. The other two social orders are the market and civil society. The State has the capacity to significantly shape the structure and scope of sport through a number of mechanisms. First, it can construct sport facilities, second, it can fund the day-to-day operations of sporting associations and clubs, third, it can deliver sport programmes to the community directly, fourth, it can establish training facilities for elite athletes to assist their ongoing development, and finally, it can control the operation of sport by introducing various laws, regulations and rules (Hylton, 2001). However, the scale of State support, and the form it takes, will vary between nations depending on the dominant political ideology, and the overall cultural importance of sport to society. In some cases the State will directly control and manage sport, while at the other end of the political spectrum the State will step back from the sport system and encourage the commercial and volunteer sectors to take up the slack.

Review questions

1. What is the role of the State?
2. How does the State go about shaping the political and economic landscape of a nation?

3. Apart from the State, what other social forces contribute to national development?
4. Explain how the State may contribute to sport development.
5. What can the State do to increase the level of sport participation and sport club membership?
6. What can the State do to increase the level of elite sport performance?
7. Why should the State want to intervene in sport?
8. Would sport development be best left to the voluntary and commercial sectors?
9. Is there any evidence that a centralized model of elite sport development is any more effective than a market-based sport development model?
10. How might the State go about increasing the scale of sport participation at the community or 'grass-roots' level?

Further reading

For a thorough analysis of the ways in which government can go about regulating a nation's economic, social and cultural affairs, see Baldwin and Cave (1999). There are now a number of publications that examine the ways in which the State has intervened in a nation's sport development. To get a detailed picture of the Australian experience you should read Bloomfield (2003) and Stewart et al. (2004). The British experience is nicely reviewed in Houlihan and White (2002) and Hylton et al. (2001). For some comparative analysis of State involvement in sport the most comprehensive treatment is contained in Chalip et al. (1996). Houlihan (1997) provides an excellent comparative study of Australia, Canada, Ireland and the United Kingdom.

Relevant websites

* To find out more about the State and Australian sport go to the Australian Sports Commission site at http://www.ausport.gov.au
* To get more details of the English experience go to the Sport England site at http://www.sportengland.org
* For a comprehensive review of the State's involvement in New Zealand sport go to the New Zealand Government Sport and Recreation site at http://www.sparc.org.nz

Chapter 3
Nonprofit sport

Overview

This chapter examines the role of the nonprofit sector in sport development. The reasons why the nonprofit sector plays such a large part in the provision of sport participation opportunities and the various ways the nonprofit sector is involved in sport are reviewed. The scope of the nonprofit sector's involvement in sport around the world is examined, with a particular emphasis on the role of volunteers in administration, officiating and coaching. The chapter also provides a summary of the relationship between nonprofit sport organizations and the State.

After completing this chapter the reader should be able to:

■ Describe the scope of the nonprofit sector's involvement in sport;
■ Understand the differences in the roles performed by the State and nonprofit sport organizations;
■ Understand the ways in which nonprofit sport organizations foster sport development around the world; and
■ Understand some of the challenges facing the nonprofit sector in delivering sporting opportunities.

Introduction

The model presented in the previous chapter outlining the organization of society between the State, the market and civil society assists us to understand the enormous variety of sporting organizations that exist in Western economies. This chapter focuses on the informal and voluntary sectors of the model, in other words, the various sport organizations that would be classified as nonprofit. Many terms have been used to refer to nonprofit organizations that operate in a variety of industry sectors and countries around the world. These terms include voluntary, not for profit, non government, community, club based, associations, co-operatives, friendly societies, civil society, and the third sector. For the purposes of this book we have chosen to use the term 'nonprofit organizations' to describe those organizations that are institutionally separate from the State, do not return profits to owners, are self governing, have a significant element of voluntary contribution, and are formally incorporated.

The nonprofit sector comprises organizations that are markedly different from State organizations discussed in the previous chapter, and also profit seeking organizations that are discussed in the next chapter. Nonprofit organizations vary in size, focus and capability and include groups as diverse as community associations, chambers of commerce, private schools, charitable trusts and foundations, welfare agencies and sporting organizations. Nonprofit organizations are a major part of many industries in health services, education, housing, welfare, culture and sport.

Nonprofit sector and society

Nonprofit organizations exist to develop communities, meet the needs of identifiable and discrete groups in those communities, and work for the benefit of public good rather than wealth creation for individuals. Nonprofit organizations have evolved to fill gaps in the provision of services such as welfare assistance that are not provided by the State or market sector, and are driven largely by the efforts of volunteers with the occasional support of paid staff.

A recent review of nonprofit organizations in Canada highlighted a number of unique aspects of nonprofit organizations and the contribution they make to Canadian life (Statistics Canada, 2004). Foremost among these was the recognition that these organizations are vehicles for citizen engagement – they enable individuals to contribute their talent, energy and time to be involved in engaging in group activities and causes that are not otherwise provided by the public or private sectors. Nonprofit organizations are in general governed by volunteers, run on the time and money contributed by volunteers, and enable volunteers to contribute to enhancing their local, regional, national and global communities.

To understand the scale of the nonprofit sector, let us examine some recent Canadian statistics. In 2003, there were more than 161 000 nonprofit organizations in Canada, that collectively utilized 2 billion volunteer hours, and received more than $8 billion in donations to deliver their services. At the same time, Canadians took out 139 million memberships in these organizations, an average of four per person (Statistics Canada, 2004). Clearly, the nonprofit sector represents a major part of the economic activity of many nations and plays a major role in people engaging in social, religious, charitable, philanthropic and sport-related activities.

Nonprofit organizations usually focus on delivering services to very specific population groups or within defined geographic areas. Many of them provide services to targeted groups and only a few focus solely on providing services to members. The variety of activities carried out by nonprofit organizations is very broad ranging, from providing sporting opportunities to funding hospital and medical services and therefore the revenue sources, cost base, numbers of paid staff and volunteers and sophistication of management systems also vary.

The nonprofit sector is not without its problems. The larger organizations such as independent schools, colleges and hospitals receive the majority of funding and almost half the funding for most nonprofit organizations comes from government. The resourcing of nonprofit organizations in some sectors continues to be inadequate as they struggle to keep up with demand, particularly in the welfare, housing and charitable sectors. By far the biggest problem facing nonprofit organizations is the inability to fulfil their missions due to problems securing adequate numbers of volunteers, finding board members, and attracting enough sustainable funding. As governments around the world seek to decrease their costs and devolve responsibility for service delivery to the private and nonprofit sectors without adequately funding such delivery, nonprofit organizations will find it increasingly difficult to operate.

Nonprofit sector and sport

The International Classification of Nonprofit Organizations (ICNPO) has a designated category for sports and recreation organizations. This category includes three broad groups: (1) sports including amateur sport, training, fitness and sport facilities and sport competition and events; (2) recreation and social clubs such as country clubs, playground associations, touring clubs and leisure clubs; and (3) service clubs such as Lions, Rotary, Kiwanis and Apex clubs. Of particular interest are those organizations that operate on a nonprofit basis in sport including professional service organizations, industry lobby groups, sport event organizations and sport governing bodies.

Nonprofit professional service organizations operate in sport in similar ways to professional associations like accrediting medical boards, or associations for lawyers and accountants. These organizations assist in setting standards of practice in their respective industries, provide professional accreditation for qualified members and offer professional development opportunities through conferences, seminars or training programmes. They operate in a business-like fashion but the aim is to return profits to members through improved service delivery rather than create wealth for owners.

In Australia, the Australian Council for Health, Physical Education and Recreation (ACHPER) is a national professional association representing people who work in the areas of Health Education, Physical Education, Recreation, Sport, Dance, Community Fitness or Movement Sciences. The role of ACHPER includes advocating for the promotion and provision of sport opportunities, providing professional development programmes for teachers, and accredits and trains people wanting to become community fitness instructors. Similar groups operate in Canada (Canadian Association for Health, Physical Education, Recreation and Dance), the USA (American Alliance for Health, Physical Education and Dance), the UK (British Institute of Sports Administration) and New Zealand (Physical Education New Zealand).

A number of industry lobby groups, representing the interests of nonprofit sport organizations, also operate throughout the world. A leading example is the Central Council of Physical Recreation (CCPR) in the UK, the representative body for National Sports Organizations. They act as the independent umbrella organization for national governing and representative bodies of sport and recreation in the UK to promote their interests to government and other players in the sport industry. This role is undertaken by Sport Industry Australia, a similar nonprofit organization in Australia.

Some of the largest and most influential sport event organizations in the world operate on a nonprofit basis, including the International Olympic Committee (IOC) and the Commonwealth Games Federation (CGF). The IOC was founded in 1894 by Baron Pierre de Coubertin, and is an independent nonprofit organization that serves as the umbrella organization of the Olympic Movement. The IOC's primary role is to supervise the organization of the summer and winter Olympic Games.

Similar to the IOC, the role of the CGF is to facilitate a major games event every four years but it also provides education assistance for sports development throughout the 53 Commonwealth countries. There are more Commonwealth Games Associations (CGA) (71) than countries (53) because some countries like the UK have seven CGAs (Scotland, England, Northern Ireland, Wales, Isle of Man, Jersey and Guernsey) that all compete in the Games as separate nations (www.commonwealthgames.com). Both the IOC and CGF fund their operations through contributions from governments that host the games, and the sale of international broadcasting rights, corporate sponsorship, ticket sales, licensing and merchandising sales.

There are also a range of specialist nonprofit organizations that focus on discrete community groups. Foremost among these is the International Paralympic Committee (IPC) which is the international representative organization of elite sports for athletes with disabilities. The IPC organizes, supervises and coordinates the Paralympic Games and other multi-disability sports competitions at elite level (www.paralympic.org). Other similar nonprofit organizations include the Cerebral Palsy International Sports and Recreation Association and the International Blind Sport Federation which facilitate major events for athletes.

Our focus for the remainder of the chapter is on those nonprofit sport organizations that provide sporting competition or event participation opportunities for their members and other members of the public – sport governing bodies and sports clubs. In countries such as Australia, the UK, Canada, New Zealand, Hong Kong and others with club based sporting systems, almost all sporting teams and competitions are organized by nonprofit sport organizations (Lyons, 2001). These organizations take many forms. They include small local clubs that may field a few teams in a local football competition; regional associations that coordinate competitions between clubs; and state or provincial organizations that not only facilitate competitions, but also manage coach development, talent identification, volunteer training, marketing and sponsorship.

They also comprise national sporting organizations that regulate the rules of competition in a country, coordinate national championships between state or provincial teams, manage elite athlete programmes, employ development officers to conduct clinics, and undertake many other tasks that facilitate participation in sport. Finally, there are international sports federations that coordinate the development of sport across the globe and facilitate rule changes and liaison between countries on issues like international competitions.

The common element amongst all these sport organizations is their non-profit focus – they exist to facilitate sporting opportunities for their members who may be individual athletes, coaches, officials or administrators, clubs, associations, or other sport organizations. They are also interdependent, relying on each other to provide playing talent, information to access competitions, resources for coach, official and player development and funding to support their activities. It is important to note that volunteers are at the heart of these organizations, playing significant roles in service delivery and decision-making at all levels of nonprofit sport organizations. At the same time though, many of the larger nonprofit sport organizations contain a significant number of paid staff who support their ongoing administration and service delivery to member associations and clubs.

To highlight the scale and scope of the nonprofit sport sector, a description of the Canadian nonprofit sport sector is presented in Case 3.1.

Case 3.1 Canadian nonprofit sport sector

In 2003, there were 33 649 nonprofit sport and recreation organizations in Canada, or 20.9% of all nonprofit organizations, making it the largest portion of organizations of this type. There are more nonprofit sport and recreation organizations in Canada than religious organizations (19%) and social service organizations (11.8%). The majority of nonprofit sport organizations deliver services in a relatively small geographic area such as a suburb, town or city. Eighty six percent of them deliver services to members rather than the general public. In other words, people who are involved in nonprofit sport organizations tend to be registered members who not only sustain the organization but consume the services the organization offers. In addition, the majority (79%) of nonprofit sport organizations tend to have individuals rather than organizations as members, which is not surprising given the fact that the majority of them service a relatively small geographic area.

Nonprofit sport organizations are also well entrenched in Canadian society with the majority of them having been in existence for more than 30 years.

However, while sport and recreation organizations are the largest portion of nonprofit organizations (20.9%) they only account for 5.4% of all revenues. They are also relatively self-sufficient with only 12% of their income being provided from government sources, and rely on membership dues and direct user-pays charges to sustain their operations.

Sport and recreation organizations rely more on volunteers than other nonprofit organizations as they account for 28% of all volunteers and 23% of all volunteer hours in Canada. Most concerning is the fact that between 2000 and 2003 sport and recreation organizations were the ones most likely to report a decline in volunteer numbers compared to all other types of nonprofit organizations. The majority of sport organizations do not employ any paid staff (73.5%), while only 11% employed greater than 5 paid staff. Of these paid staff, the majority of them tend to be in temporary positions (69%).

Given these statistics, it is not surprising that sport and recreation organizations are also more likely to report problems associated with financial difficulties and problems in engaging appropriately skilled volunteers and board members. In summary, Canadian nonprofit sport organizations, whilst making up the largest portion of nonprofit organizations, face significant problems in sustaining their operations.

Source: Statistics Canada, (2004). *Cornerstones of community: Highlights of the national survey of nonprofit and voluntary organizations*. Ottawa, Canada.

Governing bodies of sport

Sport clubs compete against other clubs in competition structures provided by regional or state/provincial sporting organizations. State-based teams compete in competitions facilitated by national sporting organizations, and nations compete in leagues or events provided by international federations of sport, such as the Fédération Internationale de Football Association (FIFA), or major competition organizations such as the International Olympic Committee or the Commonwealth Games Federation. These organizations are known as governing bodies for sport, that have the responsibility for the management, administration and development for a sport on a global, national, state/provincial level, or regional level.

The structure of the International Netball Federation Limited (IFNA) typifies the relationships between these various governing bodies of sport. The members of IFNA comprise 39 national associations from five regions: Africa, Asia, Americas, Europe, and Oceania. Each region elects 2 members to direct the activities of the world governing organization who are responsible for setting the rules for netball, running international competitions, promoting good management in the regions, striving to seek Olympic accreditation for netball, and increasing participation levels around the globe.

Netball Australia, one of the 39 members of IFNA, has more than 350 000 registered players who participate through 8 state/provincial associations. They in turn have a total of 541 affiliated associations. Each of the state/provincial associations has a delegate to the national board who, along with the staff of Netball Australia, are responsible for communicating rule changes from IFNA to their members, managing a national competition, promoting good management in the state/provincial organizations, increasing participation nationally, and bidding to host world events.

One of the largest members of Netball Australia, Netball Victoria, has 110 000 registered players who compete in 250 affiliated associations, organized into 21 regions and 6 zones across the state. Netball Victoria's role differs markedly from Netball Australia and IFNA, with responsibility for coach, official and player development, managing state competitions, promoting good management in the clubs, providing insurance coverage for players, assisting in facility development, trying to increase participation in the state, bidding to host national events, and managing two teams in the national competition. Finally, netball clubs field teams, find coaches and players, manage volunteers, conduct fundraising and may own and operate a facility.

It is important to remember that these sport governing organizations are volunteer-based, with volunteers involved in decisions at every level from clubs to international federations. As discussed in Chapter 10, nonprofit sport organizations do not operate as top down power hierarchies, with clubs always abiding by regional directives, or national governing bodies agreeing with international policy initiatives. Communication and agreement can be difficult between these organizations that may have competing priorities and localized issues. A spirit of cooperation and negotiation is required to make the nonprofit sport system operate effectively. The simple exertion of authority in a traditional organizational hierarchy is not appropriate for most nonprofit sport organizations.

The sports club environment

At the centre of sport development in countries such as Canada, New Zealand, Australia and the UK is the local or community sports club. It is worth taking some time to reflect on the role of the sports club, how volunteers and staff work in the club environment and how clubs contribute to sport development.

A background report initially prepared in 2001 and updated in 2002 for Sport Scotland provides a snapshot of sport clubs in Scotland (Allison, 2002). The most striking thing about local sport clubs is their diversity. Sport clubs have many functions, structures, resources, values and ideologies and they provide an enormous range of participation opportunities for people to be involved in sport. Most clubs provide activity in a single sport, and have as their focus enjoyment in sport, rather than competitive success. Sport clubs in Scotland come in various sizes, with an average membership size of 133, and most tend to cater for both junior and adult participants. They operate with minimum staffing, structures, income and expenditure, and often rely on a small group of paid or unpaid individuals to operate. The majority of club income comes from membership payments, so they tend to operate fairly autonomously. The management of local sport clubs in Scotland is regarded as an 'organic and intuitive process based on trust and experience rather than formal contracts and codes of practice' (Allison, 2002, p. 7).

The characteristics of local sport clubs in other countries are similar. The vast majority of sport clubs rely almost exclusively on volunteers to govern, administer, and manage their organizations and to provide coaching, officiating and general assistance with training, match day functions and fundraising.

Administrators

Administrators who fill roles as elected or appointed committee members have the responsibility for the overall guidance, direction and supervision of the organization. According to the Australian Sports Commission (2000, p. 2) the responsibility of the management committee of a sports club extends to:

- Conducting long-term planning for the future of the club
- Developing policy and procedures for club activities
- Managing external relations with other sport organizations, local governments or sponsors
- Managing financial resources and legal issues on behalf of the club
- Carrying out recommendations put forward by members
- Communicating to members on current issues or developments
- Evaluating the performance of officials, employees (if any), and other service providers
- Ensuring adequate records are kept for future transfer of responsibilities to new committee members
- Acting as role models for other club members

While governance is covered in detail in Chapter 10, it is important to note here that the ability of clubs to carry out these tasks effectively will vary according to their resources, culture and quality of people willing to be involved. The important administrative roles within local sports clubs are the chairperson or president, secretary, treasurer and volunteer coordinator. Other committee roles might involve responsibility for coaching, officiating, representative teams, match day arrangements, fundraising or marketing.

The chairperson or president should be the one to set the agenda for how a committee operates, work to develop the strategic direction of the club, chair committee meetings, and coordinate the work of other members of the committee. Club secretaries are the administrative link between members, the committee and other organizations and have responsibility for managing correspondence, records, and information about club activities. The treasurer has responsibility for preparing the annual budget, monitoring expenditure and revenue, planning for future financial needs and managing operational issues such as petty cash, payments and banking. The position of volunteer coordinator involves the development of systems and procedures to manage volunteers such as planning, recruitment, training and recognition.

Coaches

Coaches working in the sport club system may be unpaid or paid, depending on the nature of the sport and the resources of individual clubs. The role of the coach is central to developing athlete's skills and knowledge, in helping them learn tactics for success, and enjoy their sport. Coaches also act as important role models for players and athletes.

Most sports provide a structured training and accreditation scheme for coaches to develop their skills and experience to coach at local, state/ provincial, national or international levels. In Australia, for example, the National Coaching Council established a three-tier National Coaching Accreditation Scheme (NCAS) in 1978. Coaches can undertake a Level 1 introductory course, Level 2 intermediate course and Level 3 advanced courses in coaching. NCAS training programmes comprise three elements: (1) coaching principles that cover fundamentals of coaching and athletic performance, (2) sport-specific coaching that covers the skills, techniques, strategies and scientific approaches to a particular sport, and (3) coaching practice where coaches engage in practical coaching and application of coaching principles.

Officials

Sports officials include those people who act as referees, umpires, judges, scorers or timekeepers to officiate over games or events. The majority of officials are unpaid, but some sports such as Australian Rules Football, basketball, and some other football codes pay officials at all levels, enabling some to earn a substantial salary from full-time officiating. Other sports such as netball, softball or tennis rarely pay officials unless they are at state or national championship level. Sports officials are critical to facilitating people's involvement in sport but are the hardest positions to fill within the nonprofit sport system since they absorb a lot of time and often have low status.

All sports provide a structured training and accreditation scheme for officials in much the same way as coaches to develop their skills and experience at local, state/provincial, national or international levels. The Australian National Officiating Accreditation Scheme (NOAS) was established in 1994, modelled on the NCAS, but does not prescribe formal levels of officiating as these vary greatly between sporting codes. The NOAS aims to develop and implement programmes that improve the quality, quantity, leadership and status of sports officiating in Australia through training programmes that comprise three elements: (1) general principles of officiating and event management, (2) sport-specific technical rules, interpretations, reporting and specific roles, and (3) practice at officiating and applying the officiating principles.

General volunteers

Sports clubs also depend on people to perform roles in fundraising, managing representative teams, helping with match day arrangements such as car parking or stewarding, or helping to market the club. The majority of general volunteers have an existing link to a sports club through being a parent of a child who plays at the club, having some other family connection, or through friends and work colleagues involved in the club.

The nature of volunteer involvement in Australian and New Zealand sporting organizations is presented in Case 3.2 in order to illustrate the nature of people's involvement in volunteer roles in the sporting sector.

Case 3.2   Voluntary contributions in Australia and New Zealand

The Volunteering Australia 2004 publication, *Snapshot 2004: Volunteering Report Card*, provides a detailed picture of volunteer involvement in a range of activities. The report indicates that Australians are donating more time to volunteering than in previous years, in direct contrast to the declining participation trend of Canadians presented in Case 3.1. However, in terms of volunteering for nonprofit sport organizations, the data paints a different picture.

In the 12 months prior to April 2004, an estimated 4.3 million persons over the age of 15 in Australia were involved in organized sport and physical activity – 27% of the total population. Of those, 1.5 million persons were involved in non-playing roles such as coach, official, administrator, scorer, medical support or other role, and about one third of them had more than one non-playing role. Only about 12% of these people received payment for their role, which means that 88% of these 1.5 million people involved in non-playing roles were volunteers. Of these 1.5 million people, 60% also played sport. The majority of non-playing involvement was associated with junior sport.

While making comparisons between data sets is difficult due to differences in sampling methods and instruments, the data between 1993 and 2004 indicates that while the numbers of people coaching remains constant, the numbers of people involved in officiating and administration has declined. The majority of these would be volunteers, highlighting the potential fragility of a sport system dependent on volunteers to facilitate involvement.

Figures on voluntary participation in New Zealand show that just under 20% of the adult population was involved as a volunteer in the physical leisure sector in 1998. These roles included 11.1% as coaches, 8.7% as officials, and 8.8% as administrators, with people donating an average of 2.7 hours per week volunteering. This voluntary contribution was estimated to be more than 77% of the equivalent full-time workforce, and worth nearly $NZ1900 million a year.

These figures clearly illustrate the enormous contribution volunteers make in roles such as coaches, officials and administrators in order to facilitate people's involvement in sport. However, there are some worrying signs that such voluntary involvement may be on the wane and that in order to sustain current levels of involvement in sport, the management of sport volunteers needs to improve.

Sources: Volunteering Australia, (2004). *Snapshot 2004: Volunteering report card*. Melbourne, Volunteering Australia; Australian Bureau of Statistics, (2005). *Involvement in organised sport and physical activity, Australia, Cat. No. 6285.0*. Canberra, Australian Bureau of Statistics; Hillary Commission, (2000). *The growing business of sport and leisure: The impact of the physical leisure industry in New Zealand*. Wellington, New Zealand: Hillary Commission.

Government intervention

The substantial funds allocated to nonprofit sport organizations by governments to support their activities in areas of mass participation or elite performance has meant that governments are increasingly trying to influence the way in which the nonprofit sector of sport operates. Examples of these attempts include the Australian Sports Commission Volunteer Management Program and the policy of Sport England to have national organizations develop whole of sport plans. These are briefly reviewed below to highlight the increasingly interdependent nature of government and sport organizations in seeking improvements in nonprofit sport.

The Australian Sports Commission developed the Volunteer Involvement Program in 1994 in partnership with the Australian Society of Sports Administrators, the Confederation of Australian Sport, and state departments of sport and recreation. The programme aimed to improve the operation of nonprofit sport clubs and associations by providing a series of publications on sport club administration. In 2000, the Volunteer Management Program (VMP) and the Club and Association Management Program (CAMP) resources were published, and the ASC encouraged all clubs to join a Club Development Network and engage in strategic planning and other management techniques.

Another example is the policy developed by Sport England to require national sport organizations to develop 'whole of sport plans'. In 2003 Sport England identified 30 priority sports, based on their capability to contribute to Sport England's vision of an active and successful sporting nation and is now working with the national sport organizations to develop and implement these plans. The plans are designed to outline how a sport from grass roots right to the elite level will attract and keep participants, and improve their sporting experiences. The plans will drive decisions by Sport England to provide funding to sports based on clearly articulated ideas of the resources they need to drive their sport. The plans will also provide for measurable performance results and assist Sport England evaluate the benefits that accrue from funding nonprofit sport organizations.

Issues for the nonprofit sport sector

A range of challenges exist for the nonprofit sport sector around the globe. Foremost among these is the dependence on volunteers to sustain the sports system in areas such as coaching, administrating and officiating. As highlighted in Case 3.2, there is evidence to suggest that the rate of volunteerism is declining for roles such as officiating and administration in sport. Governments and nonprofit sport organizations will need to address this issue if their mutually dependent goals of increasing participation in organized sport are to be achieved.

The increasing litigious nature of society and the associated increase in costs of insurance for nonprofit sport organizations directly affects the cost of participation. In Australia fewer insurers are providing insurance cover for sporting organizations and insurance premium prices have risen significantly in recent years. For example, the public liability insurance premium for the Australian Parachute Federation increased from $127 000 to $1.1 million in two years. Public liability insurance is vital to run sport events and programmes and these costs are passed onto participants for no additional benefits, which raises the question of whether people can afford to keep playing sport in traditional nonprofit systems.

A further issue for nonprofit sport organizations is the trend away from participating in traditional sports, organized through clubs and associations, to a more informal pattern of participation. Some people are unwilling to commit to a season of sporting involvement, and are seeking ways to engage in sport and physical activity on a more casual basis, either through short-term commercial providers or with friends in spontaneous or pick up sports (Stewart et al., 2004). The increase in options available to young people to spend their discretionary leisure dollars, euros or pounds has also presented challenges for nonprofit sport organizations to market themselves as an attractive option.

As highlighted in Case 3.1, nonprofit organizations, including nonprofit sport organizations face significant capacity problems. They are often constrained by the size of their facilities or venues, and may struggle to attract enough quality people to manage the operations of their organization. They are also constrained by the interdependent nature of sport – they require other clubs, teams and organizations to provide competition – so they need to work cooperatively with other nonprofit sport organizations to expand their 'product'.

The very nature of nonprofit sport organizations requires adherence to frequently cumbersome consultative decision-making processes, often across large geographic areas and with widely dispersed and disparate groups of stakeholders. The additional complexity of the governance and management requirements of these organizations present their own set of challenges in terms of making timely decisions, reacting to market trends, being innovative, or seeking agreement on significant organizational changes.

Lyons (2001) also suggests that nonprofit organizations are unique because they have difficulty in judging performance relative to their commercial counterparts, have to be accountable to a wide range of stakeholders, and must deal with tension and possible conflict between paid staff and volunteers. These tensions are due to a lack of clarity about paid staff and volunteer roles, and are exacerbated by the lack of clear performance measures. Nonprofit sport organizations are particularly susceptible to these problems, especially where there is a coterie of paid staff in senior administrative positions.

Case 3.3   Challenges for sports volunteering in England

The peak government agency responsible for sports development in England, Sport England, commissioned a report in 2002 that (in part) identified the challenges faced by volunteers and volunteer managers in the English sports industry (Leisure Industries Research Centre, 2003). Sport volunteering in England has many of the same problems facing the sports industries of Australia, New Zealand and Canada. In short there are problems in finding and retaining enough volunteers who are appropriately skilled and motivated to deliver services to people who wish to play sport in the context of a community based club structure.

The report concluded that the sport system and its volunteers were subject to a variety of often competing pressures, driven by changes in government policy, technological change, and market competition for leisure expenditure. Core sport volunteers, those people who work, have children, and participate in sport, are most affected. As national government and sport organizations pursue policies that attempt to increase participation at the grass roots as well as drive improvements in elite performance, volunteers are being asked to deal with an ever increasing complexity and required level of professionalism in organizational procedures and systems. Government funding is increasingly tied to the ability of a sports organization to deliver measurable outcomes and be more accountable for their activities.

Improvements in technology and subsequent demands from end users for sport organizations to use the latest technology have placed increased demands on sport volunteers. An example of this is the shift to artificial playing surfaces for field hockey. These surfaces undoubtedly improve the playing and spectator experience but require volunteers at club level to fundraise continuously to meet significantly increased financial obligations.

The increasingly competitive leisure market has also meant volunteers at the club level have to manage their organizations to meet the demands of diverse 'customers' rather than the traditional member. People who are new to a sport may find it hard to differentiate between community club providers and commercial facilities and expect volunteers to meet their demands without becoming engaged in the life of the club. An example is the parent who treats the nonprofit sporting club as a cheap child minding option by dropping off and picking up their child without donating any time, energy or skills to the running of the club.

The capacity of nonprofit sport organizations and their volunteers to deal with these pressures varies enormously. Some have well established systems and resources, others flounder from one crisis to the next, continuously playing catch up. The organizations and volunteers at the community level are the ones most affected. The report recommends the use of a range of flexible and practical solutions to assist nonprofit sport organizations deal with these pressures. These include the provision of better education and training resources, simplified government funding requirements, reducing the compliance burden of reporting for sports organizations, and talking to nonprofit sports organizations in language more attuned to their core values of individual volunteer motivations and commitment than overly sophisticated business and management language.

Source: Leisure Industries Research Centre, (2003). *Sports volunteering in England 2002: A report for Sport England*. Sheffield, UK.

Summary of core principles

Nonprofit organizations were defined as those organizations that are institutionally separate from the State, do not return profits to owners, are self governing, have a significant element of voluntary contribution and are formally incorporated. Nonprofit organizations exist to develop communities, meet the needs of identifiable and discrete groups in those communities, and work for the benefit of public good rather than wealth creation for individuals. The majority of nonprofit organizations are driven largely by the efforts of volunteers rather than paid staff.

Sport organizations that operate on a nonprofit basis include professional service organizations, industry lobby groups, sport event organizations and sport governing bodies. By far the greatest number of nonprofit sport organizations are those that provide sporting competition or event participation opportunities for their members and other members of the public – sport governing bodies and sports clubs. The common element amongst all these sport organizations is their nonprofit focus – they exist to facilitate sporting opportunities for their members who may be individual athletes, coaches, officials or administrators, clubs, associations, or other sport organizations. They are also interdependent, relying on each other to provide playing talent, information to access competitions, resources for coach, official and player development and funding to support their activities.

Sport governing bodies and clubs rely almost exclusively on volunteers to govern, administer, and manage their organizations and to provide coaching, officiating and general assistance with training, events and fundraising. The substantial funds allocated to nonprofit sport organizations by governments to support their activities in areas of mass participation or elite performance has meant that governments are increasingly trying to influence the way in which the nonprofit sector of sport operates. Finally, a number of challenges exist for the nonprofit sport sector including the dependence on volunteers to sustain the sports system, the increasing litigious nature of society and the associated increase in costs of insurance for nonprofit sport organizations, the trend away from participating in traditional sports, significant capacity problems, and the additional complexity of the governance and management requirements of these organizations.

Review questions

1. What is the role of the nonprofit sector?
2. What are the unique aspects of nonprofit sport organizations?
3. Describe the role of the Commonwealth Games Council for England.
4. Explain how the State and the nonprofit sector may contribute to sport development.
5. In what way are volunteers important to the delivery of sport?
6. What are the important management roles in nonprofit sporting clubs?
7. Explain the role of a club President.
8. Why does the government attempt to intervene in the management of nonprofit sport organizations? Explain how governments do this in your own country.
9. How can nonprofit sport organizations reduce the costs to participants?
10. Explain how nonprofit sport organizations have to work cooperatively but still compete on the playing field.

Further reading

Chalip, L., Johnson, A. & Stachura, L. (Eds.) (1996). *National Sports Policies: An International Handbook*. Westport: Greenwood Press.

Chalip, L. & Thoma, J.E. (1996). *Sport Governance in the Global Community*. Morgantown, WV: Fitness Information Technology.

Lyons, M. (2001). *Third sector: The Contribution of Nonprofit and Cooperative Enterprises in Australia*. Crows Nest, NSW, Australia: Allen & Unwin.

Relevant websites

The following websites are useful starting points for further information on nonprofit sport organizations:

* Association for Research in Nonprofit Organizations and Voluntary Action at http://www.arnova.org
* Australia and New Zealand Third Sector Research Incorporated at http://www.anztsr.org.au
* Australian Sports Commission at http://www.ausport.gov.au
* Sport and Recreation New Zealand at http://www.sparc.org.nz/
* Sport Canada at http://www.pch.gc.ca/progs/sc/index_e.cfm
* Sport England at http://www.sportengland.org
* Sport Scotland at http://www.sportscotland.org.uk
* Volunteering Australia at http://www.volunteeringaustralia.org

Chapter 4
Professional sport

Overview

This chapter examines the key features of professional sport organizations and provides examples of the unique features of professional sport leagues and clubs. The chapter does not examine community, state or national sport organizations, but does comment on the relationship between these organizations and professional sport and the impact that professional sport has on the sport industry in general.

After completing this chapter the reader should be able to:

- Identify the way in which professional sport dominates the global sport industry;
- Understand the way in which the media, sponsors and professional sport organizations engage in corporate synergies to market and sell their products and services; and
- Understand the roles of players, agents, sponsors, leagues, clubs and the media in professional sport.

What is professional sport?

Professional sport, wherever it is played, is the most expensive, most visible and most watched sporting activity. It captures the lion's share of media coverage, as well as almost all sponsorship revenue and corporate support that is on offer. Professional sport is played in cities all over the world, from Kolkata (Calcutta), India to Rio de Janeiro, Brazil to Melbourne, Australia, in the very best stadiums (Eden Gardens, Maracana Stadium, Melbourne Cricket Ground), by athletes who may earn, depending on the size of the market, up to millions of dollars. Sport may once have been played exclusively for enjoyment, by amateurs in local settings, but this scenario is now a distant memory. Professional sport and the industry that surrounds it dominates world sport and those that play it are cultural celebrities on a global scale. Local, regional, state and national sport organizations are often geared around feeding professional sport leagues by developing player talent or spectator interest. These same organizations are also often forced, somewhat ironically, to compete in vain with professional sport for media coverage, sponsorship and general support (from fans, governments and communities). At its best, professional sport is the apex of the sports industry that supports those organizations below it by generating financial resources and cultural cache. At its worst, it is a rapacious commercial animal with an insatiable appetite for financial, cultural and social resources.

Professional sport leagues, such as the National Football League in the United States of America, dominate weekly media and social interests within the cities in which they are popular, with fans attracted to plots and sub-plots each week in the form of winners and losers, injuries and scandals, sackings, transfers and crisis events (financial, human or organizational). In the late nineteenth century American college football games were played on an ad hoc basis, largely special events that captured the attention of some football followers and some media outlets. College football only became a part of the national psyche and identity when games were organized around seasons, when media outlets and fans alike could plan their sport production and consumption around a weekly routine. The constancy and consistency of professional sport leagues has been the foundation upon which their popularity has been built. In many cities around the world, professional sport leagues have become an ingrained part of what it means to belong to a cultural or social group. In other words, professional sport leagues and their clubs have become, for many fans, an essential way of understanding and defining who they are.

Professional sport events, such as the Rugby Union or Cricket world cups have also become part of our cultural and commercial consumption. They are held periodically (usually every four years) and capture audience attention because they provide out of the ordinary sport action and are typically fuelled by nationalism. At a lower level, we are also exposed to annual events, such as world championships, and to circuits, such as the world rally championship, which hosts rounds in countries such as Japan, Cyprus and New Zealand. From day to day we are surrounded by saturation media coverage of these events through television, radio, magazines, newspapers and the Internet. There is no escaping the reach of professional sport.

Professional sport is now big business. It is not simply about what happens on the field of play, like it once was, often prior to the commercialization of sport in the 1970s and at times prior to the hyper-commercialization of sport at the beginning of the twenty-first century, but is also about what happens in the boardroom and on the stock exchange. Table 4.1 lists *Forbes* magazine's estimation of the football/soccer teams with the highest value in the world in 2005. It demonstrates that many of these teams are significant corporate

Table 4.1 Highest value football/soccer teams 2005

Team	Country	Value (US$)
Manchester United	England	1,251,000,000
Real Madrid	Spain	920,000,000
AC Milan	Italy	893,000,000
Juventus	Italy	837,000,000
Bayern Munich	Germany	627,000,000
Arsenal	England	613,000,000
Internazionale Milan	Italy	608,000,000
Chelsea	England	449,000,000
Liverpool	England	441,000,000
Newcastle United	England	391,000,000

Source: www.forbes.com

entities, of which a significant proportion have annual revenues in excess of US$250 million.

Circuits of promotion

In order to describe and explain the interconnections between professional sport, the media, advertisers and business, Whitson (1998) used the concept of 'circuits of promotion'. The key premise that underpins the circuit of promotion concept is that the boundaries between the promotion of sports and the use of sport events and athletes to promote products, which were previously separate, are now being dissolved. It is becoming increasingly more difficult to see where the sport organization ends and where the sponsor or media or advertiser begins. They are becoming (or have become) one, where one part of the professional sport machine serves to promote the other, for the good of itself and all the other constituent parts.

The relationship between Nike and former Chicago Bulls and Washington Wizards player Michael Jordan is a perfect example of a circuit of promotion at work. The Nike advertising campaigns that featured Jordan contributed to building the profile of both the company and the athlete, while Jordan's success in winning six NBA championships with the Bulls enhanced the corporate synergy between the two 'brands' and helped to increase the return on Nike's investment. Furthermore, the success of Jordan and the global advertising campaigns developed by Nike increased the cultural, social and commercial profile of the National Basketball Association (NBA) in America. In turn, the global promotion and advertising by the NBA, that either did or did not feature Jordan, helped to promote both Jordan, as the League's most visible and recognizable player, and Nike, as a major player in basketball footwear and apparel, either by direct or indirect association. Lastly, any advertising undertaken by Jordan's other sponsors, such as Gatorade, served to promote Jordan, but also the NBA and Nike through their association with Jordan. At its best, a sporting circuit of promotion is one of continuous commercial benefit and endless leveraging opportunities for the athletes and organizations involved.

Case 4.1   NASCAR – A circuit of promotion

NASCAR has been one of the most popular sports in the United States of America for over 50 years. It is broadcast on the FOX, SPEED, NBC and TNT television networks and stations. Like some other professional sports such as the National Hockey League in America, the Bundesliga in Germany and the National Rugby League in Australia, NASCAR operates to a seasonal calendar, with races in different American towns each week from February through to November at race tracks such as the Phoenix International Raceway, Daytona International Speedway and the Talladega Superspeedway. Scheduling races at different venues ensures good live attendances, but also enables NASCAR and its competing teams and drivers to capitalize on an array of sponsorship opportunities. Unlike the classic Daytona 500, many races have a naming rights sponsor, such as the Subway Fresh 500, the Coca-Cola 600 or the Checker Auto Parts 500.

Nextel, a telecommunications company, was the naming rights sponsor for the 2004 NASCAR season, taking over from long time sponsor Winston. Primary sponsorships for NASCAR cars are estimated to be worth between US$10–20 million, while secondary sponsorships might be worth US$500 000 to US$1 million depending on the success of the team and driver. 'This isn't just about paying US$10 million to put your logo on the hood of a car,' said Roush Racing President Geoff Smith, 'You have to realize that this goes beyond just the car – it includes uniforms, transporters and the rights to use the drivers for company marketing purposes'. To put these current sponsorship deals into an historical perspective, back in the early 1960s, Fred Lorenzen was sponsored by a Ford dealer in Fayetteville, N.C., who paid US$6000 for the entire season. By the late 1980s, it was estimated that approximately US$3 million in sponsorship was required for a team to break even over the course of the season. In 2000 UPS announced its primary sponsorship of the Robert Yates No. 88 team driven by Dale Jarrett. It was estimated that the sponsorship was worth US$15 million per year.

The 2005 NASCAR season included competing teams that were sponsored by the following companies: McDonald's, Miller Lite, Kellogg's, Budweiser, Valvoline, DeWalt Power Tools, DuPont, Target, M&Ms, Kodak, UPS, America Online and the United States Army. NASCAR claims it has a fan base of 75 million in the United States of America and the level of sponsorship is an indication that corporate America is not only willing to be associated with NASCAR, but believes it is a sound investment strategy.

Source: NASCAR website at http://www.nascar.com

Global sport circuits

Global sport circuits involve a league or structured competition. The European Champions' League is an example of a global sport circuit that is based around a league model, whereby teams play in different cities depending on who qualifies for the tournament and teams are progressively knocked out until a winner is determined. The men's and women's tennis tours are examples of a global circuit in which a series of events represent the structured competition. Each event or tournament on the tour may be entered by ranked players (who may have come through a lesser 'satellite circuit'), who compete for prize money, as well as points that go towards an overall ranking to determine the world's best player. In both the above cases, the circuit is managed or overseen by a governing body, although in the case of tennis the responsibility for managing and running individual tournaments is devolved to the host organization. For example, the Australian Open, the grand slam of the Asia–Pacific region is managed and run by Tennis Australia, the sport's governing body in Australia.

The location of events or tournaments that are part of global sport circuits are often flexible and cities or countries are able to bid for the right to host the event. In the case of the European Champions' League the teams that qualify for the tournament are entitled to host their home games (a performance based flexibility), while in tennis the grand slam tournaments of the Australian Open, the US Open, the French Open and Wimbledon are the only marquee events (no flexibility). In Formula One racing, however, cities can compete for the rights to host rounds of the championship. The Formula One season is based around Europe, but events are also held in Asia and North and South America. The races are broadcast to more than 160 countries and cities are often encouraged to bid for rights to host an event by the promise of possible economic benefits that might accrue as a result of securing a long-term contract. For example, China was added to the circuit in 2004, with racing held at the purpose built Shanghai International Circuit.

The biggest global circuits are the Olympic Games and the football (soccer) world cup. Both events are held every four years and have a complex arrangement whereby cities can bid to host the event. For a city to win the right to host the summer or winter Olympic Games it must go through a stringent two phase selection process. In the first phase – the 'candidature acceptance procedure' – national Olympic committees may nominate a city, which is then evaluated during a ten month process in which an International Olympic Committee (IOC) administrative committee examines each city based on technical criteria such as venue quality, general city infrastructure, public transport, security and government support. The cities accepted as applicants for the 2012 summer Olympic Games were Havana (Cuba), Istanbul (Turkey), Leipzig (Germany), London (Great Britain), Madrid (Spain), Moscow (Russia), New York (United States), Paris (France) and Rio de Janeiro (Brazil). The selected 'candidate' cities move through to the second and final 'candidature phase'. London, Paris, New York, Moscow and Madrid were selected as candidates for the 2012 games. In this phase the cities must submit a comprehensive candidature file to the IOC and are visited by the IOC's evaluation commission. The evaluation commission's report on the candidate cities is made available to all IOC members, who subsequently elect a host for the games at a full session of the IOC (for the election of the 2012 games the IOC session was held in Singapore in July, 2005).

Case 4.2   Global Circus – Just Add Sand

In 1987 the first International Volleyball Federation (FIVB)-sanctioned beach volleyball competition was held at Ipanema Beach in Rio de Janeiro, Brazil, with a total prize pool of US$22 000. From these humble beginnings, the world's professional beach volleyball tour has been transformed into a global travelling sand circus. In 2005, 32 tournaments were planned (16 for men and 16 for women) with a total prize pool of US$7.5 million in countries such as China, South Africa, Portugal, Indonesia, Japan, Greece, Germany, Norway, Croatia, Mexico, Russia and the United Arab Emirates. Events are held in well known locations, such as the Champ de Mars in Paris, Schlossplatz in Berlin (site of the 2005 world championships), Piazza Duomo in Milan and Bondi Beach in Sydney. In 2004, 750 000 spectators watched 26 tournaments, including grand slam events with prize pools in excess of US$500 000. Swatch is the naming rights sponsor of the world tour (2005–2008) and world championships.

The FIVB is the largest sports organization in the world in terms of its 218 member National Federations, operating at continental level through 5 Confederations based in Africa, Asia, Europe, North and Central America and South America. Under FIVB guidance, these entities provide opportunities to Volleyball and Beach Volleyball event organizers, sponsors, TV broadcasters and over 500 million participating athletes world-wide. In 2004 a total of 104 beach volleyball matches were produced for international television broadcast, and in excess of 700 hours of game and highlight programming was broadcast in 205 countries. Eurosport was the leading producer of beach volleyball television content, reaching approximately 18 million homes in five different languages.

In excess of 700 athletes from approximately 60 countries compete on the beach volleyball world tour. Many of these athletes are touring professionals. For example, in 2004 the top male pair of Emanuel Rego and Ricardo Santos from Brazil won 7 titles and prizemoney of US$260 500. Swiss pair Martin and Paul Laciga are the top all-time money winners on the world circuit with in excess of US$1 million in earnings, while Brazilian star player

Emanuel Rego has amassed US$1.3 million over the course of his career. In 2004 Brazilian pair Shelda Bede and Adriana Behar won 3 titles and US$206 000 on the women's tour, contributing to their all-time earnings of approximately US$1.8 million.

Source: International Volleyball Federation at http://www.fivb.org

Media

In 1883 Joseph Pulitzer purchased the *New York World*, a metropolitan daily newspaper with a circulation of approximately fifteen thousand and immediately set about creating the modern mass-circulation newspaper. By 1892, the *New York World* had increased its circulation to two million readers, a massive transformation even by contemporary standards (Schudson, 1978; Hughes, 1981). Pulitzer achieved this massive increase by lowering the cost of the paper, changing its layout and look, refining a sensationalist approach to news, selling advertising space on the basis of circulation and using headlines to capture the attention of audiences. Importantly, the *New York World* was also a pioneer in sports coverage throughout the 1880s and early 1890s (Oriard, 1993). One of Pulitzer's first initiatives as publisher was to establish a sports department, with its own sporting editor. The subsequent increase in the amount of space devoted to sport was a significant factor in the increased circulation of the *New York World*. Sport not only benefited from the revolution in newspaper production and content, but also contributed to the development of the print media's two-fold function of information and entertainment.

Since the 1890s the dual function of information and entertainment has not only defined newspapers, but also subsequent media forms, including radio, television and the Internet. The impact of sport news on the popularity and profitability of these new media forms has only been equalled by the transformation that sport has undergone, as a result of its interplay with the media. If, in the 1890s it was possible to construct or conceive of an image of sport without reference to the media, by the 1990s the task was impossible. It is now as if 'one is literally unthinkable without the other' (Rowe, 1999, p. 13).

The connection between professional sport and the media has become most obvious in the last ten to twenty years of the twentieth century in particular. The creation of the Mighty Ducks of Anaheim ice hockey franchise in North America's National Hockey League (NHL) is a prime example. Following in the wake of the successful Disney film of the same name, starring Emilio Estevez, the Walt Disney Corporation paid US$50 million to join the NHL as an expansion franchise in 1992. Although unusual, the Mighty Ducks are not the only professional sport team to be owned or operated by a media corporation and the phenomenon has a relatively long history. Ted Turner's Turner Broadcasting Systems (TBS), which subsequently merged with Time Warner and then with AOL to become the world's largest media company, purchased the Atlanta Braves in America's Major League Baseball and the Atlanta Hawks in the National Basketball Association in the 1970s. The Hawks have played at Turner Field since 1997, Turner is still on the board of directors in his capacity as vice chairman of AOL Time Warner, and the Braves' games are still being broadcast on TBS.

The amount of money the media is willing to pay to broadcast sport is also indicative of the intimate relationship between professional sport and the media. Again, the Olympics is an outstanding example of the growth in broadcast rights fees paid by broadcasting networks across the globe, as well as the actual and perceived popularity of sports. Figure 4.1 illustrates the magnitude of broadcast rights for the Olympics over the previous quarter of a century. Clearly, sport is effective in attracting both audiences and advertisers. Importantly, the relationship between professional sport and the media has reached a point where professional sport would not survive in its current form without the media. Broadcast revenue now provides the majority of professional sport revenue, for major events and major leagues, whereas gate or ticket revenue was once the major contributor.

Sponsorship

The amount of money available to professional sport organizations through sponsorship arrangements or deals is connected to the amount of media coverage that the club or league receives. The amount of coverage can, at a base level, be considered in terms of the official broadcast rights deal struck between a club or league and a television station or network. Sponsors are likely to want to be involved with a club or league that has very good network television coverage that reaches a broad audience. However, coverage can also refer to the general coverage that a club or league receives in a variety of media forms and outlets, including television, radio, newspapers, magazines and the Internet. This media coverage promotes the club or league and generally encourages fans to consume the sport, either by attending the game live or by accessing a mediated version. The club or league that is able to attract a greater amount of this media coverage is more likely to be embedded in the commercial consciousness of audiences and consumers. Thus, the amount of media coverage received is a measure of the audiences that can be reached by advertisers (or sponsors) through a commercial association with a professional sporting club or league and is directly proportional to the worth of the sponsorship.

The levels of sponsorship differ between sports, between leagues, between clubs and across countries. At the highest level the IOC created 'The Olympic Partner Program' (TOP) in 1985, in order to provide companies with exclusive worldwide marketing rights to the games. Coca-Cola, McDonald's, Kodak, Omega, Visa and Panasonic were among the official sponsors of the 2004 Athens Olympic Games. At other levels of professional sport the sponsorship

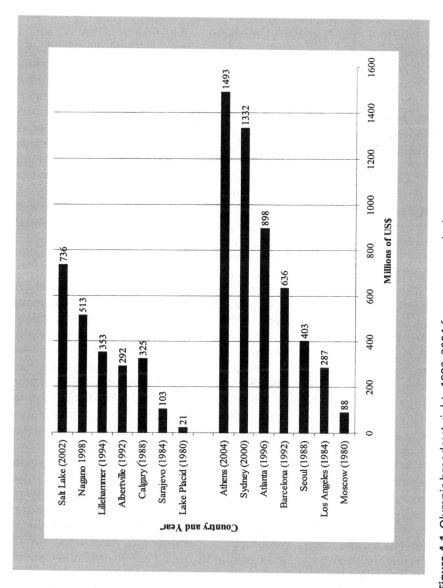

Figure 4.1 Olympic broadcast rights 1980–2004 for summer and winter games
(*Source*: www.olympic.org)

or marketing arrangements may go further, as clubs and leagues are willing to enter into sponsorship arrangements whereby commercial organizations are able to acquire naming rights or enter into arrangements that give them either exclusive or increased access to fans. The development of the Internet and online marketing has been particularly instrumental in this respect.

The English Premier League provides an example of the proliferation of sponsors within professional sport leagues and clubs. The competition is known as the Barclays Premiership, sponsored by a United Kingdom based financial service group engaged in banking, investment banking and investment management. The English Premier League also has a range of secondary or associate sponsors. For example, Budweiser is the official beer of the league, while pharmaceutical company GlaxoSmithKline is a sponsor through its Lucozade sport drink. Furthermore, the clubs that play in the Barclays Premiership have significant sponsorship deals. The primary sponsor of each club is entitled to place its brand prominently on the front of the playing strip. Manchester United's primary sponsor is Vodafone, a telecommunications company that also sponsors the English cricket team and the Ferrari Formula One racing team. Arsenal is sponsored by O$_2$, a rival telecommunications company, Chelsea is sponsored by Emirates airline, Liverpool is sponsored by Carlsberg, a Danish beer, Everton is sponsored by Chang, a Thai beer (interestingly, both are competitors with the official beer of the league) and Tottenham Hotspur is sponsored by Thomson, a travel agent.

The sponsorship of professional sport goes further than commercial agreements between clubs and leagues. Individual athletes also have sponsorship agreements that provide them with additional income to supplement their playing contracts (for team sports) or prize money (for individuals). Australian swimmer Ian Thorpe, who was Olympic champion in the 400 m freestyle swimming at the Sydney (2000) and Athens (2004) games, has an extensive list of sponsors. What is most noticeable about the companies that are associated with Thorpe is that they are not simply Australian companies that want to be associated with an Australian athlete. Qantas (an airline) is the most noticeable Australian company that sponsors Thorpe, but it has a strong global profile. Thorpe is sponsored by Adidas, a global sportswear brand, by Sony (electronic goods) in Japan and China and by TV Asahi, a Japanese broadcasting network. Well chosen brands with a global profile can enhance an athlete's overall image and in the case of more popular athletes a sponsor can establish the athlete as a brand in their own right. Sponsorship of professional athletes is not restricted to superstar athletes like David Beckham of Real Madrid (football/soccer), Lance Armstrong of the American Postal Team (cycling) or Yao Ming of the Houston Rockets (basketball). Rather, sponsorship of professional athletes exists wherever there is a market, whether it is a mass market in the case of global athletes or a niche market in the case of small or cult sports. Skateboarder Tony Hawk is sponsored by Adio footwear and Birdhouse skateboards, which appeal to a specific target market, but is also sponsored by Apple computers and McDonald's. In the case of the first two companies the sponsorship deal is primarily used to increase sales of a market specific product. In the case of the latter two companies, the sponsorship relationship with Tony Hawk is an attempt to increase awareness of global brands within the target population.

Case 4.3   The America's Cup

What started as the Hundred Guineas Cup in 1851 has become one of the biggest professional sport events in the world. Held every four years, the America's Cup is a spectacle that rivals the Olympic Games and World Cup in terms of international interest. The winner of the 1851 race was the schooner 'America', which took the cup from England to America, renamed it the America's Cup and gave it to the New York Yacht Club to be used for competition between countries. The subsequent 'deed of gift' written in 1887, set out the laws of engagement, many of which are still in operation today. Up until 1970 only single challengers were allowed and the American yachts reigned supreme. In fact it was not until 1983 that a foreign yacht (Australia II) won the America's Cup, ending the 132 year dominance of the American boats.

Australia failed to defend its win in 1987, and America successfully defended in 1991. In 1995 'Black Magic' from New Zealand won the Cup and in 2000 Team New Zealand successfully defended the title. In 2003 Swiss yacht 'Alinghi' beat the New Zealanders comprehensively. Soon after the victory, Team Alinghi announced the establishment of a commercial company (AC Management) to oversee the 2007 America's Cup. Unlike previous cups, where the winner defended in its home country, AC Management, after a selection process, announced that the 2007 America's Cup would be held off the coast of Valencia, Spain, in the waters of the Mediterranean Sea. It remains to be seen whether this new bidding process will be continued, should Team Alinghi be defeated in 2007.

The America's Cup has become one of the premier professional sport competitions in the world. Unlike the Olympic Games, however, where anyone can enter if they (the team or the individual) are good enough, a team can only enter the America's Cup if it has enough financial support to mount a challenge. Established by the Oracle Corporation's billionaire founder and chief executive officer Larry Ellison, BMW Oracle Racing is one of the challengers to Team Alinghi for the 2007 America's Cup. Oracle is one of the largest software companies, with annual revenues in excess of US$10 billion, while BMW is one of the world's leading prestige automotive manufacturers.

Each of the teams challenging for the 2007 Cup will, in all likelihood, have allocated in excess of US$100 million to the task of first, winning the right to race Team Alinghi as the challenger and second, beating the finely tuned Swiss team. Research and development can cost US$20 million depending on the team and the yacht, while tacticians are paid approximately US$200 000 per year and skippers are typically paid in excess of US$500 000. The wage bill alone can be substantial, particularly for teams such as Emirates New Zealand, who will employ a full-time staff of at least 95 from the start of 2005 to the conclusion of the competition. Sails cost up to US$100 000, while a yacht hull is approximately US$1.5 million. In total, an America's Cup yacht and its crew is an expensive piece of machinery, part of a sporting battle that is part financial muscle, part technical expertise and part sailing. In short, it is the perfect example of high stakes professional sport played at the start of the twenty-first century.

Sources: 32nd America's Cup website at http://www.americascup.com; BMW Oracle Racing website at http://www.bmworacleracing.com and Forbes online at http://www.forbes.com

Player management

Formed in the 1960s, International Management Group (IMG) is one of the world's leading player management companies, employing in excess of 2000 staff in 70 offices in 30 countries (www.imgworld.com). What began exclusively as a player management business has evolved into a complex commercial operation that includes television and publishing divisions. Golfer Arnold Palmer, winner of the US Masters golf tournament in 1958, 1960, 1962 and 1964, the US Open in 1960 and the British Open in 1961 and 1962, was the first athlete in the world to be branded by Mark McCormack, the creator and head of IMG. Back in the 1960s the 'brand-name' principle by which Palmer and McCormack approached sport was the first attempt to transform the business activities of leading athletes. Sport and business were previously related, but the scale of their operation was unique. The level of vertical and horizontal integration was essential to what became known as 'Sportsbiz' (Boyle & Haynes, 2000). McCormack took the relationship of the agent further than before, and began to handle contract negotiations, proactively sought business opportunities, and planned the sale of the Palmer brand on a long-term basis, rather than previous attempts that might be characterized as ad hoc. McCormack set an important precedent, selling people as marketable commodities.

Octagon is a global sport marketing company and competitor to IMG. It represents and promotes athletes in 35 different sports across the world. Its clients include some of the most prominent sportsmen and women, such as tennis players Lleyton Hewitt and Amelie Mauresmo. It also represents American swimmer Michael Phelps, winner of the 400 m individual medley and 200 m butterfly at the 2004 Athens Olympic Games, who Octagon claims is a perfect case study in what successful sport marketing and management can provide for an athlete in the contemporary hyper-commercial sport environment (www.octagon.com). Octagon suggests that Phelps laid the foundation with his performances in the pool, but that Octagon enhanced the Phelps story with a targeted publicity campaign, which included appearances in *Time*, *People*, the *Wall Street Journal* and *USA Today*. The result was what Octagon claims to be the creation of a connection between Phelps and corporate America, including the largest ever endorsement deal in swimming with Speedo and subsidiary deals with VISA, Omega and AT&T Wireless.

In many respects, athletes competing in individual sports are logical targets for both agents and sponsors, however athletes in team sports are often as valuable, if not more so. In the United States the term 'multiples' is used to refer to an athlete that has the ability to attract multiple media and endorsements. The multiples' play on the field is at the highest level, they help to bring fans to the game, help the team to secure broadcast contracts or sponsorship deals, help the team in merchandising and licensing and in the extreme cases have the potential to increase the net financial worth of the organization. Thus, the athlete's commercial potential can be calculated in individual earnings (through the team or an agent), but also in terms of the growth of the club or league of which they are a part. In 2002 Yao Ming led the Shanghai Sharks to the championship in the Chinese Basketball Association, averaging 32.4 points, 19.0 rebounds and 4.8 blocked shots. A member of the Chinese national team since he was 18 years old, 229 cm Ming was selected as the first pick in the 2002 NBA draft by the Houston Rockets. In his first season in the NBA Ming was voted rookie of the year and the Rockets improved their winning percentage from 34% to 52%. The Houston Rockets website is available in English or Chinese, in order to cater for Ming's enormous popularity in China (www.nba.com/rockets). Ming's success with the Rockets means that merchandising and broadcast possibilities are significant, for both the team and the league. 'The Year of the Yao', a movie about Ming's first year in the NBA and his transition from China to America was released in cinemas in 2005, further evidence of Ming's popularity and commercial value (www.yaoming.net).

Professional sport stars are well paid by any measures. Importantly, their salaries are relative to revenue of the clubs, leagues, tournaments and events of which they are a part. In fact, in some professional sports with strong player unions, the level of remuneration for players is set as a percentage of league revenue. Table 4.2 lists the highest paid football/soccer players in the world in 2005. Their annual earnings are indicative of their on-field worth and the significant investment made by their respective teams, as well as their commercial worth off the field.

Ownership and outcomes

Professional sports utilize different ownership and governance models in order to regulate and manage their businesses effectively. Some of the models have strong historical traditions, while others have been selected or adapted for their utility. One of the key distinctions is between professional sport teams and leagues that can be considered 'profit maximizers' and those that are 'win maximizers'. There is some debate as to whether these terms accurately reflect the practice of professional sport teams and franchises, but they are useful for broadly categorizing operational and financial priorities. Profit maximizing teams, such as those in the major American professional sport leagues, are typically owned by individuals or businesses and seek to maximize the financial return on investment. In some sports, however, such as English, Scottish

Table 4.2 Highest value football/soccer players 2005

Player	Team	Annual Earnings (US$)
David Beckham	Real Madrid	32 000 000
Zinedine Zidane	Real Madrid	20 000 000
Ronaldo	Real Madrid	18 000 000
Raul Blanco	Real Madrid	12 000 000
Ronaldinho	Barcelona	12 000 000
Oliver Kahn	Bayern Munich	11 500 000
Michael Owen	Real Madrid	11 000 000
Alessandro del Piero	Juventus	10 000 000
Christian Vieri	Inter Milan	9 000 000
Thierry Henry	Arsenal	8 000 000

Source: www.forbes.com

and Australian football and cricket (Quirk & Fort, 1992), the need to win is a greater priority than the need to make a profit. In fact, in some instances win maximizing teams will place the club in financial jeopardy, particularly by purchasing players it cannot afford.

In some cases, the ownership model has adapted to meet specific conditions brought about by commercial change. In the J-League, Japan's professional football (soccer) competition, teams like the Kashiwa Reysol are privately owned. The Reysol is owned by the Hitachi corporation that specializes in the manufacturing of electrical goods and equipment. Originally established as an amateur team of the Hitachi corporation, the Reysol was professionalized in order to participate in the inaugural J-League season in 1993.

Whether teams are part of a league that is win maximizing or profit maximizing, they must cooperate with each other at some level to ensure that fans, sponsors and the media remain interested and involved with the sport. Sport leagues that are dominated by one or two teams are often perceived to be less attractive to fans than leagues in which the result of games is uncertain. There is, however, a long history of leagues in which strong rivalries have maintained interest in the game (Los Angeles Lakers versus Boston Celtics in the NBA and Rangers versus Celtic in the Scottish Premier League for example), although often the teams that are part of the rivalry benefit at the expense of teams that perform poorly. A league that is not dominated by only a couple of teams and in which there is an uncertainty of outcome (of a game or season) is said to have 'competitive balance' (Quirk & Fort, 1992). Leagues across the world have instituted a range of measures to try to achieve competitive balance, which is often elusive. Perhaps the most obvious and publicized measure is the draft system that operates in football leagues such as the National Football League in America or the Australian Football League. The draft allows the league to allocate higher draft preferences (the best athletes on offer) to poorer performed teams, in order to equalize the playing talent across the league and create more competitive games.

Summary

This chapter has presented an overview of professional sport and some of the central relationships that are essential to its ongoing prosperity and survival. The media, sponsors, agents, owners, advertisers, leagues, clubs and athletes are part of a self sustaining commercial alliance, in which each of the partners promotes and supports the activities and interests of the others. Commercial networks are the binding forces that are holding professional sport together in the twenty-first century. Since the middle of the twentieth century, professional sport leagues and clubs have increasingly become willing partners in the promotion of their activities (sports and events), as well as the promotion of subsidiary products and services, and in the process have become major players in a multi-billion dollar industry.

Review questions

1. Use the circuit of promotion concept to explain the role of sponsors and the media in the professional sport industry.
2. Explain the rationale behind a company sponsoring a professional sport club, league or athlete.
3. Is the media important to the survival of professional sport?
4. Identify an international and a domestic professional circuit and examine its operation. What are the special features that attract fans and media?
5. Choose a professional sport league and identify the fees paid by television broadcasters over the previous twenty years for the broadcast rights. Has it increased or decreased over the period? Explain why.
6. Choose a sport in which the location of events or tournaments is not fixed. Imagine that the city you live in is going to bid for the right to host the event and create a list of potential benefits – consider such features as the economy, environment, transportation, public services and housing.
7. Choose a high profile athlete and identify what companies or products sponsor the athlete. Is the athlete presented by an agent or did they secure the sponsorships or endorsements themselves?
8. Choose a sporting league of the world and identify whether it should be classified as 'win maximizing' or 'profit maximizing'. Provide a rationale for your answer that includes a commentary on the ownership of teams in the league.
9. Create a list of the top 5 paid sportspeople in the world. What does the list tell you about the size of the commercial markets that the sports are played in?
10. Create a fictional international sport circuit. What cities of the world would host your events and why?

Further reading

Bellamy, R. (1998). The evolving television sports marketplace. In L. Wenner (ed.) *MediaSport*. London: Routledge, pp. 73–87.

Boyle, R. & Haynes, R. (2000). *Power Play: Sport, the Media and Popular Culture*. London: Longman.

Cousens, L. & Slack, T. (2005). Field-level change: the case of North American major league professional sport. *Journal of Sport Management*, 19 (1), 13–42.

Euchner, C. (1993). *Playing the Field: Why Sports Teams Move and Cities Fight to Keep Them*. Baltimore: John Hopkins University Press.

Fielding, L. et al. (1999). Harlem Globetrotters International, Inc. *Journal of Sport Management*, 13 (1), 45–77.

O'Brien, D. & Slack, T. (2003). An Analysis of Change in an Organizational Field: The Professionalization of English Rugby Union. *Journal of Sport Management*, 17 (4), 417–448.

Shropshire, K. (1995). *The Sports Franchise Game*. Philadelphia: University of Pennsylvania Press.

Relevant websites

Americas

* National Football League – http://www.nfl.com
* National Basketball League – http://www.nba.com
* Major League Baseball – http://www.mlb.com
* National Hockey League – http://www.nhl.com
* Nascar – http://www.nascar.com
* Professional Golfers' Association – http://www.pga.com
* Ladies' Professional Golf Association – http://www.lpga.com

Australia and New Zealand

* Australian Football League – http://www.afl.com.au
* Cricket Australia – http://www.baggygreen.com.au
* National Rugby League – http://www.nrl.com
* Super 12 Rugby Union – http://www.rugby.com.au
* New Zealand Rugby – http://www.nzrugby.com

Great Britain

* English Premier League – http://www.premierleague.com
* British Rugby League – http://uk.rleague.com/

Asia

* J-League – http://www.j-league.or.jp/eng/
* Japanese Sumo Association – http://www.sumo.or.jp/eng/index.html
* Chinese Professional Baseball League –
  http://www.cpbl.com.tw/html/english/cpbl.asp

Europe

* European Champions' League – http://www.uefa.com/
* Serie A (Italy) – http://www.lega-calcio.it/
* Real Madrid – http://www.realmadrid.com/portada_eng.htm
* Bundesliga (Germany) – http://www.bundesliga.de
* European Professional Golfers' Association Tour –
  http://www.europeantour.com

Global

* Olympics – http://www.olympic.org
* World Cup – http://www.fifa.com
* America's Cup – http://www.americascup.com
* Tour de France – http://www.letour.fr/indexus.html
* Formula One – http://www.formula1.com
* Association of Surfing Professionals – http://www.aspworldtour.com
* Association of Tennis Professionals (men) –
  http://www.atptennis.com/en
* Women's Tennis Association – http://www.wtatour.com/
* World Rally Championship – http://www.wrc.com

Part Two
Sport Management Principles

Chapter 5
Strategic sport management

Overview

This chapter reveals the processes and techniques of strategic management. Specifically, it focuses on the analysis of an organization's position in the competitive environment, the determination of its direction and goals, the selection of an appropriate strategy, the leveraging of its distinctive assets and the evaluation of its chosen activities. These processes are reviewed within the context of a documented plan.

After completing this chapter the reader should be able to:

■ Understand the difference between strategy and planning;
■ Appreciate why strategic management should be undertaken;
■ Differentiate the steps of the strategic management process;
■ Identify the tools and techniques of strategic management;
■ Specify the steps involved in the documentation of a strategic plan; and
■ Explain how the nature of sport affects the strategic management process.

Strategic management principles

In the simplest terms possible, strategy is the match or interface between an organization and its external environment (Viljoen & Dann, 2003). Looking at strategy in this way is a helpful start because it reinforces the importance of *both* the organization itself and the circumstances in which it operates. At the heart of strategy is the assumption that these two elements are of equal importance. Furthermore, strategy concerns the entirety of the organization and its operations as well as the entirety of the environment. Such a holistic approach differentiates the strategy management process from other dimensions of management.

One troublesome aspect of strategic management is its complex, multifaceted nature. Johnson and Scholes (2002), for example noted several important features associated with strategic decision-making:

1. Strategy affects the direction and scope of an organization's activities;
2. Strategy involves matching an organization's activities with the environment;
3. Strategy requires the matching of an organization's activities with its resource capabilities;
4. The substance of strategy is influenced by the views and expectations of key stakeholders;
5. Strategic decisions influence the long-term direction of the organization.

With Johnson and Scholes' points in mind, it might be concluded that the management of strategy requires a keen understanding of the organization, the environment, as well as the consequences of decisions. But these points miss one vital outcome in the strategy process. Porter (1996) argued that the central purpose of strategy is to become different to the competition. From this viewpoint, strategy should help explain how one football club is different from the next, or why a customer should choose to use one recreation facility over another in the same area. To Porter, the match between an organization and its environment should result in a competitive advantage that no other organization can easily copy.

Before we proceed, it is necessary to make several important distinctions in definition. The first point to make is that strategy and planning is not the same thing. Strategy can be defined as the process of determining the direction and scope of activities of a sport organization in light of its capabilities and the environment in which it operates. Planning is the process of documenting these decisions in a step-by-step manner indicating what has to be done, by whom, with what resources and when. In short, strategy is a combination of analysis and innovation; of science and craft. Planning identifies, in a systematic and deductive way, the steps and activities that need to be taken toward the implementation of a strategy. Strategic management marries strategy and planning into a process.

The second point to make about terminology is concerned with the generic use of the word strategy. The term can be legitimately used to explain three levels of decision-making. The first is the identity level where a sport organization is faced with the task of establishing clarity about what business it is actually engaged in. For example, is the core business providing sport competitions, managing facilities, developing players, winning medals, championships and tournaments, selling merchandise, making a profit or improving shareholder wealth? At the second level, the term strategy is commonly used to identify how the organization is going to be competitive against others. Strategy here is an explanation of how competitive advantage is going to be created and sustained. Strategy is also used at an operational level to identify how daily activities are to be undertaken and how resources are to be deployed to support them. For example, a broader strategy to improve player scouting methods might be supported by an operational strategy specifying the purchase of some computer software.

Why undertake strategic management?

Surprisingly, the need for management of the strategy process is not always considered necessary. Some managers believe that the fast-paced nature of the sport industry precludes the use of a systematic strategic management process. Strategy for these managers is developed 'on the run' and in response to emerging circumstances and events. However, this approach is fundamentally contradictory to the principles of strategic management, which emphasize the importance of actively shaping the future of one's own sport organization rather than waiting for circumstances to prompt action. Pro-activity is at the heart of good strategy because it helps to reduce the uncertainty that accompanies chaotic and changeable industries like sport, where on-field performance can have such a radical effect on the organization's success. Those versed in the concepts of strategic management would argue that with more uncertainty comes the need for greater strategic activity. Thus, a sport club that can generate a sizable surplus with a performance at the top of the ladder but a dangerous deficit with a performance at the bottom of the ladder should engage in the strategy process in order to seek new ways of managing its financial balance. In addition, those who favour reactive approaches to strategy assume that opportunities are always overt and transparent. This is seldom true. Identifying new opportunities that have not already been leveraged by competition is rarely easy and requires thorough analysis and innovative thinking. Neither of these can be achieved easily without the investment of time and energy on strategy development.

Allied to the notion of pro-activity is the importance of coordination. In other words, without a broad approach to the strategy process, different parts of the organization are likely to pursue their own agendas. It is therefore essential that scarce resources are deployed in a coordinated and integrated manner that is consistent with an overarching strategy. Such a coordinated approach to strategy ensures that new strategy represents change. For many sport organizations for which change is a necessary condition for survival, strategy represents what Lewis (1993) calls the 'cognitive component' of change management; the intellectual part that can be planned. The result of this process should be a coordinated attempt to achieve goals that have been agreed upon by organizational stakeholders that takes into account a balance between the achievement of goals and the resources required to do so. This is another way of saying efficiency is an important organizational goal.

Strategic sport management

One of the biggest issues in sport strategy comes in finding the balance between two or more divergent obligations. For example, it is common in sport organizations to seek both elite success as well as improved participation levels. Deploying resources to both of these commitments is troublesome from a strategic viewpoint because they are not necessarily as compatible as popular assumptions would suggest (Stewart et al., 2004). It is commonly assumed that international success for a particular sport serves as a motivator for people to participate. The success of Pieter van den Hoogenband, the Dutch Olympic swimming champion, might be the trigger for Dutch people to become involved in swimming. Similarly, tennis participation in Australia increases after the Australian Open. However, in both of these examples, the retention of new participants has been poor in the medium term and negligible in the longer term.

Assumption is a dangerous activity in strategic decision-making. To make matters more complex, the choices of direction inherent in sport can be distracting, from the necessity to develop players or increase participation, to the pressure to make more money or win at all costs.

Case 5.1 International Cricket Council shifts to Dubai

One of the most traditional sports in the world has made a key strategic decision to shift its base of international operations from its home of nearly 100 years to a location where the sport is little known. The International Cricket Council (ICC), the governing organization for the national cricket boards, has voted to move from its base at Lords in London to Dubai in the United Arab Emirates (UAE).

The move was overwhelmingly approved by the ICC Board, made up of representatives from the 10 full member test-playing nations and three associate member nations. Given the single abstention and only one vote against the decision, what would motivate such a unanimous but significant strategic re-direction?

Two factors precipitated the extraordinary decision. First, the ICC has been under significant pressure to demonstrate its commitment to a more global representation of cricket. In other words, the sport's international governing body feels that it is time to encourage the international distribution of cricket by distancing itself from the traditional Commonwealth centrality of England.

Allied to the resolution that cricket needs a governing body removed from its traditional home and more equitably positioned for other nations, was the specific choice of Dubai, one of seven emirates in the oil-rich Middle Eastern country of the UAE. Although cricket is popular in the Northern emirate of Sharjah, it is not prominent in Dubai. As a result, the choice of location is politically neutral and geographically equitable between the cricket powers in Australia and New Zealand, England, the West Indies, Pakistan and India, and South Africa. In addition, the ICC was enticed by the development of Dubai Sports City, which when completed, will host the ICC's first global cricket academy.

Intended as a centre for international excellence, the ICC Academy in Dubai Sports City will have a 30 000 seat cricket stadium, three cricket fields, indoor and outdoor facilities, a gymnasium, pool, sport science facilities, medical rooms and lecture theatres for education. Dubai Sports City is also touted to be host to other sport brands seeking to enhance their international profile, including a Manchester United Soccer Academy, an Ernie Els Signature Golf Course, a David Lloyd Tennis Academy and a Butch Harmon School of Golf.

The second factor is more mundane, but equally powerful from a strategic viewpoint. The United Kingdom Treasury has declined ICC requests for tax concessions. With the UAE's attractive taxation conditions, Dubai was an important location for the strategic financial position of the organization. The ICC has already attempted to avoid United Kingdom taxation by establishing a company in Monte Carlo. Combined with an enticing deal offered to use Dubai Sports City, the ICC determined that the UAE is the best base from which international cricket can be cultivated.

The strategic management process

Strategic management (Figure 5.1) is the process that achieves an overlap between preparation and opportunity. This way of thinking has emerged from the first uses of the strategy concept, which came from the military. On the battlefield, the importance of imposing conditions that disadvantage the enemy in combat is paramount. For example, one of the key principles of military strategy is to manoeuvre your adversary into a position where

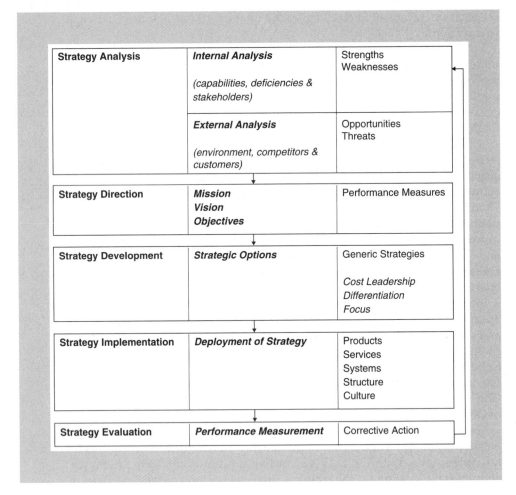

Strategy Analysis	*Internal Analysis* *(capabilities, deficiencies & stakeholders)*	Strengths Weaknesses
	External Analysis *(environment, competitors & customers)*	Opportunities Threats
Strategy Direction	*Mission* *Vision* *Objectives*	Performance Measures
Strategy Development	*Strategic Options*	Generic Strategies *Cost Leadership* *Differentiation* *Focus*
Strategy Implementation	*Deployment of Strategy*	Products Services Systems Structure Culture
Strategy Evaluation	*Performance Measurement*	Corrective Action

Figure 5.1 The strategic management process

they are outnumbered at the point of conflict. Variables like terrain and the opportunity to outflank, or attack the enemy from both the front and side simultaneously, make strategic decisions more complicated. These principles are also applied in the strategic sport management process.

Like a general, the sport manager must first make an assessment of the 'battle' conditions. They do this by studying the capacities and deficiencies of their own organization, competing organizations, stakeholder groups and the business environment – the battlefield. This first stage in the strategic management process is known as *Strategy Analysis*.

Next, and in light of the information obtained from the first stage, the sport manager must make some decisions about the future. These are typically concentrated into a 'mission' statement recording the purpose of the organization, a 'vision' statement of the organization's long-term ambitions, and a set of objectives with measures to identify the essential achievements along the way to the vision. This second stage of the strategic management process is called *Strategy Direction*.

Setting a direction only determines what an organization wants to achieve. In the next step, the sport manager must consider how the direction can be realized. This is the most creative part of the strategic management process. Here, the sport manager, and his or her team, must work together to imagine the best methods or strategies for the organization. At this time, the key challenge is to match the unique circumstances of the organization to the unique environmental conditions. When this is undertaken well, opportunities worth exploiting are found. This stage is called *Strategy Development*.

With a clear direction and a sharp idea of how that direction can be achieved, the task of the sport manager becomes one of implementation. It is at this point that the range of products, services and activities that the organization is engaged with, and the systems that support them, are adjusted in line with the overarching strategy that was developed in the previous step. This is known as the *Strategy Implementation* stage.

Finally, it is important to note that strategy is rarely perfect the first time around. Modifications are always essential. Mostly this means a minor adjustment to the way in which the strategy has been implemented. However, sometimes it does require a re-think about the suitability of the strategy itself. Neither of these can be successfully undertaken without some feedback in the first place about the success of what has been done. That is why the final stage in the strategic management process, *Strategy Evaluation*, is necessary. In this stage, the organization reviews whether objectives have been achieved. Most of the time, some corrective action will need to be taken. It is not unusual that the catalysts for these changes are unexpected events that affect the environment in which the sport organization operates. This necessitates a return to strategy analysis. In this sense, the strategic management process never stops. In fact, it is also quite normal to move back and forth between the stages in order to develop the best outcomes. The strategy process works best when management takes the view that it is not linear or discrete but rather a circular and continuing activity.

Stage 1: Strategic analysis

One of the biggest challenges facing sport managers is in combating the desire to set strategy immediately and to take action without delay. While a call to action is a natural inclination for motivated managers, many strategies can fail because what Dess and Lumpkin (2003) call the 'advance' work has not been done properly. This advance work entails a comprehensive review of the internal and external environments. The tools for doing this include 1) SWOT analysis; 2) stakeholder and customer needs analysis; 3) competitor analysis; and 4) the five forces analysis.

SWOT analysis

One of the basic tools in the environmental analysis is called the SWOT analysis. This form of analysis is used to examine an organization's strategic position, from the inside to the outside. The SWOT technique considers the strengths, weaknesses, opportunities and threats that an organization possesses or faces.

There are two parts to the SWOT analysis. The first part represents the internal analysis of an organization, which can be summarized by its *strengths* and *weaknesses*. This analysis covers everything that an organization has control over, some of which are performed well, and can be viewed as capabilities (strengths), while others are more difficult to do well, and can be seen as deficiencies (weaknesses). The second part of the SWOT technique is concerned with external factors; those which the organization has no direct control over. These are divided into *opportunities* and *threats*. In other words, issues and environmental circumstances arise that can either be exploited, or need to be neutralized.

The purpose of the SWOT technique is to find the major factors that are likely to play a role affecting the organization's direction and the success of its strategy. With this in mind, the sport manager should be looking for overarching issues. A good rule of thumb is to look for no more than five factors under each of the four headings. This way, the more important issues are given higher priority.

Given that the strengths and weaknesses part of the analysis is a consideration of what is inside the organization, it has a time-orientation in the present; what the organization does right now. Strengths can be defined as resources or capabilities that the organization can use to achieve its strategic direction. Common strengths may include committed coaching staff, a sound membership base or a good junior development programme. Weaknesses should be seen as limitations or inadequacies that will prevent or hinder the strategic direction from being achieved. Common weaknesses may include poor training facilities, inadequate sponsorship or a diminishing volunteer workforce.

In contrast, the opportunity and threats analysis also has a future-thinking dimension, because of the need to consider what is about to happen. Opportunities are favourable situations or events that can be exploited by the organization to enhance its circumstances or capabilities. Common opportunities tend to include new government grants, the identification of a new market or potential product, or the chance to appoint a new staff member with unique skills. Threats are unfavourable situations which could make it more difficult for the organization to achieve its strategic direction. Common threats include inflating player salaries, new competitors or unfavourable trends in the consumption of leisure such as the increased popularity of gaming consoles with young people.

Stakeholder and customer needs analysis

Before an analysis of the environment is complete, an assessment of the organization's stakeholders and customers is essential. Stakeholders are all the people and groups that have an interest in an organization, including its employees, players, members, league or affiliated governing body, government, community, facility-owners, sponsors, broadcasters and fans. The constant question that a sport manager has to answer is concerned with whom they are trying to make happy. Either deliberately or inadvertently serving the interests of some stakeholders in preference to others has serious implications for the setting of strategic direction and the distribution of limited resources. For example, some professional sport clubs tend to focus on winning at the exclusion of all other priorities, including sensible financial management. While this may make members and fans happy in the short term, it does not reflect the interests of governing bodies, leagues and employees, for whom a sustainable enterprise is fundamental.

Sponsors and government sport funding departments are prepared to withdraw funding if their needs are not met. A careful analysis of the intentions and objectives of each stakeholder in their affiliation with the sport organization must therefore be completed before a strategic direction can be set. The substance of strategy is influenced by the beliefs, values and expectations of the most powerful stakeholders.

Competitor analysis

Opportunities and threats can encompass anything in the external environment, including the presence and activities of competitors. Because the actions of competitors can greatly affect the success of a strategic approach, *competitor analysis* is used to ensure that an investigation is done systematically.

There are many forms of competitor analysis, and they can range in detail considerably. However, most competitor analyses consider the following dimensions, as summarized in Table 5.1. For each competitor, these eight dimensions should be considered. Time and care should be taken in assessing a competitor's strategies, their strengths, vulnerabilities and resources, as well as their next likely actions.

Five forces analysis

An extension of the competitive environment analysis is the *five forces analysis*, which was developed by Michael Porter (Figure 5.2). It is the

Table 5.1 Competitor analysis dimensions

Dimension	Description
Geographic Scope	Location and overlap
Vision and Intent	Ranges from survival to attempts at dominance
Objective	Short- to medium-term intentions
Market Share and Position	From small player to virtual monopolist
Strategy	Methods of gaining a competitive advantage
Resources	Volume and availability
Target Market	To whom the products and services are directed
Marketing Approach	The products, services and the promotions, pricing and distribution behind them

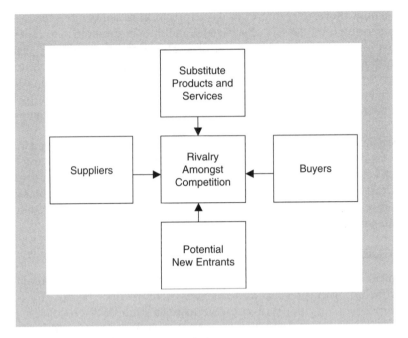

Figure 5.2 Five forces competitive analysis

most commonly used tool for describing the competitive environment. The technique does this by focusing upon five competitive forces (Porter, 1980).

The threat of new entrants: Every organization is faced with the possibility that new competitors could enter their industry at any time. In some forms of professional sport, this is unlikely as the barriers preventing entry are very high. For example, it would be extremely difficult for a private independent league to enter the market against any of the professional football leagues in Europe. On the other hand, new sport facilities, events, sport apparel companies and new equipment manufacturers are regular entrants in the sport industry.

The bargaining power of buyers: Buyers are those individuals, groups and companies that purchase the products and services that sport organizations offer. The nature of the competitive environment is affected by the strength or what is known as bargaining power of buyers. For example, most football fans in the UK hold little power, if the price of football tickets is an indication. When there is buying power, prices are lower. Despite some extravagant sums paid by broadcasters for the media rights of certain sports, the bargaining power of media buyers should be relatively strong. For most sport organizations, however, the chief buyers – fans – do not work together to leverage their power, and therefore the bargaining power of buyers is limited.

The bargaining power of suppliers: When suppliers of raw materials essential to sporting organizations threaten to raise prices or withdraw their products or services, they are attempting to improve their bargaining power. This may come from suppliers of the materials necessary in the building of a new facility or from sporting equipment suppliers. The most important supplier issue in sport has come about with the unionization of professional players in an attempt to increase their salaries and the salary caps of clubs. Where player groups have been well-organized, their bargaining power has proven significant. A potential strike in 2002 by players in Major League Baseball in the United States of America (USA) was avoided, but the failure to resolve a similar dispute has recently led to the cancellation of an entire season of the US National Hockey League.

The threat of substitute products and services: Increasingly, the traditional sport industry sectors are expanding, and it is more common for different sports to compete against each other. When this threat is high a sport organization is faced with the problem of being out-competed by other kinds of sports, or worse, by other forms of leisure activity.

The intensity of rivalry among competitors in an industry: The more sport organizations offering virtually identical products and services, the higher the intensity of rivalry. For example, in the sport shoe marketplace, the rivalry between Nike and Adidas is extremely intense. Rivalry is more ambiguous between sport clubs in the same league that share a general geographical region. London football clubs, Melbourne Australian football teams and colleges in the same state in the United States, are examples. In these cases, it is unlikely that one club would be able to 'steal' supporters from another local club. Nor is the alumnus of one college likely to start attending home games of another college team. However, these clubs do intensely compete for media exposure, corporate sponsorship, players, coaches, managers and management staff. Of course, they also compete with the most intense rivalry imaginable for the championship.

Case 5.2   SWOT analysis and the International Judo Federation

Like other sports that have emerged from a traditional or practical part of life, judo has faced many challenges in formulating strategy to enhance its global profile and participation. However, the International Judo Federation (IJF) has worked hard to find leverage points for its strategic goals. For example, the technical and organizational aspects of the sport have radically improved in the last decade, and the successful official inclusion of women's judo into the Olympics has been a major achievement.

To bolster the development of the sport and the achievement of its next set of objectives, the IJF has introduced a strategic management approach, including the establishment of a direction and vision. Furthermore, as part of the strategic analysis preceding the process, the IJF instituted an environmental audit. In this stage, the IJF recognized that with the new millennium and increased competition from other combat sports, they needed an honest assessment of their internal capabilities and deficiencies, as well as the external possibilities and obstacles they face. The result was a SWOT analysis, which is reproduced below. Each point is explained in sentence form to allow the reader to better appreciate the context of the essential point.

Strengths

1. Emphasizes both the physical and mental aspect.
2. As an indoor sport, judo can be practised throughout the year.
3. Judo is practised by all ages, men and women.
4. The diffusion of medals in judo is widespread.

Weaknesses

1. There is difficulty in understanding the rules of judo for the average spectator, and the winner can be hard to determine.
2. Financial weakness within the IJF due to a lack of commercial support.
3. Large differences in technical abilities amongst the Continental Unions and National Federations.
4. Underdeveloped nations have no means of obtaining corporate sponsorships.

Opportunities

1. Opportunities for the promotion and development of judo due to its Olympic status.
2. Opportunities due to the worldwide trend in health consciousness and spirituality.
3. Opportunity to promote stars at a top level of competition.
4. Support of government and the Olympic Movement to become a part of the education system.

Threats

1. Limited media exposure.
2. Possibility of elimination as an Olympic sport.
3. The decline in popularity within nations which do not perform well in tournaments.
4. To the lay spectator it is hard to distinguish between judo and other combat sports due to their similarities.

Stage 2: Strategic direction

Once the strategic analysis has been completed, the strategic direction can be set. There are four conventional tools that are used to clarify and document this direction: 1) mission statement; 2) vision statement; 3) organizational objectives; and 4) performance measures.

Mission statements

A *mission statement* identifies the purpose of an organization. While it may seem strange to need to put this in writing, such a statement is important because it reduces the risk of strategic confusion. For example, it is not uncommon for players, members, spectators, staff, coaches, media, sponsors and government representatives to hold different interpretations of the purpose of a sport organization. The mission statement should define why an organization was set up, what services and products it provides, and for whom it provides them. When reduced to a single statement, this mission is a powerful statement of intention and responsibility. It usually does not exceed one paragraph.

Vision statements

It goes without saying that behind the idea of setting a strategic direction is the need to be visionary: to look into the future and form a clear mental image of what an organization could be like. Thinking in this manner means being able to interpret the information collected during the analysis stage and find the opportunities they present. A *vision statement* is the culmination of this kind of thinking. It is a statement that declares the medium to long-range ambitions of an organization. The statement is an expression of what the organization wants to have achieved within a period of around three to five years. The statement is normally no longer than a sentence.

Organizational objectives

Given that the vision statement is a reflection of the medium to long-term ambitions of an organization, *organizational objectives* serve as markers on the way to this destination. Objectives reflect the achievements that must be made in order to realize the vision. For example, if a club is situated at the bottom of the championship ladder, their vision might be to finish in the top three. However, achieving this vision inside a single season is unrealistic, so an objective might be set to indicate the ambition to improve by three places by next season, as a progression toward the overarching vision. Objectives are normally set in each of the major operational areas of an organization, such as on-field performance, youth development, finances, facilities, marketing and human resources. However, it is essential that objectives are measurable.

Performance measures

Key Performance Indicators (KPIs) are used in combination with organizational objectives in order to establish success or failure. KPIs are therefore inseparable from objectives and should be created at the same time. Each time a performance measure is used, care should be taken to ensure that it can indeed be measured in a concrete way. For example, a marketing objective of 'improving the public image' of an organization is meaningless unless it is accompanied by something that is quantifiable. It is worth noting that measures do not have to focus exclusively on outputs like volumes, rankings and trophies. They can also be used to measure efficiency; that is, doing the same with less or doing more with the same.

Case 5.3   The Australian Sport Commission Strategic Plan 2002–2005

The Australian Sport Commission (ASC) manages the deployment of government resources for elite development and participation in sport in Australia. The ASC developed a plan detailing its strategic intentions up until the period 2005. Parts of this plan are reproduced below to allow the reader to see how a large and successful sport organization has recorded some of its strategic decisions. This plan and other useful planning examples can be found at http://www.ausport.gov.au/publications/ascstrat.asp.

Our mission

To enrich the lives of all Australians through sport.

Our vision

To continue to be recognized as the world leader in developing high performance and community sport.

Our stakeholders

Our stakeholders include:

- The Australian community;
- Our people;
- Employees and contractors;
- AIS scholarship holders, their families and coaches;
- Government;
- The Minister;
- Federal, state and local government;
- Other Federal Government agencies;
- The sports sector;
- National sporting organizations;
- Sporting clubs and associations;
- Athletes and sports participants of all ages and capabilities;
- Coaches, administrators and volunteers;
- Officials and referees;
- The sports industry;
- The media;
- Australian and international sports bodies;
- Countries in receipt of Australian sport development assistance.

Our objectives

Our mission will be achieved through key objectives which seek:

1. To secure an effective national sports system that offers improved participation in quality sports activities by Australians.
2. To secure excellence in sports performance by Australians.

Objective 1

An effective national sports system that offers improved participation in quality sports activities by Australians.

Critical result areas

1. Greater grass-roots sports participation, particularly by youth, indigenous Australians and people with disabilities.
2. Increased sports participation, particularly in rural and regional communities.
3. Increased membership and reach of local sporting clubs.
4. Best practice management and governance of sport within and through national sporting organizations.
5. Increased adoption of values of fair play, self improvement and achievement.
6. Recruitment, retention and, where appropriate, accreditation of people within the sports sector.
7. Improved economic efficiency within and commercial return to the ASC and national sporting organizations.

Strategies

1. Through Active Australia Partnerships, develop and implement targeted initiatives that encourage national sporting organizations to expand the membership, reach, business capability and sustainability of grass-roots clubs and associations.
2. Through Active Australia Partnerships, provide more effective pathways for participation by all Australians especially young and indigenous people, women and people with disabilities.
3. Encourage best practice in the management of Australia's national sporting organizations by providing leadership, funding, support, consultancy services, information, education and training, and business tools that promote improved efficiency, effectiveness and outcomes.
4. Continue to develop and make available education and accreditation programmes that assist national sporting organizations to recruit and retain administrators, coaches, officials and volunteers.
5. Ensure that national sporting organizations embrace the values of fair play and implement policies and guidelines to ensure a quality sport experience for all participants.

6. Demonstrate leadership and act as a role model in the development of initiatives to increase sources of and opportunities for non-government funding.
7. Encourage contestability and a higher level of commercial activity on the part of national sporting organizations, the ASC and its facilities.

Stage 3: Strategy formulation

Strategic analysis reveals the competitive position of a sport organization and setting the strategic direction plots a course for the future. The next question is how to get there. In the strategy formulation stage of the strategic management process, the sport manager and his or her team are charged with the task of positioning their organization in the competitive environment. This necessitates a combination of imagination and scenario thinking. In other words, they must consider the implications of each potential strategic approach. To help matters, however, from a strategic positioning viewpoint there are a finite number of strategies available to the sport manager. These are called *generic competitive strategies*.

Generic competitive strategies

Porter (1985) contended that there are only three fundamental or generic strategies that can be applied in any organization, irrespective of their industry, products and services, environmental circumstances and resources. Generic competitive strategies answer the most basic of questions facing a sport manager in forming a strategic choice: What is going to be our source of *competitive advantage*? To put it another way, every sport organization must take a position somewhere in the marketplace. The challenge is to find a position that is both opportune *and* advantageous. As a result, some sport organizations try to out-compete their adversaries because they can provide their products and services cheaper; others compete on the basis of a unique product or service that is hard for others to replicate; others still attempt to position themselves as the exclusive supplier to a small but loyal niche in the marketplace. These three strategic positions are described below:

Cost leadership: To become a cost leader by supplying products and services at the lowest possible cost to as many customers as possible. The logic of this strategic approach is driven by volume and market share where more sales than any other competitors lead to greater profitability. Essential to this generic competitive strategy is efficiency and the ability to keep costs to a minimum. While this approach is common in consumer products like shampoo, it is less common in sport. However, some equipment and sport apparel manufacturers do provide their products at the cheap end of the market in the hope that they can significantly outsell their more expensive competitors. Similarly, many leisure facilities try to attract customers on the basis of their lower prices.

Differentiation: To provide a differentiated set of products and services that is difficult for competitors to replicate. The logic of this strategic approach is underpinned by an assumption that consumers will place a high value on products and services that are unique. Typically, this approach is supported by an attempt to build a strong brand image, incorporate regular innovations and new features, as well as responsive customer service. Many sport organizations are thrown into this position almost by default because of the nature of their offerings. A tennis club, for example, offers a range of services that are by definition differentiated, at least when compared to other sports or leisure activities. However, when two tennis clubs compete in a similar area, it may become necessary for one to take a new strategic position. One option is to further differentiate their services, perhaps by offering something new or innovative like a creche for mid-week players or a gym for conditioning the more seriously competitive players.

Focus: To provide a set of products and services to a niche in the market with the intention of dominating market share. The logic guiding this strategic approach is that being dominant in a small section of a larger market is a way for an organization to have early success, without having to compete with much larger and better resourced organizations. To succeed with this strategic approach it is necessary to choose the market segment very carefully, aware that the products and services provided must fill particular needs in customers very well. Many sport organizations take this approach as well. Examples include specialist sport equipment and less mainstream sport clubs and associations like rock climbing and table tennis.

The key to making a decision between these alternatives returns to the analysis and direction stages of the strategic management process. A strategy-savvy sport manager is always looking for a way to position the organization in a cluttered market. Part of the choice is in determining what the sport organization is likely to be able to do better than others – their competitive advantage (like keeping costs low or delivering great customer service). The other part is in finding the opportunity in the environment that is worth exploring. Where there is a match between these factors consistent with strategic direction, strategic formulation is born. It is worth remembering that the worst place to be is 'stuck in the middle' between strategies, but that combining strategic options can be advantageous if managed effectively.

Stage 4: Strategy implementation

Strategy implementation represents the introduction of the organization's choice of competitive strategy. For example, if a differentiation strategy has been selected, the implementation stage considers how it can be brought about across the organization's products, services and activities. There is an important distinction to be made here between the strategic level of decision-making and the implementation level. To return to the military analogy, strategy is concerned with how a whole army is deployed. At the implementation level, tactical and operational decisions are made as well. These are like the choices of what each battalion does and what each unit or platoon does, respectively. Always the overarching goal is a reflection of the army's objectives, but each smaller part of the army works towards smaller achievements that will eventually bring about success in the battle.

Once decisions have been finalized concerning the strategy that will be employed to achieve organizational objectives, the task of converting them into action begins. This means that representatives from each major area or department of the organization must become involved in deciding how they can contribute toward the generic strategy. For example, if one objective in a club is concerned with on-field performance, it is likely that the leaders of the developmental programmes will play a role in planning. Equally, an objective associated with financial performance will require marketing staff responsible for sponsorship to become involved. As a result, the strategy implementation process should permeate the organization including junior development, community liaison, coaching, facilities, governance, marketing, finance and human resources, for example. In each of these areas a plan should be developed that illustrates the set of activities that will be performed at the tactical and operational levels to support the generic strategy. Like objectives, each of these actions requires a measure or KPI of some sort. Often the implementation process also requires changes to resource allocation, organizational structure, systems for delivering products and services, organizational culture and leadership. These areas are considered in subsequent chapters.

Stage 5: Strategic evaluation

One of the more difficult aspects of strategic management is the control or evaluation of what has been done. In sport there are numerous issues that make this process more complicated including the obvious one that on-field performance can have a tendency to overwhelm the other elements of strategy. Chapter 11 Performance Management considers these important issues in detail.

The *strategic evaluation* stage requires an assessment of two related aspects of the strategy. First, the KPIs associated with each organizational objective need to be compared with actual results, and second, the success of the implementation actions needs to be ascertained.

Summary of principles

This chapter is concerned with the process of strategic management. This process is founded on the principle that opportunity is discovered by analysis rather than luck. Strategic management, we have argued, is therefore at the heart of the success of a sport organization.

Five stages in the strategic management process have been identified. The first stage is strategy analysis, which demands the assessment of both internal organizational capacities as well as external environmental conditions. The second stage is strategy direction, which sets the vision and objectives of an organization. The third stage is strategy formulation, where a definitive strategic position is selected for an organization. The fourth stage is strategy implementation, where the strategy is directed to action across organizational areas. The final stage, strategy evaluation, involves the control and measurement of the process so that improvements can be made.

Strategic management in sport organizations requires preparation, research and analysis, imagination, critical thinking and decision-making. It demands an equal balance of systematization and innovation. This chapter is weighted heavily toward the system side, but that is simply a necessity to convey the principles and techniques of strategic management. It is up to the reader to provide the imagination in their own strategic management activities.

Review questions

1. Why is strategic management important in the turbulent world of sport?
2. What is the basic principle that underpins strategic management?
3. Name the five stages of strategic management.
4. In what ways might strategic management be troublesome in sport organizations compared to corporations?
5. What is the relationship between a SWOT analysis and competitor analysis?
6. How do stakeholders influence the setting of strategic direction?
7. Explain the differences between a focus strategy and a differentiation strategy.
8. What is the relationship between KPIs and strategy evaluation?
9. Select a sport organization that has a strategic plan on its website. Conduct an analysis of this plan, and comment on its approach to each of the five steps of strategic management explained in this chapter.
10. Select a sport organization that you know well and that does not have a strategic plan available. Based on your background knowledge, make point form comments under the headings of the five steps in strategic management to illustrate your approach to forming a plan.

Further reading

Chappelet, J.L. (2005). *Strategic and Performance Management of Olympic Sport Organizations*. Human Kinetics Publishers Inc., Champaign, Illinois, US.

Kaplan, R.S. & D.P. Norton. (2001). *The Strategy-focused Organization*. Harvard Business School Press.

Porter, M. (1985). *Competitive Strategy: Creating and Sustaining Superior Performance*. Simon & Schuster, New York.

Whittington, R. (2001). *What is Strategy and Does it Matter?* London: Routledge.

Relevant websites

The following websites are useful starting points for further information on strategic management:

* For sport planning at Sport England:
  http://www.sportengland.org/index/get_resources/resource_ps.htm.
* For 'Game plan: A strategy for delivering government's sport and physical activity objectives'
  http://www.sportdevelopment.org.uk/html/gameplan.html.
* For Sport Canada: http://www.pch.gc.ca/progs/sc/index_e.cfm

Chapter 6

Organizational structure

Overview

The study of organizational structure has spawned a large number of textbooks devoted to explaining the minutiae of organizational structure, its impact on performance, theories of employee behaviour linked to structure and design, and what are the drivers of change in relation to organizational structure. Rather than replicate existing material, this chapter attempts to highlight the unique aspects of the structure of sports organizations. Consequently, this chapter reviews the key concepts of organizational structure, provides examples of the unique features of how sport organizations are structured, and summarizes the key research findings on the structure of sport organizations. The chapter also provides a summary of principles for managing organizational structures within community, state, national and professional sport organizations.

After completing this chapter the reader should be able to:

- Describe the key dimensions of organizational structure;
- Understand the unique features of the structure of sport organizations;
- Understand the various models of organization structure that can be used for sports organizations;
- Identify the factors that influence the structure of sport organizations; and
- Understand some of the challenges facing managers and volunteers involved in managing the structure of sport organizations.

What is organizational structure?

An organizational structure is the framework that outlines how tasks are divided, grouped and coordinated within an organization (Robbins et al., 2004). Every sport organization has a structure that outlines the tasks to be performed by individuals and teams. Finding the 'right' structure for an organization involves juggling requirements to formalize procedures whilst fostering innovation and creativity. Finding the 'right' structure ensures adequate control of employee activities without unduly affecting people's motivation and attitudes to work, and it clarifies reporting and communication lines while trying to reduce unnecessary and costly layers of management.

An organization's structure is important because it defines where staff and volunteers 'fit in' with each other in terms of work tasks, decision-making procedures, the need for collaboration, levels of responsibility and reporting mechanisms. In other words, the structure of an organization provides a roadmap for how positions within an organization are related and what tasks are performed by individuals and work teams within an organization.

Dimensions of organizational structure

When designing any organization's structure, managers need to consider six elements: work specialization, departmentalization, chain of command, the span of control, centralization and formalization (Robbins et al., 2004).

Work specialization

Creating roles for individuals that enable them to specialize in performing a limited number of tasks is known as work specialization. This concept can easily be applied in organizations that manufacture things such as sporting goods, or need to process a large volume of resources such as distributing uniforms and information to volunteers for a large sporting event. The advantage of breaking jobs down to a set of routine repetitive tasks is an increase in employee productivity and reduced costs for a lower skilled labour force. This advantage must be balanced against the risks of making work too boring or stressful for individuals which can lead to accidents, poor quality, lower productivity, absenteeism and high job turnover.

The majority of sports organizations do not have large numbers of staff, and staff are often required to perform a diversity of tasks over a day, week or year. In these cases, the structure of the organization will require a low level of work specialization. A good example would be a sport development officer for a state or provincial sporting organization whose role may involve conducting skills clinics with junior athletes, designing coach education courses, managing a database of casual staff, or representing the organization to sponsors or funding agencies. These roles require very different skill sets and in such an organization the structure would benefit from a low level of work specialization.

Departmentalization

Departmentalization is the bringing together of individuals into groups so that common or related tasks can be coordinated. In essence, people are assigned to departments in order to achieve organizational goals. Organizations can departmentalize on the basis of functions, products or services, processes, geography or customer type.

The most common form of departmentalizing is based on assigning people or positions to various departments according to the function a person may perform. For example, a state or provincial sporting organization might group their staff according to athlete development, competition management, special events and corporate affairs departments, with each department having a very specific function to perform.

Alternatively, a sport organization that manufactures cricket equipment may group their staff according to the product line they produce with groups of people handling the manufacturing, sales and service for cricket apparel, cricket bats, and training aids. In this case, the functions of marketing, human resource management, financial management and production are all replicated in each department. These criteria can also be applied to service-based sport organizations. For example, an athlete management firm may offer a range of services under financial planning, career development, life skills and public relations training. Again each department would manage their own marketing, human resource management, and financial management systems.

Sport organizations can also design departments on the basis of geography. For example, the operations for a sports law firm may be split into departments for capital city offices or regions. Each of the offices or regions would have responsibility in regard to their operations in a designated geographical region. Finally, sport organizations can arrange their departments on the basis of their various customer types. This approach could be used by an organization like the Australian Institute of Sport creating departments that support individual athletes or team sports.

It is important to note that organizations may choose to use more than one criterion to devise departments and their choice will depend on organizational size, capabilities and operational requirements.

Chain of command

The chain of command is the reporting trail that exists between the upper and lower levels of an organization. In essence it is the line of authority that connects each position within an organization to the Chief Executive.

It encompasses the notions of establishing clear authority and responsibility for each position within the organization. Authority refers to the rights managers have to give orders to other members in the organization and the expectation that the orders will be carried out. If managers at certain levels of an organization are provided with the authority to get things done, they are also assigned a corresponding level of responsibility. Having a single person to whom an employee is responsible is known as the unity of command. Having a single 'boss' avoids employees having to deal with potential conflict when juggling the demands of two or more managers and it helps clarify clear decision-making.

Robbins et al. (2004) argue that the basic tenets of the chain of command are less relevant today due to the increase in use of information technology, and the corresponding ease with which most employees can communicate with each other at all levels of the organization and access information that was previously restricted to top level managers. Nevertheless, managers of sports organizations should be cognizant of the basic principle of the chain of command when designing their organizational structure.

Span of control

Span of control refers to the number of staff which any manager can directly supervise without becoming inefficient or ineffective. The exact number which any manager can effectively control is determined by the level of expertise or experience of the staff – the logic being that more experienced and skilled staff require less supervision. The complexity of tasks, the location of staff, the reporting mechanisms in place, the degree to which tasks are standardized, the style of managers and the culture of an organization also play a role in determining what the ideal span of control might be for an individual manager in an organization. The span of control impacts on how many levels of management are required in any given organization. The wider the span of control, the more employees can be supervised by one manager which leads to lower management costs. However, this reduced cost is a trade off with effectiveness as this single manager must devote more of his or her time to liaison and communication with a large number of staff.

The trend over the past 10 years has been for organizations to introduce wider spans of control and a subsequent flattening of organizational structures. This must be done in conjunction with providing more employee training, commitment to building strong work cultures and assisting staff to be more self-sufficient in their roles.

Centralization and decentralization

Centralization refers to the degree to which decision-making is located at the top of an organization. An organization is deemed to be highly centralized when the majority of decisions are made by senior managers with little input from employees at lower levels. Alternatively, an organization is decentralized when decisions are able to be made by employees and lower level managers who have been empowered to do so. Robbins et al. (2004) makes the important point that the concepts of centralization and decentralization are relative, an organization is never exclusively one or the other. Organizations could not function if all decisions were made by a small group of top managers or if all decisions were delegated to lower level staff.

Nonprofit sport organizations tend to be more centralized than decentralized due to the influence of their traditional structures. Decision-making is often concentrated at the board level, where volunteers make decisions related to strategy for paid staff to implement at an operational level. This can lead to problems (see Chapter 10) of slow decision-making or politics. On the other hand, the nature of nonprofit sport organizations that are often made up of disparate groups, spread over a wide geographical area, requires local level decision-making to make clubs, events, and sporting competitions operate effectively.

Formalization

Formalization refers to the extent jobs are standardized and the degree to which employee behaviour is guided by rules and procedures. These rules and procedures might cover selection of new staff, training, general policies on how work is done, procedures for routine tasks, and the amount of detail that is provided in job descriptions. Formalizing an organization increases the control managers have over staff and the amount of decision-making discretion individual staff may have. An organization such as a local sport club may have very few procedures or rules for how things are done, but the tribunal for a professional sports league will have a very detailed set of procedures and policies in regard to how cases are reported, heard and prosecuted.

Netball Victoria uses a typical nonprofit sport organizational structure. The core concepts of work specialization, departmentalization, chain of command, the span of control, centralization and formalization are reflected in its structure.

Case 6.1   Netball Victoria

Netball Victoria (NV) is the State Sporting Organization responsible for the management and development of netball across Victoria, one of the major states of Australia. Netball is the largest female participation sport in Australia and has more than 110 000 registered participants in Victoria. NV provides a range of programmes and services for netball players, coaches, umpires, administrators, associations and clubs with the aim of increasing and enhancing participation experiences. NV manages a variety of programmes for the development of players, coaches, umpires and administrators including accreditation courses, special interest clinics and workshops. In addition to facilitating participation opportunities, NV holds the license for the two Victorian teams that compete in the Commonwealth Bank Trophy (the national league) – Melbourne Phoenix and Melbourne Kestrels. As such NV is responsible for the management and marketing of the teams, and staging the Commonwealth Bank Trophy games in liaison with Netball Australia. NV also has the opportunity to host or tender for a range of National and International events including National Championships, International Series, World Youth Cup and World Championships.

More than 250 associations or groups affiliate with Netball Victoria which provides access to netball events, programmes and services as well as a pathway to State, National and International representation. These Associations are geographically grouped into one of twenty-one (21) Regions, and then Regions are grouped into one of six (6) Zones. A team of 30 staff work with a board of management and an extensive network of volunteers to deliver these programmes, services and events across Victoria. The organizational structure for the state office staff developed by NV to enable this to happen is presented in Figure 6.1.

Note that the structure is based around the key functional departments of marketing, development, association services, high performance and finances and administration. Each of these departments has a designated manager, meaning the Chief Executive has a span of control of 5 staff. Each of the department managers in turn has between 2 and 4 staff under their control. The structure allows individuals to be appointed to carry out specialized tasks and for the establishment of a clear chain of command between the lower levels of the organization and the Chief Executive. To judge the degree to which NV is centralized or formalized, you should visit the NV website at www.netballvic.com.au.

Sources: Netball Victoria website at http://www.netballvic.com.au/

Structural models

The types of structure adopted by sports organizations can be categorized into four common types: simple structure, the bureaucracy, the matrix structure, and the team structure (Robbins et al., 2004). Let's examine each of these briefly and what is their relevance for sport organizations (Figures 6.2–6.5) .

The simple structure has a low degree of departmentalization and formalization, wide spans of control, and would most likely have decisions centralized to few people. Such a structure would be used by a small sporting goods retail store that might have 10 casual and full time staff and an owner/manager. There would be no need for departments, as most decisions and administrative tasks would be performed by the owner/manager and all other staff on the sales floor. The majority of procedures would be execcuted according to a simple set of rules and the owner/manager would have all staff reporting directly to him or her. The advantages of the structure in this case are obvious: decisions can be made quickly, it ensures a flexible workforce to cater for seasonal needs and busy periods, and accountability clearly rests with the owner/manager.

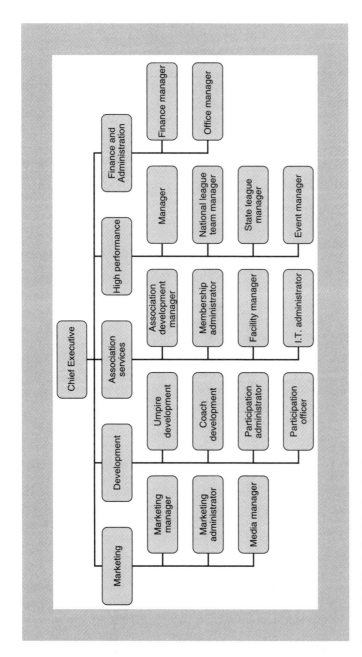

Figure 6.1 Netball Victoria structure

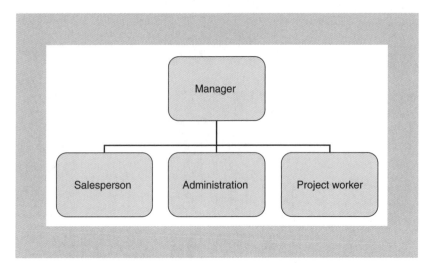

Figure 6.2 Simple structure

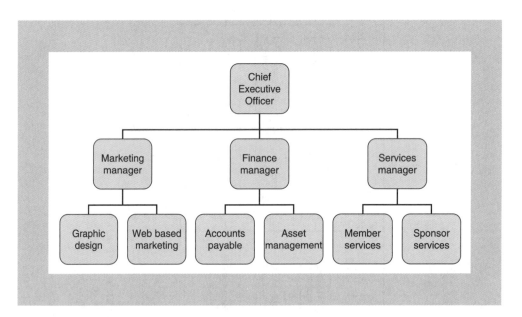

Figure 6.3 The bureaucratic structure

If the owner/manager wanted to expand the operation and open other stores in other locations, he or she would require a different structure to cope with the added demands of controlling staff in multiple locations, making decisions across a wider number of operational areas, and ensuring quality products and services are provided in each store or location. The owner/manager might consider adopting a bureaucratic structure.

The bureaucratic structure attempts to standardize the operation of an organization in order to maximize coordination and control of staff and

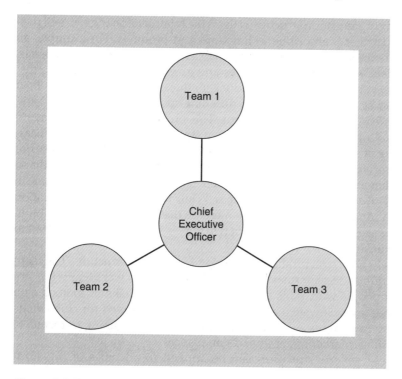

Figure 6.4 Team structure

	Football operations division	Corporate services division	Marketing division
Team 1	Manager 1	Project worker 1	Worker 1
Team 2	Manager 2	Project worker 2	Worker 2
Team 3	Manager 3	Project worker 3	Worker 3

Figure 6.5 The matrix structure

activities. It relies on high levels of formalization, the use of departments to group people into discrete work teams that deal with specific functions or tasks, highly centralized decision-making and a clear chain of command. An organization such as Sport England, the Australian Sports Commission, or a state or provincial government department of sport would be structured along these lines. Obviously, as an organization expands in size, increases the number of locations it delivers services, or diversifies its range of activities, the more likely it is to reflect some elements of bureaucratization.

The matrix organization structure reflects the organization of groups of people into departments according to functions and products. For example, an elite institute for sport might group specialists such as sports psychologists, biomechanists, skill acquisition coaches and exercise physiologists into discrete teams. At the same time, individuals in these teams might be involved in providing services to a range of different sporting groups or athletes, effectively creating two bosses for them. This breaks the unity of command principle but allows an organization to group specialists together to maximize sharing of expertise while facilitating their involvement in a number of projects or service delivery areas. The argument for this arrangement is that it is better to have the specialists work as a team than to appoint individuals to work in isolation to provide their services. While this allows the organization to provide a range of services, it does increase the potential for confusion in regard to managing the demands from two bosses, which in turn may lead to an increase in stress.

A relatively new structural design option is the team structure. The team structure requires decision-making to be decentralized to work teams that are made up of people with skills to perform a variety of tasks. A football club franchise might employ such a structure with teams formed for club events or marketing campaigns as it will allow quick decision-making in regard to finance, staffing, marketing, or impacts on players.

While these generic structures can be applied to all types of organizations, there has been some research that has attempted to categorize the various structures that exist within nonprofit sport organizations. Kikulis et al. (1989) developed a structural taxonomy for provincial (state) Canadian amateur sport organizations based on the organizational dimensions of specialization, standardization and centralization. The evolution of Canadian sport organizations in the 1980s to a more professional and bureaucratized form prompted the researchers to attempt to establish exactly what form this evolution had taken. Kikulis et al. (1989) identified eight structural designs for voluntary sport organizations, ranging in scale of complexity for the three structural dimensions. Theodoraki and Henry (1994), in a similar study defined a typology of structures for British sport governing bodies. They too utilized the structural elements of specialization, standardization and centralization to distinguish between various structural designs.

Identifying design types for national level sport organizations was the focus of a study by Kikulis et al. (1992) who used organizational values and organizational structure dimensions to identify three distinct designs – kitchen table, boardroom and executive office. Each design represents a distinct mix of organizational values comprising their orientation toward private or public interests; the domain of activities conducted (ranging from broad participation based to a focus on high performance results); the degree of professional involvement in decision-making; and the criteria used to evaluate effectiveness.

Now that we have explored what are the elements of structure and the various ways they can be used, we can examine the factors that influence the structure adopted by a sport organization.

What influences the structure of a sport organization?

There are generally four factors that influence the structure of an organization: strategy, size, technology and environmental uncertainty. Each of these is briefly reviewed.

Strategy

In a perfect world, an organization's structure would be designed purely around the requirement to maximize the chances of an organization's strategic goals being achieved. This is rarely possible, but strategy does play a important part in determining the structure adopted by a sport organization. Whether an organization is pursuing an overall strategy of innovation, cost minimization, or imitation would necessitate the design of a specific organizational structure (Robbins et al., 2004).

An important trend to note in the development of structure for nonprofit sport organizations has been the impact of the introduction of paid professional staff, a very deliberate strategy in response to increases in government funding in sport in most club based sporting systems around the world. The impact of such a strategy on the structure of Canadian provincial VSOs was explored by Thibault et al. (1991). They found that specialization and formalization increased after the introduction of professional staff, but that centralization, after initially increasing, actually decreased over time. It was suggested that centralization increased because volunteer board members sought to retain control over decisions, and then decreased as the relationship between board members and staff stabilized. Such resistance to changes in structure were noted by Kikulis et al. (1995) who studied the changes in specialization, standardization and centralization of Canadian NSOs over a four year period. They found that incumbent volunteers resisted change across all three elements of organizational structure, highlighting the role of human agents and personal choice in determining organizational change outcomes.

Size

The size of an organization also plays an important part in the determination of what will be its best possible structure. Larger organizations tend to be more formalized, with more specialist roles and departments and more levels of management than smaller organizations. This makes sense as managers need to implement greater control measures to manage the volume and communication of information in a large organization. Amis and Slack (1996) state that much of the research into the relationship between organizational size and degree of centralization suggest that as 'organizations become larger, decision-making becomes more decentralized' (p. 83). In terms of nonprofit sport organizations they also found that with an increase in size of the organization, control over organizational decision-making remains at the voluntary board level and they concluded that a 'central role of decision-making as a means of control and the desire for volunteers to retain this control' (Amis & Slack, 1996, p. 84) meant that the boards of many sport organizations were reluctant to relinquish control to professional staff.

Technology

Technology does have an impact on organizational structure. Robbins et al. (2004) argue that if organizations predominantly undertake routine tasks then there is a high degree of departmentalization, and a high level of centralized decision-making. This would appear to be logical because non-routine tasks would require decisions to be made at the level of organization where they actually happen. In regard to a sport organization such as a professional sport club, the increased use of information and communication technology would seem to require additional specialist staff such as video technicians, statisticians, and network programmers who may have replaced staff that used to perform tasks manually. The net effect is a higher level of departmentalization and specialization amongst the workforce.

Environmental uncertainty

Environmental uncertainty for sport organizations can be influenced by the actions of suppliers, service providers, customers, sponsors, athletes, volunteers, staff, stakeholder groups, government regulatory agencies, as well as general changes in economic or market conditions. For example, if a group of professional athletes behave inappropriately, their actions can affect the ability of their club or team to maintain or develop sponsorships, which in turn may affect their ability to retain staff and hence require a structural adjustment. Similarly, a downturn in the economy can directly affect sales of sporting merchandise, and organizations may have to adjust their structure accordingly to reduce costs or change product lines.

The case of the Hong Kong Sports Institute Limited highlights how the four generic factors of strategy, size, technology and environmental uncertainty can influence the structure of a sports organization.

Case 6.2   Hong Kong Sports Institute Limited

The Hong Kong Sports Institute Limited (HKSI) was created on 1 October, 2004 when its predecessor, the Hong Kong Sports Development Board (HKSDB), was dissolved. The HKSI performs a similar role to equivalent organizations such as the Australian Institute of Sport or Sport England in managing the training and development of elite athletes. The objectives of the HKSI are to provide an environment for elite athletes in Hong Kong to excel at international level through the provision of coaching, sports science, management and education services and to promote interest in elite sport.

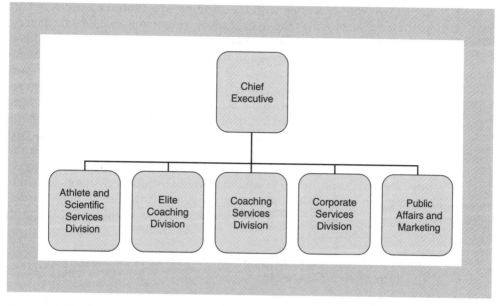

Figure 6.6 The Hong Kong Sports Institute structure

The HKSI splits its service delivery between two categories of sports: Elite Sports which have individual athletes or teams with realistic opportunities to win medals in international competitions, and Development Sports where athletes have demonstrated potential to produce significant performances in the international arena. Elite Sports receive guaranteed funding from the HKSI on a four year cycle and includes sports such as athletics, badminton, cycling, fencing, rowing, squash, swimming, table tennis, tennis, tenpin bowling, triathlon, windsurfing and wushu. The funding extends to providing world-class coaching staff, access to facilities, local and overseas training and competition and full technical support. Development Sports received targeted funding for individual athletes to further their prospects of international success. The HKSI also provides elite athletes with disabilities with support on facilities, training, coaching and funding.

The HKSI is a government-owned enterprise, controlled by an appointed group of 13 prominent individuals in the Hong Kong sports industry who fill positions on a Board of Directors. The Board has five standing committees in areas such as elite athlete affairs, finance committee, operations and planning, marketing and sponsorship, and fundraising. The management structure for the paid staff is presented below. The staff are split into five departments with responsibilities for athlete and scientific services, coaching of athletes, coach development, corporate services, and marketing.

In terms of the four contingency factors that have impacted on the structure of the organization, the most obvious one is strategy. The HKSI has a very clear mandate to deliver services and coaching for elite athletes and to raise the profile of elite athletes in Hong Kong. Accordingly the structure reflects these core functions with the addition of a central corporate affairs department that provides the usual human resource management, finance, information technology and administration support to facilitate the delivery of core services. An increase in the number of Elite Sports or athletes supported would not necessarily lead to a change in structure, rather each department would simply expand to cater for the increased service requirements. Similarly, the HKSI is well placed to utilize improvements or changes in technology with a dedicated information technology department and sports science group. As a government-owned enterprise, its structure is in part determined by its mandate to deliver services to a discrete group in the sports industry, and is unlikely to be unduly affected by environmental uncertainty. The drivers of change in structure would include any significant shifts in strategy or client group, such as a move to also promote mass participation in community sport, which would require a significant redesign in organizational structure.

Source: Hong Kong Sports Institute Limited website at
    http://www.hksi.org.hk

There are some additional drivers of structural change in sport organizations that are worth noting. These include poor on-field performance, changes in personnel due to politics, competition and market forces, government policy changes, and forced change via mergers and amalgamations. Poor on-field performance by professional sporting teams or clubs can lead to an end of season purge of playing or coaching personnel, and may entail a review of how the group of staff involved in coaching, athlete support or allied health services is organized. The political nature of some sport organizations that elect individuals to govern their activities can lead to structural change being implemented due to personal preferences of elected leaders or a mandate for change. Competition and market forces affect all organizations, but the interdependent nature of clubs operating within a league or competition necessitates them sharing information. Consequently, these organizations tend to be structured in similar ways, making structural change difficult. Governments may also change the way they fund high performance programmes or tie funding levels to the performances of international teams or individuals. Poor international performances may consequently reduce funding and therefore the capability of an organization to sustain their organizational structure. Finally, structural change may be forced upon sports organizations, either by economic conditions (such as population loss in rural areas forcing clubs to merge) or government policy (such as forcing single gender sport organizations to merge).

Challenges for sport managers

An ongoing challenge facing sport managers is the need to strike a balance between lowering costs by using fewer staff and increasing productivity.

This can be achieved through a greater use of technology for communication, data management and analysis, the appointment of skilled staff able to use technology, and the development of semi-autonomous work teams who are able to make operational decisions quickly. This requires the use of a more flexible organizational structure than perhaps is the norm for the majority of sport organizations today.

A further challenge for sport managers is to ensure that their organizations are flexible enough to quickly react to opportunities in the market or to the demands of their stakeholders while at the same time maintaining adequate forms of control and accountability. Sport managers will need to establish clear guidelines for decision-making and acceptable levels of formalization for standard procedures without unduly constraining the flexibility to modify those guidelines and formal procedures.

An aspect of managing organizational structures that is relatively unique to sport is the presence of both paid staff and volunteers, often with volunteers directing the work of paid staff. Sport managers will need to be cognizant of the need to maintain close links between these two significant parts of their workforce and maintain a suitable structure that allows these groups to communicate effectively and work to achieve organizational outcomes.

Sport managers also need to ensure the structure can enable strategy to be realized. If strategic plans are devised, new markets identified, or new product and service offerings developed in the absence of concomitant changes to the organizational structure, then the ability of the organization to deliver such planned changes is questionable. It is imperative that sport managers pay attention to designing their structure to enable specific strategic directions to be achieved.

As illustrated in the previous chapters, organizations that work within the sport industry must work within a myriad of other organizations from the public, private and nonprofit sectors. Often, sport organizations have many stakeholders involved in setting the strategic direction of the organization. The organizational structure should therefore facilitate decision-making processes that engage all relevant stakeholders.

Finally, the interdependent relationships that exist between sports organizations that may be involved in a league, a collection of associations, a joint venture, or a funding agreement with multiple partners and sponsors, necessitates organizational structures that reflect these connections. This may extend to establishing designated roles for external liaison within the structure or incorporating representation from members of external organizations on internal decision-making committees.

The structure adopted by the British Basketball League represents an attempt to deal with many of these challenges.

Case 6.3   British Basketball League

The top men's professional basketball league in the UK is the British Basketball League (BBL). The BBL is an independent company owned by its member clubs, each with an equal shareholding in BBL. Each club has a representative on the BBL Board of Directors who oversee the operation of a central BBL office in Birmingham which manages administration, marketing and media functions. The interesting aspect of the structure of the BBL is that each club operates as a franchise in designated areas across the UK in order to maximize commercial and media value within their local community.

Unlike other sports where second division champions are promoted to replace the bottom ranked team in the top league, the BBL operates independently of the second tier competition, the English Basketball League (EBL). There is no promotion and relegation between the BBL and the EBL, and EBL clubs cannot join the BBL based on their performances in official competition alone. However, EBL clubs and any other organizations can apply for a franchise from the BBL.

The organizational structure or franchise system used by the BBL is used because of the significant costs of running a team in the BBL compared to running any other team in the UK. The structure attempts to provide financial security and protect investment into clubs by removing the threat that comes with relegation. A salary cap and income distribution policy amongst BBL clubs also assists with competitive balance and financial management.

Clubs can apply to join the BBL by submitting a detailed business plan to the BBL Franchise Committee that specifies venue details, proof of an acceptable level of financial backing, and an explanation of how the club will be sustainable. Because government funding for basketball goes to England Basketball, the BBL receives no government financial support. Instead, it derives its income from sponsorship, media partnerships, merchandising and ticket sales. Commercial and media rights generate the largest portion of income for the league and clubs.

The challenge of organizing a viable professional basketball league in a country dominated by football, rugby and cricket is significant. Competition for sponsorship dollars, access to appropriate venues, securing media rights, and maintaining market share in a crowded professional sport market are all challenges for the directors of the BBL and the managers of their member clubs. The organizational structure adopted by the BBL in using the US style franchise system is an attempt to combat these challenges. The structure allows the league and clubs to plan for future expansion, manage income and costs across all elements of the organization, and ensure equitable decision-making amongst the member clubs.

Source: British Basketball League website at http://www.bbl.org.uk

Summary

Organizational structure was defined as the framework that outlines how tasks are divided, grouped and coordinated within an organization. An organization's structure is important because it defines where staff and volunteers 'fit in' with each other in terms of work tasks, decision-making procedures, the need for collaboration, levels of responsibility and reporting mechanisms.

Six key elements of organizational structure were reviewed: work specialization, departmentalization, chain of command, the span of control, centralization and formalization. In addition, four basic models for how an organization may use these six elements to design an appropriate structure were reviewed: the simple structure, the bureaucracy, the matrix structure, and the team structure.

The generic contingency factors that influence organizational structure – size, strategy, technology and environmental uncertainty – were reviewed as well as some unique drivers of change to the structure of sport organizations. Finally, a number of unique challenges for sport managers in dealing with structure were presented. Sport managers should be aware of these factors that drive structural change and the specific structural elements they can influence that are likely to deliver improved organizational outcomes and performance.

Review questions

1. Define organizational structure in your own words.
2. If you were to manipulate any of the six elements of structure, which do you think could have the most impact on the day-to-day role of the chief executive of a sports organization?
3. Why do staff in small sports organizations have a low degree of work specialization?
4. Which structural model would suit a large sports event such as the Commonwealth or Olympic Games? Why?
5. How does a change in size affect the structure of a sports organization?
6. Compare the organizational structure of a sport manufacturing organization and a local community sports facility. How do each of the six elements of organizational structure differ? Which elements are similar?
7. Explain how environmental uncertainty can force change to the structure of a sports organization.
8. Interview the CEO of a medium sized sports organization. What is their most significant challenge in managing their organizational structure?

Further reading

The use of organizational theory in the analysis of structures for non-profit sport organizations is well established. Three broad questions have been addressed in these studies. These are; first, investigating the relationship between organizational structure and organizational effectiveness; second, attempts to categorize organizational types; and third, exploring the impact of professionalization on various elements of organizational structure.

Students interested in reading further should consult the following journal articles:

Amis, J. & Slack, T. (1996). The size-structure relationship in voluntary sport organizations. *Journal of Sport Management*, 10, 76–86.

Frisby, W. (1986). The organizational structure and effectiveness of voluntary organizations: The case of Canadian national sport governing bodies. *Journal of Park and Recreation Administration*, 4, 61–74.

Kikulis, L.M., Slack, T. & Hinings, B. (1992). Institutionally specific design archetypes: A framework for understanding change in national sport organizations. *International Review for the Sociology of Sport*, 27, 343–367.

Kikulis, L.M., Slack, T. & Hinings, B. (1995). Toward an understanding of the role of agency and choice in the changing structure of Canada's national sport organizations. *Journal of Sport Management*, 9, 135–152.

Kikulis, L.M., Slack, T., Hinings, B. & Zimmermann, A. (1989). A structural taxonomy of amateur sport organizations. *Journal of Sport Management*, 3, 129–150.

Theodoraki, E.I. & Henry, I.P. (1994). Organizational structures and contexts in British national governing bodies of sport. *International Review for the Sociology of Sport*, 29, 243–263.

Thibault, L., Slack, T. & Hinings, B. (1991). Professionalism, structures and systems: The impact of professional staff on voluntary sport organizations. *International Review for the Sociology of Sport*, 26, 83–97.

Other useful texts:

Robbins, S.P., Bergman, R., Stagg, I. & Coulter, M. (2004). Management (3rd edn). Pearson Education, Sydney: Australia.

Robbins, S.P., Millett, B., Cacioppe, R. & Waters-March, T. (2001). Organizational Behaviour: Leading and managing in Australia and New Zealand (3rd edn). Pearson Education, Sydney: Australia.

Relevant websites

The following websites are useful starting points for further information on the structure of sport organizations:

* University of Calgary Scholarly sport sites web page for sport structures at http://www.ucalgary.ca/library/ssportsite/natorg.html
* Australian Sports Commission at http://www.ausport.gov.au
* Sport and Recreation New Zealand at http://www.sparc.org.nz/
* Sport Canada at http://www.pch.gc.ca/progs/sc/index_e.cfm
* Sport England at http://www.sportengland.org
* Sport Scotland at http://www.sportscotland.org.uk

Chapter 7

Human resource management

Overview

This chapter will review the core concepts of human resource management, provide examples of the unique features of human resource management within sport organizations, such as volunteer and paid staff management, and summarize the key phases in the human resource management process. The chapter will examine human resource management within community, state, national and professional sport organizations, in order to illustrate core concepts and principles.

After completing this chapter the reader should be able to:

- Identify the key concepts that underpin human resource management within sport organizations;
- Explain why human resource management in sport organizations can be different to non-sport organizations;
- Identify each of the phases within the human resource management process; and
- Explain the ways in which each of the human resource management phases would be implemented in different sport organization contexts.

What is human resource management?

Human resource management, in business or sport organizations, is essentially about first, finding the right person for the right job at the right time, and second, ensuring an appropriately trained and satisfied workforce. The concepts that underpin effective human resource management are not particularly complex. However, the sheer size of some organizations, as well as the difficulties in managing unusual organizations in the sport industry, make human resource management a complex issue to deal with in practice. At the same time, successful sport leagues, clubs, associations, retailers and venues all rely on good human resources, both on and off the field to get their jobs done. Conversely, organizations with staff who lack motivation, are ill-suited to their work, under-paid or under-valued will struggle to perform.

Human resource management is a central feature of an organization's planning system. It cannot be divorced from other key management tools, such as strategic planning, financial planning or managing organizational culture and structure. Human resource management can both drive organizational success, and is a consequence of good management and planning. Human resource management involves a process of continual planning and evaluation and is best viewed as part of a cycle in which an organization aims to meet its strategic goals. Human resource management is therefore an holistic management function in that it can be 'both person-centred and goal-directed' (Smith & Stewart, 1999).

Human resource management can mean different things to different organizations, depending on their context and outlook. For professional sport organizations that are profit driven, such as the American National Basketball Association (NBA), Major League Baseball (MBL) or National Hockey League (NHL), successful human resource management is equated with profitability, long-term growth and success (on and off the court, diamond and rink). This is not to suggest that these things are sought after at the expense of employees, but rather that the success of the employees is measured by dispassionate business indicators and human resource management is a tool for driving the business towards its goals. For example, player welfare and development programmes within professional sport organizations are designed to produce socially, morally and ethically responsible citizens. This is viewed as a good human resource strategy, not only because of the intrinsic value to the athletes, but for the extrinsic value that results from better public relations and sponsor servicing. In other words, better behaved athletes mean greater profitability and overall success for professional sport teams and franchises.

For not-for-profit sport organizations, successful human resource management is usually not always about bottom line financial performance. It can also encompass a range of strategies and outcomes depending on the organizational context. A local sporting club that has had a problem with alcohol consumption among its junior players may develop a range of programmes to educate its players, coaches and administrators (who may be paid or volunteer staff) in order to encourage a more responsible club culture. This player welfare programme may actually be part of a human resource management strategy, as the inappropriate club culture may have been making it difficult to attract and retain volunteers with expertise and commitment. In the case of the professional team context the player welfare programme can be used to manage image and maintain brand credibility. In the case of the local community sport the player welfare programme can be used to retain volunteers who were being driven away from the club by poor behaviour and a dysfunctional culture. From these two examples it is clear that human resource management can be both person-centred and goal-directed at the same time.

Is human resource management in sport special?

Many of the core concepts that underpin human resource management apply to all organizations, whether they are situated in the world of business, such as soft drink manufacturer Coca-Cola or mining company BHP Billiton, or in the world of sport, such as the South African Rugby Football Union or the Canadian Curling Association. This is not surprising, given that all these organizations employ staff who are expected to perform a range of designated tasks at an appropriate level of performance. These staff will manage finances, undertake strategic planning, and produce products like *Fanta*, iron ore, coaching clinics and national championships. There are, however, significant differences between business and sport organizations, which result in modifications to generic human resource management practices.

In particular, professional sport organizations have special features, which present a unique human resource management challenge. Sport organizations, such as the Cincinnati Bengals in America's National Football League, revolve around three distinct types of employees. First, the Bengals employ people in what they call 'the front office', such as the business development manager or the director of corporate sales and marketing. Second, the Bengals employ people in what can be referred to as the 'football operations department', such as the coaches, trainers and scouts. Finally, the Bengals employ people that comprise 'the team', the players, who are the most visible people of any professional sport organization. It could be argued that non-sport businesses operate in the same way, with different levels of management, from the chief executive officer all the way through to the employee on the factory floor. The obvious difference in the sporting context is that the human resources at the bottom of the staffing pyramid are the highest paid employees in the entire organization. The difference between sport and non-sport organizations is illustrated in Figure 7.1. It should be noted that sport organizations have employees that could be considered 'the lowest paid', but relative to non-sport organizations they are not equivalent, and as such a

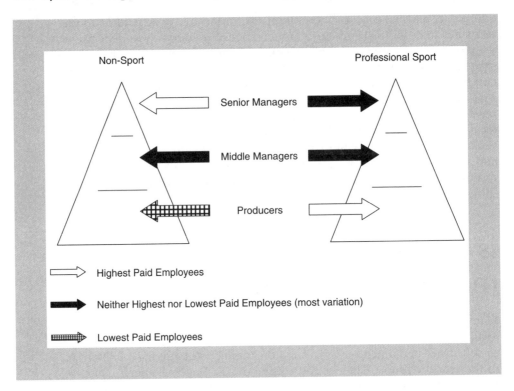

Figure 7.1 Pay and organization levels in professional sport and non-sport organizations

checkered arrow has not been included for the sport organization pyramid (sport organizations are not completely unique in this respect, however, for in many forms of entertainment, such as film or television drama, the actors are the highest paid).

In non-sport organizations, chief executive officers, general managers and other senior executives often receive performance bonuses and have access to share options that allow them to share in the wealth and profitability of the company. The workers producing the product (at the *Fanta* bottling plant or the iron ore mine for example) do not have access to performance schemes and bonuses that might be worth millions of dollars. In professional sport organizations the situation is reversed and the performance bonuses are available to those who produce the product, the players. It is important to keep this special feature of sport in mind when considering the human resource management needs of professional sport organizations specifically and sport organizations more generally.

Additionally, a significant proportion of staff in semi-professional and not-for-profit sport organizations are volunteers. The distinction between volunteers and paid staff in the effective management of these groups is a challenge for human resource management in sport organizations.

Because sport is often played in a community environment (at a state, regional or local level), it necessarily requires the support of volunteers to maintain services, facilities and events. Some national sport organizations, like the South Africa Rugby Football Union or the Canadian Curling Association mentioned earlier, have paid staff at the national level, whose job is to coordinate and develop programmes, events, championships and national teams. Equivalent state or regional associations for sports like these might, depending on the size, popularity and government funding afforded the sport, also have paid staff in key management, development and coaching positions. In some instances these state or regional associations will have more staff than the national body because of the requirement to deliver programmes and services, as well as manage and provide strategic direction for the sport. Local associations, again depending on the size and popularity of the sport, might also have some paid staff, however, at this level sports are supported by a significant core of volunteers. In Australia it has been estimated that sporting activities are supported by 1.5 million volunteers who collectively contribute in excess of 150 million volunteer hours per year, while in the United Kingdom it has been estimated that volunteers contribute in excess of 1 billion hours of labour (www.sportengland.org).

A significant proportion of sport is played on a weekly basis within leagues and associations across the world. Depending on whether the sport is played indoor or outdoor, the sport might have a winter season (football or ice hockey), a summer season (baseball) or might be played all year (basketball). The regularity of the season and the competition, whether at the elite or community level, means that the staffing requirements of sport organizations are predictable and remain relatively stable. There are, however, a range of sporting events and championships for which staff planning is difficult and staffing levels fluctuate greatly. These events are either irregular (a city might get to host the Olympics once in 100 years) or big enough that they require a large workforce for an intense period of time (the annual Monaco Grand Prix). The staffing for major annual sport events can be referred to as 'heavily skewed' or 'strongly peaked' as illustrated in Figure 7.2. In essence, major events need a large workforce, often composed primarily of volunteers or casual workers, for a short period of time prior to the event, during the event and directly following the event, and a small workforce of primarily paid staff for the rest of the year (events such as the Olympic Games or world championships will require a permanent paid staff for many years prior to the event, but most staffing appointments will conclude within six months of the event finishing). The rapid increase and decline in staffing within a one or two week period is a complex and significant human resource management problem. It requires systematic recruitment, selection and orientation programmes in order to attract the staff, and simple yet effective evaluation and reward schemes in order to retain them.

Large organizations with a large workforce have both the capacity and responsibility to engage in sophisticated human resource management. Often there is a dedicated team or department that manages human resources, led by a senior member of staff. In small to medium sized organizations, however, there is not always the human or financial capacity to devote to human resource management practices in a formal system. Human resource management in small to medium sized organizations is often the responsibility of the most senior staff member, such as the chief executive or general manager or

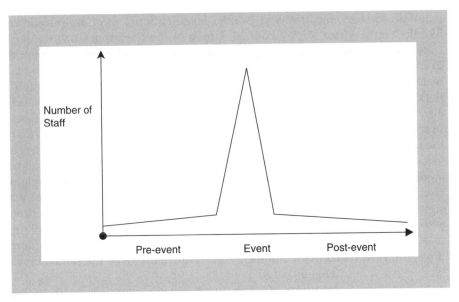

Figure 7.2 Heavily skewed/strongly peaked sport event staffing

is combined with roles performed by another senior manager responsible for finances, planning or marketing, for example.

Sport leagues, clubs, associations and venues rarely have enough staff to warrant employing someone to be responsible solely for human resource management. Often the other key management roles, such as marketing, events or sponsorship are considered essential and human resource management is considered either as a luxury or peripheral to the core management functions. Furthermore, human resource management can be confused with personnel management, which encompasses more mechanistic functions such as payroll and record keeping (leave, sick pay, etc.).

Australian Swimming, the national body responsible for managing one of Australia's biggest and most popular sports has approximately 30 staff, with a chief executive officer and four functional divisions (sport services, events, corporate services and finance/employee relations). The finance/employee relations division is the smallest, with two employees, a manager and an assistant. Australian Swimming is a good example of a medium sized organization in which the human resource management responsibilities have been merged with another significant management responsibility, in this case finance.

The essentials of human resource management

Human resource management in sport organizations aims to provide an effective, productive and satisfied workforce. Human resource management

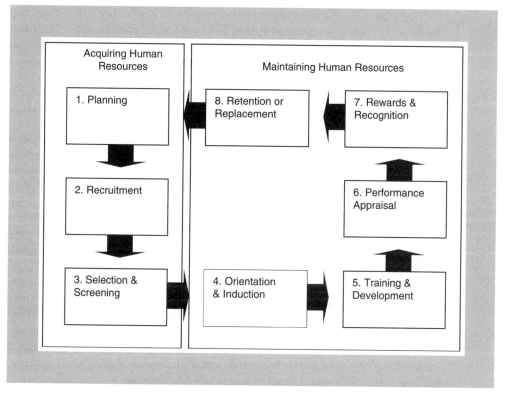

Figure 7.3 The traditional human resource management process

refers to the design, development, implementation, management and evaluation of systems and practices used by employers to recruit, select, develop, reward, retain and evaluate their workforce. The core elements of the human resource management process are represented in Figure 7.3. The following phases are considered the core functions of human resource management, although it is important to keep in mind that these functions will differ significantly depending on the size, orientation and context of the sport organization in which they are implemented.

Phase 1: Human resource planning

Human resource management planning is essentially about assessing and forecasting the staffing needs of the organization and is often referred to as the most important phase for effective human resource management (Smith & Stewart, 1999). The planning phase of human resource management is short and fairly static for organizations in which the staffing levels remain fairly constant and the types of jobs performed by staff members vary little. For organizations that are dynamic or in a state of flux (as a result of economic pressures or opportunities for example), human resource planning is a cycle of ongoing development.

In the planning phase an organization must assess whether current staffing needs will be adequate to meet future demand (or alternately, whether fewer staff will be required), whether staff turnover is predictable and can be accommodated, whether the ratios of paid, full-time, part-time, casual and volunteer staff are appropriate or adequate, whether there are annual or cyclical fluctuations in staffing that need to be met and managed, and whether specific capabilities will be required in the future that the organization is currently lacking.

Once an organization decides that a new staff member is required or a new position is to be created, the organization must undertake a job analysis, in order to determine the job content (primary and implied tasks), requirements (skills, competencies, qualifications and experience) and context (reporting relationships and job characteristics). Once the job analysis has been completed in as much detail as possible, the organization is ready to develop a job description (a document that covers the job content and context) and a job specification (a document that covers the job requirements, especially skills and knowledge base).

There are four management principles that can be applied to job design. They are most useful for considering how a job might be positioned within an organization, as well as for identifying different types of organizations. These themes are job simplification, job rotation, job enlargement and job enrichment (Chelladurai, 1999). Job simplification refers to the process in which a job (and the organization) is broken down into a series of simplified and specialized tasks. This simplification is intended to increase the specialization of employees, thereby increasing efficiency and productivity. Job simplification can be viewed as a positive management tool, particularly when it comes to evaluating the performance of an individual employee, however, job specialization, depending on the context, can lead to workers becoming bored and subsequently dissatisfied with their work.

The second principle, job rotation, is partly a remedy to the boredom and dissatisfaction that can result from simplification. Job rotation involves workers swapping jobs on a periodic basis, in order to keep fresh and stimulated, although clearly a sport organization will only have a finite range of jobs through which employees can rotate.

Job enlargement refers to the process by which employees are encouraged to enlarge their work and add tasks, even if they are simplified and specialized. The benefit of this approach is a happier workforce, but the downside is the perception of overwork.

Finally, job enrichment refers to the structuring of the job so that it maximizes employee motivation and involvement. This process relies on being able to design jobs that are flexible and have the capacity for growth and change, as well as the employment of people that can work autonomously.

Phase 2: Recruitment

Recruitment refers to the process by which an organization tries to find the person most suited to the job that has been designed. The greater the pool of applicants, the greater the chance the organization will find a suitable candidate. Generating a pool of applicants is not always simple, however, particularly if the job requires specific skills, knowledge, qualifications or experience that are in demand or short supply. Thus, for the chief executive position in a major professional club with responsibility for a multi-million dollar operation, the search might be extensive and costly. However, recruiting an attendant to check membership tickets at home games of the professional club might only require a small advertisement in a local newspaper. Finally, recruiting 10 000 people to act as volunteers for a major hallmark event might require a nationwide or international advertising campaign across various media forms. Increasingly, recruitment processes are becoming more sophisticated as organizations take advantage of rapidly developing communication technologies (see Case 7.1).

Case 7.1   Rebel Sport

Rebel Sport is Australia's leading retailer of sporting equipment, apparel and footwear. What began as a single store in Sydney in 1985 has grown into a business that is listed on the Australian stock exchange, has 55 stores Australia wide and employs in excess of 2,500 people.

Rebel Sport's human resource management practices are extensive, including what the company claims is Australia's most extensive online training facility – 'RebelUni'. All staff undertake an online and face-to-face induction training course that covers product knowledge, merchandising and excellence in customer service.

The online feature of Rebel Sport's human resource management is not limited to the people that it employs, however, for all prospective employees are also required to undertake a 'pre-employment' induction and training. In this respect, Rebel Sport has combined some of the key human resource management practices – recruitment, selection and induction – into a single online process. People who wish to apply for a job with Rebel Sport, whether it is as the marketing manager in head office or as a cashier in the Townsville store, are required to complete a two phase online induction process. Phase A gives the prospective employee a broad understanding of what Rebel Sport considers as important, including the customer service philosophy and company culture. After the prospective applicant has completed the introductory module, they complete an assessment which is graded based on the position that is being sought. Once this stage has been completed the applicant is able to apply for a specific position via an online application form. The application is then assessed and the applicant, if successful, is contacted by the human resources department (with a possible interview) and asked to complete phase B of the induction process, an online product knowledge and selling module. This process is all before the person has gained employment with Rebel Sport.

Once employed, employees are encouraged to complete a range of accredited training programmes, while a 'management development programme' identifies team members with ability that can be trained for store management roles.

Source: Rebel Sport website at www.rebelsport.com.au

Phase 3: Selection

Selection and screening is the process condensing the candidates that applied for the position during the recruitment phase to a short-list. The selection phase will usually include at least one interview of the short-listed candidates, which will supplement the application form and curriculum vitae submitted by the applicants in order to determine whether they are appropriate in light of the job analysis and which of the applicants is the best person for the job. Depending on the geographic location of the applicants, the interview might be conducted in person, via telephone, via video conferencing or via an Internet link. Industrial relations legislation covers a range of organizational and employment issues in most countries. It is important to comply with these laws and regulations throughout the human resource management processes, such as the recruitment and selection phase, so that the organization is not exposed to claims of discrimination or bias (on the basis of race, colour, country of birth, ethnicity, disability, religion, sex, age, marital status, pregnancy or sexual preference). In this respect Smith and Stewart (1999) refer to the types of questions not to ask in an interview:

- How old are you?
- Do you have a problem working with younger people?
- Are you married?
- Do you have any children?
- How will you care for your children when at work?
- How long have you been a single parent?
- Do you intend to have any more children?
- Where do you attend church?
- Do you have a Christian background?
- What are your views on taking prohibited drugs?
- Please send a recent photo with your application form.
- What are you going to do about your weight problem?
- Do you have a communicable disease?
- What clubs do you belong to?
- Do you belong to a trade union or professional association?
- Tell us about your political affiliations.
- Have you undertaken any military service?

An interview is the most common way of determining whether a prospective employee will be best suited to the organization and the position. However, other techniques, such as sophisticated personality and intelligence tests, are increasingly being used to determine whether the applicant has the job requirements identified in the planning phase (skills, competencies, qualifications and experience). For example, the Myers-Briggs Type Indicator (MBTI) is a personality test which, based on questions about psychological processes such as the way people like to interpret information or make decisions, categorizes people into one of 16 personality types. Based on the psychological theories of Carl Jung, the MBTI can be used by sport organizations to determine whether an applicant not only has the appropriate skills and educational qualifications for the job, but also whether their personality, attitudes and values will be a good 'fit' for the organization.

Phase 4: Orientation

Once the employee has successfully navigated the recruitment and selection processes, they are ready to begin work in their new job within the sport organization. Before they start, however, they need to be orientated and inducted. This phase of human resource management is important, as a good quality orientation and induction programme can make an employee feel both welcome and empowered, but a poor programme, or no programme, can make a new employee feel as if they have travelled to a foreign country, in which they can't speak the language, don't know where to go and can't read any of the signs. In short, being in a new organization can be a daunting and frightening experience. The implementation of successful orientation and induction programmes can ameliorate some of the difficulties, concerns and anxieties. Potential problems are compounded if the employee is a volunteer and can be exacerbated further if the volunteer does not have any direct supervision from a paid employee of the organization. This is a recipe for disaster, both for the organization and the employee.

Successful orientation and induction programmes revolve around forthright and effective communication of information about the organization and its operations. This information might include a general overview, policies and procedures, occupational health and safety regulations, industrial relations issues, a physical tour of the organization's facilities, an overview of the training and development programmes available to employees or an explanation of the performance appraisal process (Slack, 1997). The focus on orientation and induction is usually magnified when a large number of volunteers are required by the organization, such as at an Olympic Games. A total of 60 422 volunteers participated in running the Atlanta Olympics in 1996, 47 000 in Sydney in 2000 and the Athens Olympics in 2004 received in excess of 160 000 volunteer applications from all over the world.

Case 7.2   Volunteer management

In the early 1990s the Australian Sports Commission, in conjunction with the Australian Society of Sports Administrators, the Confederation of Australian Sport and state departments of sport and recreation, developed the 'Volunteer Involvement Program'. The original programme was designed to encourage sport organizations to adopt professional volunteer management practices, which was viewed as essential given the large numbers of volunteers involved in sport organizations and the increasing professionalization of the industry.

The programme has since been revised and improved to provide sporting clubs and associations with resources and training modules for volunteer management ('recruiting volunteers', 'retaining volunteers', 'volunteer management: a guide to good practice', 'managing event volunteers', 'volunteer management policy' and 'the volunteer coordinator'). The six modules that form the new 'Volunteer Management Program' (VMP), written by Graham Cuskelly and Christopher Auld from Griffith University, Australia, encourage Australian sporting clubs and associations to adopt a human resource management approach to volunteers. For example, the first module, 'Recruiting Volunteers' contains a section on orientating volunteers, a core function of human resource management. The module encourages sport organizations to develop systematic processes and practices.

The following checklist, reproduced from the 'Recruiting Volunteers' module, is a clear example that without a professional approach to volunteer management (orientation in this case), volunteers may not feel part of the organization, might not do their job properly (often through a lack of adequate training or knowledge) and in all likelihood leave the organization.

Orientation Programme Checklist

- ✓ Provide an orientation guidebook or kit
- ✓ Provide copies of current newsletter, annual report and recent marketing/promotional material
- ✓ Provide a copy of the constitution
- ✓ Enter the name, address and contact details of each volunteer into database
- ✓ Gather and file copies of qualifications and accreditation certificates from each volunteer
- ✓ Introduce the organization's culture, history, aims, funding, clients/members and decision-making processes
- ✓ Introduce key volunteers and/or staff (and organization chart)
- ✓ Outline the roles and responsibilities of key volunteers and staff
- ✓ Detail the roles and responsibilities and accountabilities of the volunteer in their new position
- ✓ Familiarize volunteers with facilities, equipment and resources
- ✓ Explain and 'walk through' emergency and evacuation procedures
- ✓ Familiarize volunteers with the organization's day-to-day operations (safety and risk management, telephone, photocopier, keys, filing system, tea/coffee making, office processes and procedures, authorizing expenditure)

Source: Australian Sports Commission website at www.ausport.gov.au/clubs/volunteer_prog.asp#3

Phase 5: Training and development

Training and development is at the heart of an organization that seeks continual growth and improvement. Sport organizations that do not engage in systematic training and development programmes are destined to operate far below their optimum, not only because they will fall behind in current trends, practices and skills, but because they will not see themselves as learning organizations (Senge, 1990). At its most basic, training and development is a process through which new and existing employees learn the skills required for them to be effective in their jobs. At one end of the spectrum these skills could be associated with learning how to operate automated turnstiles at a professional sport arena (training for the novice employee), or learning how to creatively brand the organizations in order to compete in a hostile marketplace (training for the experienced existing employee). Where training was once a fairly mechanistic activity, it now includes more generic organizational skills that require development and implementation, such as when a major league sport franchise ensures product or service quality, or when a national sport organization develops an organizational culture that encourages compliance from state or regional sport organizations.

Dressler (2003) outlines five-step training and development process that is useful for sport organizations. Step one is to complete a 'needs analysis', in which the organization identifies the necessary skills for its employees, analyses the current skills base and develops specific training objectives. Step two involves developing the actual training programme, which may be done internally or externally. Most sport organizations, as previously noted, are too small to have sophisticated human resource management departments that have the skill and experience to design, develop and implement sophisticated training programmes. Sport organizations will most often use external training providers, such as universities or consultancy firms, to provide tailored or standard programmes, depending on the needs analysis. Step three, validation, is an optional step in which the organization is able to validate that the training programme that has been developed or contracted satisfies the needs analysis. Step four is the implementation of the programme, during which the staff are trained (this could be anything from a one day short course, through to a two year Masters programme). In the fifth and final step the training programme is evaluated. The successful programme might be expanded to include more employees or more skills, while the unsuccessful programme needs to be discontinued or re-worked, which requires the organization to re-assess the needs analysis. Like the entire human resource management process, the training and development process is best viewed as cyclical.

Phase 6: Performance appraisal

This phase of the human resource management process is potentially the most dangerous, as it has the inherent ability to pit 'management' against 'employees' at the macro level, and at the micro level cause managers to feel uncomfortable in judging others or cause employees to feel unworthy, as part of a negative appraisal. The performance appraisal process must be approached carefully by sport organizations and human resource managers within an organization must seek to develop a collaborative process in which the employee, as well as the manager, feels empowered. Managers and leaders need the ability to review performance and suggest improvement, as a way of developing overall organizational capacity. On the other hand, employees need a forum in which they feel comfortable identifying the things they did well and the things they could have done better, as part of a process of ongoing professional and career development. In this respect the performance appraisal process within any sport organization, whatever its size or type, must be seen within the simple, but effective 'plan, do, review, improve' scheme, which is usually associated with the quality assurance agenda (Deming, 1993: 134–136).

In professional sports organizations in particular, the performance appraisal process is often very public, if convoluted. Athletes and coaches are constantly rated on their performance. In basketball the number of points, rebounds, assists, turnovers, steals, fouls and blocked shots are recorded meticulously. From year to year, goals are set for athletes and their ability to meet targets in key performance indicators can result in an extended contract with improved conditions. On the other hand, not meeting the targets can mean a player in a sport like baseball has to return to the minor leagues, to return to form or to see out their playing days. For coaches, performance appraisal is often based on one statistic alone, the win-loss record. The fact that the coach is adept at making the players feel good about themselves or has a great working relationship with the administrative staff, will count for very little when it comes to negotiating a new contract if he or she has posted a losing record.

Phases 7 and 8: Rewards and retention

Once a sport organization has planned for, recruited, selected, orientated, trained and appraised its staff, it makes good sense that it would try to retain them. Retaining good quality staff, whether they are in a paid or volunteer capacity, means that the organization will be better off financially and strategically. Organizational knowledge and intellectual property is lost when a sport organization fails to retain its staff. Constantly losing staff will mean that the organization may have the opportunity to encourage and develop new ways of thinking, but the more likely scenario is that it will lead to wasted resources, unnecessarily diverted to rudimentary induction programmes.

The first six phases of the human resource management process all contribute to retaining staff. Poor orientation, training and performance appraisal programmes in particular can all have a negative impact on staff retention. On the other side of the retention equation, rewards and compensation can encourage employees to remain with an organization. At a professional sport organization this may mean, rather than attempting to keep wage costs low, the senior managers will be prepared to pay the 'market rate' (Smith & Stewart, 1999). In a primarily voluntary organization, the reward may take the form of a letter of appreciation for being part of a successful event and an invitation to participate next year. In other words, the reward and retention strategy will depend greatly on the context in which it is being implemented and the existing level of job satisfaction.

Case 7.3   NBA Rookie Orientation and Induction

Most professional league sports in the United States of America (USA), such as the National Football League and National Hockey League have what are called 'rookie' camps, where players fight for a place on the roster. These camps are equivalent to the selection and screening process for off-field administrative positions. The recruitment process has usually taken place over years of high school and college competition, with scouts travelling across the nation in search of talent. Once a rookie has made it through the recruitment and selection processes they are invariably faced with the completely new world of professional sport and all the demands that accompany it.

The National Basketball Association (NBA) in the USA recognized that this was a difficult time for many young athletes and developed a comprehensive orientation and induction programme. Since 1986, the rookie players of the forthcoming season have been required to participate in a week long training and development camp in the month prior to the season's start. The rookie transition programme is designed so that these young athletes can develop better life skills, which in turn will hopefully prepare them for the particular and peculiar stresses of a professional athletic career. Through the transition programme, which includes a diverse range of topics such as sexual health, nutrition and anger management, the NBA hopes that its young players will be able to make better decisions.

The transition programme also includes role-play sessions where common scenarios are acted out for the rookies. These scenes invariably involve relationship issues, which are important to a group of young men, most of whom are 22 years old or younger, have annual salaries of approximately US$1million, are likely to attract the attention of the opposite sex during their sporting career and lack the maturity to navigate the difficult transition from amateur to professional sport. The mantra that is preached to these young athletes as part of the orientation programme is 'choices, decisions, consequences'. The programme is complemented by ongoing support provided through the player development department of the NBA and the National Basketball Players Association.

Source: NBA website at www.nba.com

Summary

Effective human resource management in sport organizations relies on the implementation of an interdependent set of processes. At one level this can be viewed as quite mechanistic, yet on another more positive level it can viewed as a blueprint for the successful management of people through a clearly delineated set of stages. Human resource management planning, recruitment, selection, orientation, training, performance appraisal, rewards and retention strategies are essential for an organization to operate successfully in state, non-profit or commercial sport environments, because good people management is at the core of every successful sport organization, irrespective of the context. Good human resource management allows sport organizations to deal with some of its unique and particular challenges, such as the place of athletes in professional sport organizations and the large casual and semi-permanent workforces required by major events (annual or periodic). On the other hand, poor human resource management can result in a workforce that is not only uncommitted, but also subject to low levels of morale and job satisfaction. In short, effective and systematic human resource management should be seen as an important management tool in any sport organization, whatever the size or type.

Review questions

1. Which is the most important phase of the human resource management process? Why? Refer in your answer to organizations with primarily paid staff and organizations with primarily volunteer staff.
2. Is human resource management important for the effective management of sport organizations? Why?
3. Examine the human resource management processes of a local sport organization. Are the processes adequate?
4. Examine the staffing levels of a major annual event in your city/province/region. Are the staffing levels stable?
5. Should the human resource management role within sport organizations be combined with another functional division?
6. Should different human resource management strategies be applied to volunteers and paid staff?
7. Does the place of athletes in professional sport organizations make the need for effective human resource management practices more or less important?
8. Compare the orientation and induction processes of a sport organization and a non-sport organization. How and why do they differ?
9. Does the often public appraisal of employees in sport organizations diminish the integrity of the human resource management process?
10. Choose a small to medium sized organization without a human resource management specialist. Perform a job analysis for a new employee in the role of human resource management.

Further reading

Chelladurai, P. (1999). *Human Resource Management in Sport and Recreation*, Champaign: Human Kinetics.

Doherty, A. (1998). Managing Our Human Resources: A Review of Organizational Behaviour in Sport. *Journal of Sport Management*, 12 (1), pp. 1–24.

Robinson, L. (2004). Human Resource Management. In Robinson, L. *Managing Public Sport and Leisure Services*. London: Routledge.

Relevant websites

The following websites are useful starting points for further information on the human resource management of sport organizations:

* Australian Sports Commission Resources at
  http://www.ausport.gov.au/clubs/volunteer_club_mngmt.asp
* Sport England Resources at
  http://www.sportengland.org/index/get_resources/resource_downloads/funding_information.htm
* Sport and Recreation New Zealand Sport Administrator Resources at
  http://www.sparc.org.nz/sports_admin/

Chapter 8
Leadership

Overview

When asked about great leadership, we can all list the men and women who made their mark. High on anyone's list would be Julius Caesar, who was the ruler of the Roman Empire two thousands years ago, Queen Elizabeth the First who ruled England throughout the 1500s and Napoleon Bonaparte who was in charge of most of continental Europe 200 years ago. More contemporary leaders include the likes of Nelson Mandela, Bill Gates and Michael Jordan. But, why Michael Jordan, you may wonder? How does Michael Jordan qualify as a leader when he clearly was not in charge of a country or corporation?

Leadership is probably the most researched yet least understood topic in the context of management. What we define as excellent leadership and who are great leaders remain points of serious and widespread academic debate. For example, the *Handbook of Leadership: Theory, Research and Managerial Applications* (Bass, 1990) contains over 7500 citations about the concept of leadership and is certainly not a light read. In the United States alone, more than 2000 books on the topic of leadership are published every year. Irrespective of the diversity of opinion in both academic and popular writings most leadership authors agree on one of the most basic of leadership principles: Leadership implies direction. One cannot lead if there is no destination or anticipated outcome. Even if the followers do not exactly know the destination or anticipated outcome, the leader should at least have some understanding of where he or she will lead towards. As already noted, leadership also implies followership, and without someone following, even Michael Jordan will not be a leader. However, with people believing and following in the direction that Jordan sets out, he automatically becomes a leader. Followership therefore gives the leader the power to influence the behaviour of others.

In the remainder of this chapter we will provide a broad outline of the different approaches that can be taken towards describing and implementing good leadership. We will also use a number of cases to further explore what best describes leadership. Much of this discussion will take place in reference to the leadership challenges that confront sport organizations.

By the end of this chapter the reader should be able to:

■ Describe the need for leaders and for leadership;
■ Distinguish between leadership and management;
■ Outline the different levels (in the organization) that leaders can work at and how this impacts upon their approach to leadership;
■ Outline the specific challenges that leaders in sport organizations are confronted with; and
■ Provide an overview of your personal leadership development needs.

What is leadership?

As noted previously it is not easy to define leadership in such a way that all readers will accept as a true and complete reflection of what leadership entails. Sometimes leadership is described as 'getting things done through people'. Others argue that leadership is about 'exercising power in order to influence others' or that true leadership is about 'envisioning a bright future and taking others by the hand towards it'.

In other words, leadership can be many things to different people. Cotton Fitzsimmons, former coach of the Kansas City Kings argues that 'if you're a positive person, you're an automatic motivator. You can get people to do things you don't think they're capable of' (Westerbeek & Smith, 2005). Vince Lombardi, the famous coach of the Green Bay Packers of the 1950s and 1960s once said that 'leaders are made, they are not born; and they are made just like anything else has been made in this country – by hard effort. And that's the price that we all have to pay to achieve that goal, or any goal' (Westerbeek & Smith, 2005). According to former US President Theodore Roosevelt 'the best executive is the one who has sense enough to pick good men to do what he wants done, and self-restraint enough to keep from meddling with them while they do it', and Lou Holts, a former coach of the Notre Dame football team argued that 'all winning teams are goal-oriented. Teams like these win consistently because everyone connected with them concentrates on specific objectives. They go about their business with blinders on; nothing will distract them from achieving their aims' (Westerbeek & Smith, 2005). A few things stand out from all these quotes. According to these experienced, but very different leaders, leadership is:

• goal oriented;
• about influencing others;

- about empowering others;
- about seeing the big picture;
- about needing others; and
- about strength of character.

We can use these different components of leadership to construct a leadership definition that we will use for the remainder of this chapter. For the purposes of this book we define leadership as 'skilfully influencing and enabling others towards the attainment of aspirational goals'. We do appreciate that we may not do justice to the many aspects one can argue that need to be incorporated in a complete definition of leadership, but as an introduction to the topic in this book the above definition will serve its purpose. In the next section of this chapter we will further outline the ways that leadership can be viewed.

Case 8.1 Mark McCormack and the International Management Group

The International Management Group (IMG) is headquartered in Cleveland, Ohio and currently has 70 offices in 30 countries around the globe. The company's businesses include the number one modelling agency in the world, the largest independent licensing agency, a literary agency, a representative agency for world-renowned classical music artists, a golf course development division, a consulting arm in the area of sport marketing and sponsorship, the largest independent television sports production company and rights distributor (Trans World International) and of course IMG is the world leader in athlete, celebrity and sport organization representation (such as Tiger Woods, Ernie Els, Jennifer Capriati, John McEnroe, Michael Schumacher, Kate Moss, Liv Tyler, Manchester United, the US Olympic Committee, Oxford University). IMG also own numerous (sporting) events and represent others (such as Wimbledon, Rugby World Cup, the Australian Rally Championship) to the extent that the company, on average, is involved in 11 major sport and cultural events around the world every day.

Meeting Arnold Palmer at university when they were playing golf against each other, Mark McCormack saw an opportunity in representing excellent athletes in their efforts to maximize their earning capacity outside the field of play, when no one else saw this as a possibility. Rather than focusing on athletic ability, McCormack quickly realized that building the athlete's profile through continued, intensive positive exposure was the key to success. What now seems common knowledge was a visionary realization more than 40 years ago. After shaking Arnold Palmer's hand as his first 'contract', he signed up Gary Player and Jack Nicklaus, effectively locking in golf's 'big three'. The success of the company that he was building was based on 'celebrity' not by merely signing the best athletes or in later years, the most beautiful model or best musicians. Although the big boom of sport-specific television production only started in the late 1980s, McCormack set up TWI, the television production arm of IMG in the late 1960s. Setting up (dream) confrontations between athletes that he controlled and exposing them through IMG owned media launched the company globally.

McCormack himself commented on the reasons for IMGs tremendous success by stating that 'I think what we tried to do was to use sports in a way that it had never been used before and to enable us to get companies to be able to use it to entertain customers and to sell their products, because, as you well know, in the last 30 or 40 years, the people that are most looked up to in most parts of the world are sports personalities'. One of his personal friends out of the racing industry, Jackie Stewart summarizes the secret to the success of IMG succinctly: 'The automotive industry is the third largest manufacturing industry in the world, and it had potentially more commercial ramifications and opportunities than any other sport I could think of. Here I was just embarking on that, so I knew I needed someone very good. Mark was incredibly strong as a visionary because he could have stayed in golf and just done very well. Skiing for example, was not a big sport at that time'. Jean-Claude Killy was very well known in the early days of the sport because he had won three Olympic gold medals. McCormack picked up Killy because he was a celebrity, not because skiing was such a popular sport. Throughout his career McCormack maintained friendships with most of the athletes he signed. Personal service was everything. IMG currently has two CEOs who share the job. McCormack's shoes were simply too big to fill.

Source: www.imgworld.com, and www.cbn.com

Theories of leadership

Personality or trait theories form the basis of the earliest approaches to studying leadership. These theories were underpinned by the assumption that certain traits and skills are essential for leadership effectiveness.

Trait or personality approaches

Although the personality and trait approaches to leadership stem from the earliest of leadership research times, popular leadership literature continues to stress the importance of personality and innate ability in the demonstration of leadership. Locke (1991) argues that trait theories (or great man theories as they are also called), are incomplete theories of leadership, irrespective of traits and/or personality of the leaders being important contributors to, or detractors from excellent leadership. Locke (1991) suggests that the possession of certain traits, such as energy and honesty, appear to be vital for effective leadership. Basketball legend Michael Jordan, for example, has been credited with having an impressive range of innate leadership traits that will put him in good stead of being an excellent leader in many different contexts. Leaders must use their traits to develop skills, formulate a vision, and implement this vision into reality. This being the case, it appears that traits only form part of the picture.

Although empirical evidence linking the personality of leaders with their success is weak, it is still valuable examining leadership personalities from a wide range of sources (e.g. popular literature) to provide a better understanding of leadership. In general, the trait theories are based on the assumption that social background, physical features and personality characteristics will distinguish good from not so good leaders.

Behavioural approach

When it became clear that good leadership could not simply be explained on the basis of the innate characteristics of the leaders, organizational research began to focus on discovering universal behaviours of effective leaders. Behaviouralists argued that anyone could be taught to become a leader by simply learning the behaviours of other effective leaders.

Behavioural strategy takes behaviours as signs of learned responses to contingencies. If research shows that to behave in a certain manner results in success for a leader, then one can learn to discharge those behaviours in particular leadership situations. The behavioural approach to leadership was also a response to early approaches to management as a whole. Frederick Taylor was an early spokesman and champion of the idea that managers should use science to improve efficiency. This approach became known as Taylorism or Scientific management, a philosophy in which there was limited attention for the human side of the mass production movement. Rather, under Taylorism humans were simply 'part of the larger machines' and standardization of human labour would lead to great efficiency and higher profits. Managers, according to Taylor, should begin by studying the tasks workers performed, break jobs down by analysing, measuring and timing each separate element of the job in order to determine the most efficient manner of doing the job. The most efficient method for each job became both the standard method that workers were supposed to adopt and a means for measuring worker productivity.

In response to Taylor's ideas, behaviouralists demanded a new 'human relations' approach to management of organizations involving an examination of the interaction between managers and workers. In the Hawthorne experiments, which were originally designed to study the effects of lighting upon factory workers, Elton Mayo discovered that human relations between workers, and between workers and supervisors was most important in ensuring efficiency. In other words, to focus on interaction between humans, and by studying the best ways of interacting, managers could better lead the people that worked for the organization. Another behavioural approach to the study of leadership is the so-called Theory X and Theory Y, developed by Douglas McGregor. The theories are formulated based on the assumptions that leaders have about individuals. Managers that have Theory X assumptions argue that the typical employee dislikes work and needs direction at all times. They also think that employees need to be coerced to perform their duties. Theory Y managers believe that employees are self-motivated and committed to work and to the company. They naturally seek responsibility for the work they perform. As a result, Theory Y leaders would behave in quite different ways from Theory X leaders.

Another behaviouralist approach was formulated by Blake and Mouton. They developed the managerial grid model along two dimensions; one with a concern for people and one with a concern for production. Blake and Mouton argued that differing levels of concern along those dimensions would lead to different styles of leadership. For example, managers with low levels of concern for people and production will have an impoverished style of leadership whereas those leaders with high concern for people and production can be typified as having team style leadership qualities. The Blake and Mouton approach has also been used to differentiate person-centred leaders from task-centred leaders. Ultimately it is important to conclude that the behaviouralist approach to leadership leads to the identification of different styles that can be described as more or less successful.

Contingency approach

It became increasingly clear to those studying leadership that traits and behaviours of leaders were often observed in relation to the situation at hand, or in other words, according to situational contingencies. Isolated behavioural and trait approaches failed to take account of how situational variables, such as task structure, the characteristics of the environment, or subordinate characteristics could impact and moderate the relationship between the behaviour of a leader and the different outcomes.

In contingency theories of leadership, the core argument is that different leadership styles and approaches will apply to a range of possible management situations. This is why, for example, the on-field leadership brilliance of Diego Maradona with the Argentinian team resulted in winning the 1986 World Cup, but when Diego was required to achieve similar results with club teams in different cultures (Napoli in Italy and Barcelona in Spain), he failed dismally, also resulting in the exposure of a number of personal leadership flaws. The centrality of leader behaviour and/or personality needs to be de-emphasized, and in the contingency approach we turn our attention to the leader in conjunction with circumstances that are specific to the situation at hand, including characteristics of the subordinates and the work setting. In the next section we will present three situational theories of leadership that have influenced the ways in which leadership is understood and practised. They are:

- Fiedler's Least Preferred Co-worker Approach
- Hersey and Blanchard's Situational Leadership Theory
- Path Goal Theory

Fiedler's least preferred co-worker approach

Fiedler's (1967) model is based on the following three axioms:

1. the interaction between the leader's personal characteristics and some aspects of the situation determines the effectiveness of the leader
2. leaders are either 'task oriented' or 'person oriented'

3. effectiveness of the leader is determined by the leader's control of the situation.

Fiedler comes to his classification of task or person oriented leadership by the use of a measurement scale called the 'Least Preferred Co-worker' (LPC) scale. The instrument asks leaders to assess co-workers on a series of bi-polar descriptors including pleasant-unpleasant, cold-warm, and supportive-hostile in order to assess to what degree they think they would not work well together with that co-worker. A leader who obtains a low LPC is more motivated by task achievements and will only be concerned about relationships with subordinates if the work unit is deemed to be performing well. A leader who obtains a high LPC score will be more motivated to develop close interpersonal relations with subordinates. Task directed behaviour is of a lesser concern, and only becomes important once sound interpersonal relations have been developed. According to Fiedler, if the least preferred co-worker still scores relatively high it indicates that the leader derives a sense of satisfaction from 'working on good relationships', indicating a person oriented leadership style.

The model further suggests that control is dependent on three combined contingency variables:

1. the relations between the leader and the followers
2. the degree of task structure (or the degree to which the followers' jobs can be specified clearly)
3. the leader's position of power or amount of authority, yielding eight possible conditions presented in Figure 8.1.

Condition	Situational favourability			
	Leader-Member relations	Task Structure	Position Power	Effective leadership
1	Good	High	Strong	Low LPC
2	Good	High	Weak	Low LPC
3	Good	Weak	Strong	Low LPC
4	Good	Weak	Weak	High LPC
5	Poor	High	Strong	High LPC
6	Poor	High	Weak	High LPC
7	Poor	Weak	Strong	High LPC
8	Poor	Weak	Weak	Low LPC

Figure 8.1 Fiedler's Situational favourability factors and leadership effectiveness. Adapted from Fiedler, F.E. (1967), *A theory of leadership effectiveness*, New York: McGraw Hill, p. 34.

Hersey and Blanchard's situational leadership theory

A theory claiming that as maturity of the group changes, leader behaviour should change as well is known as the Situational Theory of Leadership. Hersey and Blanchard (1977) argued that as the technical skill level and psychological maturity of the group moves from low to moderate to high, the leader's behaviour would be most effective when it changes accordingly. When low levels of maturity are enacted in relation to the tasks being performed, a high task-behaviour of the leader should be exhibited, or in other words, a 'selling' and 'telling' approach to communicating with the subordinates. At medium levels of maturity, leaders need to be more focused on relationship-behaviours and at the highest levels of subordinate maturity, the leader needs to offer little direction or task-behaviour and allow the subordinate to assume responsibilities, or in other words, a 'supportive' and 'delegation' driven style of leadership communication.

According to sport organization theory researcher Trevor Slack (1997), there have been few attempts to empirically test the concepts and relationships that Hersey and Blanchard (1977) have outlined in their work, even in the management and organizational literature. Some attempts have been made to apply the theory directly in sport settings, but results have been inconsistent.

The path-goal theory

The path-goal theory (House, 1971) takes a behavioural and situational approach to leadership. There are many roads that lead to Rome and therefore the path-goal theory suggests that a leader must select a style most appropriate to the particular situation. The theory in particular aims to explain how a leader's behaviour affects the motivation and satisfaction of subordinates.

House (1971) is cited in Wexley and Yukl (1984), arguing that 'the motivational function of the leaders consists of increasing personal payoffs to subordinates for work-goal attainment, and making the path to these payoffs easier to travel by clarifying it, reducing roadblocks and pitfalls, and increasing the opportunities for personal satisfaction en route' (p. 176). In other words, characteristics of the subordinates and characteristics of the environment determine both the potential for increased motivation and the manner in which the leader must act to improve motivation. Subordinate preferences for a particular pattern of leadership behaviour may also depend on the actual situation in which they are placed (Wexley & Yukl, 1984). Taking those different perspectives, consider the path-goal theory proposes four styles of leadership behaviour that can be utilized to achieve goals (House & Mitchell, 1974). They are:

- Directive Leadership (leader gives specific instructions, expectations and guidance);
- Supportive Leadership (leader shows concern and support for subordinates);

- Participative Leadership (subordinates participate in the decision-making);
- Achievement Oriented Leadership (leader sets challenges, emphasizes excellence and shows confidence that subordinates will attain high standards of performance).

The theory is principally aimed at examining how leaders affect subordinate expectations about likely outcomes of different courses of action. Directive leadership is predicted to have a positive effect on subordinates when the task is ambiguous, and will have a negative impact when the task is clear. Supportive leadership is predicted to increase job satisfaction, particularly when conditions are adverse. Participative leadership is predicted to promote satisfaction due to involvement (Schermerhorn et al., 1994). Achievement-oriented leadership is predicted to encourage higher performance standards and increase expectancies that desired outcomes can be achieved.

From transactional to transformational leadership

As already noted earlier in this chapter, the Scientific approach to management (Taylorism) reduced the individual to performing machine-like functions. The human relations approach to management took into consideration the human part of the labour equation, appreciating that much better results can be achieved if people's individual needs are taken into consideration when leading them towards achieving certain work outputs.

One of the most recent thrusts in leadership research is that of transactional and transformational leadership. Transactional leadership encompasses much of the theories based on rational exchange between leader and subordinate, such as the theories presented above, but transformational leaders, according to Bass (1985), are charismatic, and develop followers into leaders through a process that transcends the existing organizational climate and culture. The transactional leader aims to create a cost-benefit economic exchange, or in other words, to meet the needs of followers in return for 'contracted' services that are produced by the follower (Bass, 1985). To influence behaviour, the transactional leader may use the following approaches:

- Contingent Reward (the leader uses rewards or incentives to achieve results)
- Active Management by Exception (the leader actively monitors the work performed and uses corrective methods to ensure the work meets accepted standards)
- Passive Management by Exception (the leader uses corrective methods as a response to unacceptable performance or deviation from the accepted standards)
- Laissez-Faire Leadership (the leader is indifferent and has a 'hands-off' approach toward the workers and their performance).

However, leadership theorists have argued that transactional leadership merely seeks to influence others by exchanging work for wages. It fails to build on the worker's need for meaningful work and it does not actively tap into their sources of creativity. A more effective and beneficial leadership behaviour to achieve long-term success and improved performance therefore is transformational leadership. Sir Alex Ferguson, the long time Manchester United (Man U) manager can be described as a transformational leader. He envisioned a future for the club and the Board repaid him with the trust of keeping him at the helm at Man U for more than 1000 games. Under his guidance and supervision the club became the most successful team in the new English Premiership and he prepared the likes of Eric Cantona, Ryan Giggs, Roy Keane, David Beckham, Ruud van Nistelrooy and Wayne Rooney for the world stage of football leadership.

What is transformational leadership?

It has been argued by Bass and Avolio (1994) that transformational leadership is the new leadership that must accompany good management. In contrast to transactional models, transformational leadership goes beyond the exchange process. It not only aligns and elevates the needs and values of followers, but also provides intellectual stimulation and increased follower confidence. Bass and Avolio (1994) identified four 'I's' that transformational leaders employ in order to achieve superior results. These are:

- Idealized Influence: Transformational leaders behave in ways that result in them being admired, respected and trusted, and ultimately becoming a role model. The transformational leader demonstrates high standards of ethical and moral conduct.
- Inspirational Motivation: By demonstrating enthusiasm and optimism, the transformational leader actively arouses team spirit and motivates and inspires followers to share in and work towards a common goal.
- Intellectual Stimulation: By being innovative, creative, supportive, reframing problems and questioning old assumptions the transformational leader creates an intellectually stimulating and encouraging environment.
- Individualized Consideration: Transformational leaders pay special attention to each individual's needs for achievement and growth by acting as a coach or mentor.

Looking closer at the four 'I's' it can be argued that charisma (the ability to inspire enthusiasm, interest, or affection in others by means of personal charm or influence) is an important component of transformational leadership. Purely charismatic leaders may be limited in their ability to achieve successful outcomes, due to their need to instill their beliefs in others which may inhibit the individual growth of followers. However, transformational leaders are more than charismatic in that they generate awareness of the mission or vision of the team and the organization, and then motivate colleagues and followers towards outcomes that benefit the team rather than merely serving the individual interest.

Case 8.2   Right to Play

The primary objective of *Right To Play*, formerly known as *Olympic Aid*, the legacy project of the Lillehammer Olympic Organizing Committee, is to engage leaders in sport, business and media in the betterment of living conditions and developmental opportunities for children all over the world. In March 2001, *Olympic Aid* became an implementing NGO (Non-Governmental Organization) and by organizing child development programmes and engaging in research and policy development it works towards improving the chances that all children are guaranteed their right to play.

Four time Olympic gold medallist Johann Olav Koss, the current CEO and President of the organization was the driving force behind the transition of *Olympic Aid* into *Right to Play*. Having visited the country of Eritrea during his sporting career, as an athlete ambassador, he was so affected by the living conditions of the local children in particular, that he decided to donate the majority of his Olympic winnings to *Olympic Aid*. In the process he challenged other athletes and the public to do the same, leading to the raising of US$18 million. Between 1994 and 2000, *Olympic Aid* continued to raise funds for children in disadvantaged situations, building on the momentum of subsequent Olympic Games.

In early 2003, *Olympic Aid* evolved into *Right To Play* in order to meet the growing demands of programme implementation and fundraising. Building on the founding legacy of Lillehammer, this transition allowed *Right To Play* to include both Olympic athletes and other high profile sportsmen and women as athlete ambassadors, but also increase relationships with non-Olympic Sports, partner with a wider variety of private sector funding agents, and to deepen involvement at the grass-roots level of sport. The vision of leading athlete Johan Olav Koss has been translated into a highly successful organization that he continues to head up today as an organizational leader, developing and delivering its own child and community development programme using sport and play as its vehicles of communication and fundraising. To a large extent, sport leads the way as well.

Source: http://www.righttoplay.com

Leadership and management

At this stage of the chapter it will be useful to briefly consider the debate about the relationship between leadership and management, and how to distinguish between the two. Kotter (1990) has conducted extensive research work in order to find out how to differentiate managers from leaders. He concluded that management effectiveness rests in the ability to plan and budget; organize and staff; and control and solve problems. Leadership, however, is principally founded upon the ability to establish direction; align people; and to motivate and inspire. According to Kotter, leaders achieve change whilst managers succeed in maintaining the status quo. Bass (1990), however, states that 'leaders manage and managers lead, but the two activities are not synonymous' (p. 383). It goes beyond the scope of this book to further elaborate on the distinction between leadership and management. Suffice to say that in the context of discussing management principles in sport organizations, management without leadership is much less likely to be successful than a capable manager who can also provide excellent leadership. In the next section we will therefore put forward what can be described as the five key functions of leadership, functions that need to be managed well! These functions are:

- To create a vision
- To set out strategy
- To set objectives and lead towards performance
- To influence and motivate people
- To facilitate change and nurture culture

To create a vision

A vision can be described as 'a state of the future that lies beyond the directly imaginable by most people'. This view of the future, in the context of an organization, is a positive and bright state of being that only the 'visionary' (one who is characterized by unusually acute foresight and imagination) can see at that time. In other words, the leader is responsible for envisioning a future for the organization that can become reality if the people working in the organization can be aligned towards achieving that 'envisioned state'. It is often said that good leaders distinguish themselves from good managers because they do have a vision whereas managers do not. How to achieve the vision through strategy is the next function of the leader.

To set out strategy

The process of strategic planning is all about the different ways that a vision can be achieved. It constitutes two principal perspectives; that of the organization and that of the individuals making up the organization. Visionary leaders are not necessarily successful leaders if they are not capable in translating the vision into action strategies. The process of strategic management is therefore concerned with carefully managing the internal organization, including considering the individual needs of workers, and the external environment in which many opportunities and threats impact the ability of the leader to achieve the vision. To be better prepared for action, the leader needs to be involved in setting measurable objectives.

To set objectives and lead towards performance

Setting objectives is the next function of the leader. Once the broad strategies have been set out (and these strategies are never set in concrete, they need constant updating), it is time to link measurable outcomes to these strategies. In other words, what do we want to achieve in the short term, in order to work towards our visionary objectives that lie ahead in the distant future. Stated differently, the leader often is involved in setting objectives at different levels of the organization, ranging from 'visionary' and strategic objectives to mostly delegating the responsibility to set more operational objectives at lower levels of the organization. Only when SMART (specific, measurable, achievable, resources available, time bound) objectives are set, the leader will be in a position to manage the performance of the organization and its employees effectively. An important part of the performance of an organization is achieved through the people management skills of the leader.

To influence and motivate people

In our overview of the different approaches to leadership, we have already commented on the different styles that leaders chose to develop (because they better fit their skill set) in order to influence groups of people and communicate with individuals or teams. Where setting objectives is important in making people aware of the targets of performance, the actual activation and application of people skills is critical when trying to steer people in a certain direction. This is where leaders with charismatic appeal will have an easier job. Their natural ability to inspire enthusiasm, interest, or affection in others by means of personal charm or influence will put these leaders in a favourable position in regard to achieving the objectives that were set.

To facilitate change and nurture culture

Finally it is important to acknowledge that in this day and age, change is constant. Leaders who are incapable of assisting others to understand why 'change' is needed and how this change can be achieved with minimal disruption and maximum outcomes will have a difficult time surviving in the organizations of the 21st century. Most organizations are required to keep close track of the market conditions that they are working under and the impact changes in market conditions will have on their structures and strategies. Often a rapid response to changing market conditions is needed and this is where the interesting relationship with the organization's culture comes into play. Ironically, a strong and stable organizational culture can contribute to the need to constantly modify direction and changing the systems and structures of the organization. It is the leaders' responsibility to create and nurture a culture in which change is accepted as part of the natural way of organizational life. A strong culture is the backbone of any successful organization and the maintenance of culture is therefore one of the primary areas of leadership responsibility.

Case 8.3 'Envisioning' a future for the Al Jazira Sport and Cultural Club

The Al Jazira Sport and Cultural Club is one of the major multi-sport organizations residing in Abu Dhabi, the capital of the United Arab Emirates. Al Jazira is Arab for 'the island' and refers to the island that the city of Abu Dhabi is built on. At the start of 2004 the club embarked on a massive change management strategy that was initiated by the production of a strategic plan for the club as a whole by a group of outside consultants. At that time the club had a Board of (volunteer) Directors, was heavily supported (in terms of finance and superb facilities) by the Abu Dhabi government (approximately 2/3 of total income) and as a consequence of funding, was also pushed in a particular direction by government. Furthermore, the club employed a number of professionals ranging from highly qualified coaches and facility managers to non-qualified administrative and operational personnel, all of whom have their own ideas about where the club should be going. The club had as many as 400 people on its payroll employing approximately the equivalent of 100 full-time staff. The club had no CEO, General Manager or Executive Director. Irrespective of the fact that Al Jazira is a multi-sport club (including handball, volleyball, tenpin bowling, swimming, table tennis and football), most attention and resources went (and still go) into the football department (soccer). The club presently participates in the nation's premier football competition and is a regular contender for the championship. It therefore will come as no surprise that one of the most important objectives for the club is to have a high performing first team. This objective outranks all other objectives in terms of perceived importance.

From the perspective of a vision for the club as a whole, the relative importance of a high performing first football team limited the visionary scope. In other words, although Al Jazira is a multi-sport club, the perceived vision was limited to expressing ambitions in regard to future international success in football. There was limited interest for the future potential of the club in becoming a major tool and meeting place for community cohesion and development.

There was a clear need to establish a 'common core direction' for the Al Jazira club as a whole, which was expressed in a vision statement, focusing on the highest profile sport that could 'draw' the rest of the club in its slipstream. At the level of what the club wanted to contribute to its stakeholders and customer communities, a mission statement was formulated to further outline the services the club has on offer.

Vision statement

The Al Jazira club will be considered THE benchmark for performance on and off the football field for football clubs in the Middle East. Al Jazira will *always* be a contender for domestic and international championships.

Mission statement

The Al Jazira club wants to be a multi-sport organization that caters for school children (boys and girls), local citizens and a diverse range of ethnic communities. Enabling participants to play high quality sport is at the core of activities of the club. Playing football at a high level is of critical importance as it offers the club high exposure and credibility in the Abu Dhabi and UAE community. The Al Jazira club wants to be an international contender. The club is made up of passionate people, who are active in sport, business and the educational system, and it prides itself in having a strong administrative structure of full-time professionals with qualifications in the area of sport business.

These vision and mission statements were used by the executive of the club to initiate a process of strategy formulation and organizational change and the first thing that happened to kick start this process was the appointment of an interim CEO, a person with a significant change management track record. This person should be a short-term leader for change, who should prepare the club for new enduring leadership towards efficiency, effectiveness and ultimately, sustainable success on and off the football field.

Leadership challenges in sport organizations

So far we have mainly been talking about generic leadership theory and principles, simply, because it applies to sport organizations in the same way as it does to non-sport organizations. We have also discussed the interrelationship between leadership and management and how leadership is largely about establishing visionary direction, and then to motivate and align people and structures towards that direction. In Case 8.3 it is shown that sometimes, visionary direction needs to be supplied from outside. However, there will also be specific challenges for leaders (and managers) of sport organizations that are based on the unique characteristics of (some) sport organizations. In our discussion of these characteristics we will take a closer look at the leadership and management challenges of three types of sport organizations:

- Small Community Sport Clubs and Regionally Based Sport Associations
- National Sporting Organizations
- International Federations and Professional Sport Organizations

Small community based sport clubs and regionally based sport associations

Small community based sport clubs are traditionally set up and run by the same people; those who share a passion for a particular sport and are interested in participating in some form of organized competition. Regional volunteer associations are similar in their structure and processes in that they largely coordinate the competitions that the community clubs are playing in and as such, they represent the interests of the individual clubs. Most of these clubs and associations are run by volunteers leading to relatively low levels of professionalism and standardization of organizational processes. They operate in suburban or regional communities with little desire or incentive to expand and grow beyond their identified community base. The main challenge for the leaders of small clubs, and their representatives at the regional level, is first and foremost, to survive in an environment of decreasing levels of volunteer labour and commitment. Increasing competition for the scarce leisure time of members leads to a diminishing supply of free labour. Consumer (not member!) expectations about services delivered are also on the increase. Club and association leaders need to envision how they can transform their ways of operating into more professional and competitive ways of sport service delivery, but they have to do that without the abundant volunteer resources they had in the past. Most of these challenges are of a tactical or operational nature. Typical leadership questions that club and association leaders are faced with today are:

- Can small clubs survive or should they consider merging or relocating?
- How can we retain our younger members and our most valued volunteers?
- How can we attract new resources to the club in order to pay for professional services?
- How can we maintain the culture of the club?

National sporting organizations

Many national sporting organizations have already successfully negotiated and adapted to the changing community landscape of sport, and are now in a position to face the next set of challenges. In much the same way as community and regionally based sport organizations, national governing bodies are confronted with higher levels of customer expectations in combination with fewer resources to deliver services. In a better position than community organizations to lobby for resources at the different levels of government, many of the national governing bodies have increased their levels of professionalism and standards of service delivery by employing professionally educated staff in their organizations. Leaders are now facing increased competition for paying customers to become affiliated to the sport's governing bodies. A major dilemma for national governing bodies is the fact that they only have one core product, their sport, which only offers limited strategic scope to expand into existing or new markets. The leaders of national sporting organizations also face the issue of the increasing gap between the 'haves' (i.e. the popular television and Olympic sports) and the 'have nots' (i.e. minority sports). In other words, do leaders want 'all sports for all' or rather, let the market decide about the sports that will stay and grow and those that will fade into insignificance? The answer to this question also impacts where leaders of NSOs will focus much of their attention; on elite or mass participation sport. Most of these challenges are of a strategic nature. Typical leadership questions that the leaders of national sport governing bodies are faced with today are:

- Are we a national or international sport or in other words, what is our marketplace?
- What is best for our sport: a focus on elite; on mass participation; or an equal balance between the two?

- How can we better deliver our sport through the regional and local associations and clubs? (this is a systems question)
- How can we change our systems of governance to be better prepared for radical (short term) changes in the sport market?

International federations and professional sport

Although there may be quite significant differences in size and structure between the International Federations (IFs) and professional sport organizations (ranging from clubs to the governing bodies), the leaders of these organizations are largely confronted with the same leadership challenges. If NSOs were already concerned with questions about what their marketplace is, then the IFs and professional sport organizations should be able to answer those questions now. As with the lead that NSOs are taking in relation to the community and regional sport organizations below them in the hierarchy, the IFs are leading the way for NSOs in regard to their leadership challenges. Both the IFs and professional sport organizations are required to make genuinely visionary decisions in that competition is forcing them to think outside the square of previous operations. The World Wrestling Federation (now WWE) had to make a decision about operating in the sport or entertainment market, Manchester United and the New York Yankees are working on market expansion beyond football and baseball, and the world governing body for football, FIFA, is seriously considering its options beyond simply organizing a few football competitions (albeit a few very profitable ones). Europe's governing body for football, UEFA, has major headaches about the possibility that the strongest European clubs will create a competition of their own, which will virtually eliminate the highly lucrative Champions' League that is owned and operated by UEFA. The leaders of IFs and professional sport organizations face truly visionary leadership challenges. Typical leadership questions that these leaders are confronted with today are:

- Are we in the business of sport or are we simply competing for people's leisure time?
- How much control do we need to exercise in terms of our chain of distribution? For example, do we need to own our sporting facilities and broadcast centres rather than contracting with other owners?
- How will the market for sport, entertainment and leisure develop over the next decade? Where do we need to be placed in order to become and remain major players in those markets?
- Who will be the leaders for the sport of the future?

Summary

In this chapter we described what it takes to be a leader. We argued that irrespective of leadership type or style, leaders are goal oriented; they influence others; they empower others; they need to remain focused on the big picture; they need others to achieve their goals; and they have strong characters. Based on these components of leadership we discussed a number of theoretical approaches to leadership including the trait/personality, behavioural and contingency approaches, ultimately resulting in a discussion about transactional versus transformational leadership. Prior to looking at the future challenges for leaders in sport at the end of the chapter, we highlighted the differences between managers and leaders by outlining what are the functions of leaders. These functions were the creation of a vision; the setting out of strategy; setting objectives and measuring performance; influencing and motivating people; and finally, to facilitate change and nurture organizational culture.

Review questions

1. Are leaders born or can they be made? Justify your answer by comparing the different leadership theories discussed in this chapter.
2. Does sport offer valuable leadership lessons to business? What are the specific characteristics of sport organizations that challenge leaders in sport organizations more than leaders in business and how can this knowledge be transferred to a non-sport context?
3. 'A good manager is also a good leader'. Do you agree or disagree with this statement? Justify your answer.
4. Explain how leadership is important for the performance of a sport organization.
5. Interview the leader of a small sport organization. How would you describe their leadership style?
6. Is there any difference in the leadership skills required to be the CEO of a major professional sport franchise versus the manager of a community sports club?
7. What criteria would you use to evaluate the leadership skills of a sport manager?
8. Is it possible to compare the performance of leaders of two different sport organizations? Why or why not?

Further reading

Bass, B.M. (1990). *Bass & Stogdill's handbook of leadership: Theory, research, and managerial applications* (3rd ed.). New York: The Free Press.

Kotter, J.P. (1990). *A force for change: How leadership differs from management.* New York: The Free Press.

Locke, E.A. (1991). *The essence of leadership: The four keys to leading successfully.* New York: Lexington Books.

Slack, T. (1997). *Understanding sport organizations: The application of organization theory.* Champaign, IL: Human Kinetics.

Relevant websites

* Olympic Aid (now Right to Play) at http://www.righttoplay.com/
* The Centre for Creative Leadership at http://www.ccl.org/
* The Test Café Leadership Test at http://www.testcafe.com/lead/

Chapter 9
Organizational culture

Overview

This chapter explores the influence of organizational culture in sport. It examines why organizational culture is pivotal, highlights its impact and explains how it can be diagnosed. Several cases and numerous examples will be used throughout the chapter to help explain the role of culture in a sport organization's performance.

By the end of this chapter the reader should be able to:

- Define the meaning of organizational culture;
- Specify why culture is important to sport organizations;
- Explain how different contexts can affect an organizational culture;
- Identify how sport organizational cultures can be diagnosed;
- Show the dimensions across which sport organizational cultures can be measured; and
- Discuss how sport organizational culture can be changed.

What is organizational culture?

Culture was originally defined by anthropologists as the values and beliefs common to a group of people. These researchers set themselves the task of investigating, interpreting and translating the behavioural and social patterns of groups of individuals by trying to understand the manner in which they relate to their environment. From an organizational perspective, researchers like Miles (1975) and Pettigrew (1979) observed that while people in organizations run the technology and invent the processes, they in turn, as part of the process, have much of their behaviour determined by the system they operate. In other words, there are underlying forces that impact upon behaviour. The concept of culture is a way of putting a name to these forces.

There is no single accepted definition of organizational culture. For example, organizational culture is viewed by some as the 'personality' of an organization, while for others it represents the things which make an organization unique. Several assumptions about organizational culture are well-accepted though. These are:

1. Culture tends to be inflexible and resistant to easy or rapid change.
2. Culture is shaped by an organization's circumstances, its history and its members.
3. Culture is learned and shared by members of an organization and is reflected in common understandings and beliefs.
4. Culture is often covert; the deep values and beliefs causing behaviour can be hidden from organizational members making them difficult to identify.
5. Culture is manifested in a variety of ways that affect the performance of an organization and its members.

Although elements of commonality exist in the way in which researchers conceive and define culture in organizations, much inconsistency and controversy can still be found. However, for the purposes of this chapter, we shall discuss organizational culture in a way consistent with the view of Schein (1984, 1997), who invokes a more psycho-dynamic view. This means that he believes culture is, in part, an unconscious phenomenon, driven by deep level assumptions and beliefs, and where conscious views are merely artefacts and symbolic representations. For example, most sport clubs members would report that on-field winning is important. Schein's interpretation of organizational culture would lead to questions about *why* winning is important. Does it have to do with a need to belong to a successful group, the pressure of peers, or some other more mysterious explanation? While many people involved in sport would think this question easy to answer, it is less easy to specify the underpinning values that drive unusual rituals, ceremonies, myths, legends, stories, beliefs, memorabilia and attitudes.

In current and former nations of the British Commonwealth, cricket is played with enormous enthusiasm, but can take up to five, six-hour days to complete a single match, which often ends in a draw. Similarly, to the uninitiated, American football seems quite strange with each team comprising separate players for offensive and defensive manoeuvres. Off the field can be just as odd. In Australia, many (Australian Rules) football clubs have 'sausage-sizzles' (BBQs), 'pie-nights' (involving the traditional meal of a meat pie) and a host of rituals associated with drinking beer. In addition, many sport organizations are packed with memorabilia and expect their employees to work during evening training sessions and weekend games. Sport organizations are rich with strong, meaningful cultural symbols, which on the surface seem easy to interpret, but sometimes are only superficial symptoms of deeper issues.

What Schein searches for is not the superficial, but rather the unconsciously held fundamental concepts of right or wrong; what an organization might perceive as correct or incorrect values. These values, which are the foundation of an organization's culture, do not simply exist or come into being by their own volition. Instead, they are painstakingly built up by members of the organization as they gradually learn to interact and achieve their collective and individual aims (Schein, 1984). The originators of the organization, together with the more powerful of the organization's past and present members, are usually the most influential in determining the culture. Thus, Schein prefers to examine the long-held assumptions and beliefs in an organization, believing that they will more likely explain the organization's culture.

For the purposes of this chapter, we shall define sport organizational culture as follows:

Sport organizational culture is a collection of fundamental values, beliefs and attitudes that are common to members of a sport organization, and which subsequently set the behavioural standards or norms for all members (Ogbonna & Harris, 2002, Pettigrew, 1979; Schein, 1985). This definition reflects the view that sport organizations have ways of approaching things that have evolved over time. In many ways, organizational culture therefore holds answers to questions about solving problems. Culture is how 'things are done around here' and how we 'think about things here'. Culture is a subtle form of 'brainwashing'.

Case 9.1   Cultural change at the Japan Sumo Association

Amongst the most illuminating cultural markers are the myths and legends perpetuated within sport, and no professional sport in the world has more than sumo. The Japanese legend goes that it was in fact a sumo match between two gods that created the Japanese islands. Originally a ritual act dating back to 712 AD as a dedication to the gods in exchange for a beneficial harvest, sumo became part of the imperial court, and later a form of combat training. The professional sport of today is still fixed in ceremony, ritual and strict codes of conduct. Young wrestlers enter training 'stables' from the age of 15, beginning daily practice at 4.30 am. They work hard to bulk up and rise through the rigid hierarchy of ranks with the dream of performing well in one of the six, 15 day-long Grand Tournaments held each year.

Sumo today, however, is changing. Like all sports, sumo's governing body, the Japan Sumo Association, has been faced with pressures from globalization, social change and professionalism. In fact, the Japan Sumo Association is one of the most insular sport organizations in the world, particularly considering it presides over a sport that is a national obsession. Sumo champions are superstars, beamed to over 60 percent of households during Grand Tournaments, a staggering figure considering that only 40 percent of households in the United States watch the Super Bowl each year. The Japan Sumo Association has in the past been notorious for its hierarchy, secrecy, chauvinism, xenophobia and total resistance to change. Although still extremely slow, some of these values are softening.

Unlike martial arts, which have thoroughly inculcated the Western world, sumo has remained a Japanese sport. However, in the last 50 years, a number of foreign participants have slowly made progress in opening the sport to other nationalities. This has partly been because young Japanese men have become increasingly interested in more global sports like soccer and golf. In addition, the traditional system of sponsorship for young sumo has diminished. Sumo training stables have subsequently been more open-minded to training non-Japanese wrestlers. There are now over 50 foreign-born sumo wrestlers from a dozen different countries. Although one Hawaiian sumo whose results were sufficient was disqualified from reaching the highest ranking in the sport – the prestigious Yokozuna – because the Sumo Association considered him morally unfit, now several non-Japanese have become Yokozuna.

The Sumo Association is grappling with other cultural changes as well. The sport has periodically been subject to negative media associated with allegations of match fixing; what the officials refer to as 'spiritless' fights. The Japan Sumo Association has also caved in to pressure for women's sumo to gain greater recognition. While women's sumo is strictly amateur, the New Sumo Association has been set up to promote it as a potential Olympic sport. However, according to Shinto beliefs which lie at the heart of sumo culture, a woman is rendered impure by her menstrual cycles, and should not be allowed to even touch the sumo ring, and certainly not fight in it. This rule still holds to the point where recently a female provincial governor was precluded from presenting prize money to the winning sumo in her own region, a tradition begun by her male predecessors. More positively, the Japan Sumo Association has spearheaded initiatives banning smoking in venues and fat-testing sumo participants to discourage rampant obesity and weight-related injury and ill-health common in the sport.

The importance of culture to sport organizations

In many countries sport has for some time been regarded as a particularly important social institution. Sporting heroes are often national heroes as well. Examples include Michael Jordan and Vince Lombardi in the United States, Roger Bannister and David Beckham in the United Kingdom, Shigeo Nagashima and Hanada Katsuji (sumo name, Wakanohana) in Japan, and Sir Donald Bradman and Ian Thorpe in Australia. Although these names are not the definitive sporting heroes of the nations identified, their sports and personal profiles are illustrative of the national cultural pressures that influence the sport organizations they host. This quick list, for example, excludes women; a trait common to many sport organizational cultures, and one that many are seeking to change. However, the influence of the national culture means that such changes are more likely to occur in some nations than others (Hofstede, 1991).

We can expect that different types of sport organizations will possess different kinds of cultures. For example, professional clubs and major national leagues are more likely to emphasize dispassionate business values, while smaller, not-for-profit associations are more likely to value participation and fun. Some sport organizations like Italian and Spanish football (soccer) clubs are geared almost exclusively to winning and are prepared to go heavily into debt in order to do so. Others, like the company Formula One Holdings, manage the commercial rights to major events and have little other interest than to make money. While the Fédération Internationale de l'Automobile seeks to regulate motor sport, others still, like the International Olympic Committee, are interested in developing sport around the world, and in so doing acquire vast sums of money and spend it liberally.

Sports organizations are increasingly compelled to join the commercial world, and are under great pressure to adopt the operational and structural characteristics of business enterprises. The influence of modern communication has been profound, with sporting results being available from overseas as readily as domestic results. Many sporting organizations have realized that in order to remain competitive they must provide similar entertainment value to that provided by other sports on television as well as the wide array of alternative leisure options available. Subsequently, corporate boxes line major sporting venues, sport is blanketed across pay or cable and free to air television, high profile athletes earn extraordinary sums, and politicians associate themselves with certain teams. The commercial and competitive pressures placed upon sport organizations from local football clubs, universities and colleges, to professional leagues and teams, has encouraged sport managers to embrace business tools and concepts like organizational culture. Culture is important to sport organizations because a better understanding of it can help to bring about change. Since organizational culture is so influential on the performance of its members, it is critical that cultural traits are both appropriate and strong. In the case of sport, it is common to have strong cultures that have been forged by tradition and a fierce sense of history, but some cultural characteristics like excessive drinking and on-field violence may no longer suit the more professional management approach that needs to be assumed.

Commentaries on organizational culture, while as disparate as the number of researchers pursuing its investigation, generally emphasize its most superficial manifestation. Moreover, organizational culture is frequently seen as mono-cultural; that is, it is perceived at one level, and as one entity. The organization is distinguished as a giant cultural mass, constructed equivalently throughout, and with little or no internal variability. However, this methodology is difficult to sustain when analysing a sporting organization. Sporting club cultures are inherently poly- (multi-) cultural, and can be perceived readily at several levels, or as several entities. For example, as an organizational or administrative unit comparable to other business organizations; as a supporter organization, whose aims, objectives and traditions may be different (such as winning matches in preference to making a financial profit); and as a player unit, where motivation may vary from glory to money. While a player may perform for a club because of loyalty or remuneration (or any number of other reasons), the supporters are usually passionately attached to the clubs' colours and traditions, expecting only on-field success in return.

Sub-cultures and sport

In sporting organizational cultures there is the additional hurdle of translating and adopting a culture directly from traditional business theory. It is dangerously simplistic to assume that a sporting organization should adopt the methods and practices of a traditional business without addressing the cultural variables. While business methods can be transferred to accommodate the organizational strategies of a sporting club, a direct transfer fails to confront the issue of what it is that makes the culture of a sporting organization differ from that of a traditional business enterprise.

Ideal business culture tends to reflect a willingness by an organization's employees to embrace a standard of performance that promotes quality in the production of goods and services, in the attempt to generate a financial profit. This cultural ideology, while cognizant of business necessities, is unable to cater for the more diverse structures that exist in a sporting organization. In any business, fiscal realities must be acknowledged, but in a sporting business, additional behavioural variables require recognition and respect. While different businesses have different cultures, they are less variable than the cultural differences between individual sports. It cannot be assumed, for example, that a single unified culture exists for all sports.

Fighting during a sporting context is an example of the variability of sporting culture. While in just about every ball game it is illegal to punch people, it is acceptable behaviour in some cases. The situation could not be clearer in terms of official rules and regulations. An overt punch in soccer is an immediate red-card, sending-off offence. In contrast, a punch in rugby-union will only get the player a warning, and the opposition a penalty in their favour. In soccer, punching is unacceptable. In rugby, it is merely discouraged. The identical behaviours have quite different cultural meanings. Furthermore, in ice-hockey, fighting is virtually considered an inherent and accepted part of the game, and charging the pitcher, although illegal, is considered to be almost within the batter's moral right should they be struck by a wayward pitch in baseball. Consider the ramifications of a punch thrown at the Wimbledon Tennis Championships or on the eighteenth green of Augusta. Sport managers must be aware of the cultural nuances of their respective sports and the influence they have upon players, employees, members, fans and the general public.

Culture is not a simple matter within a single sport either. Professional players, for example, have a different cultural attitude from some amateurs and spectators. This variability of attitudes is symptomatic of a wider, more troublesome area: the clash of cultures within sports. This is illustrated best at an international level, where players from different countries have been brought up with profoundly different ideologies of the game, and how it should be played. Soccer – the 'world game' – is indicative of this culture clash, in addition to the immense cultural significance inherent in the game. Like all living cultures, sport is incessantly changing, dynamic in nature and subject to constant reinterpretation by its participants and viewers. The only apparent consistency in sporting culture is the pursuit of competition, the love of winning, and the ability to summon strong emotional responses in both victory and defeat.

Clearly, there is a need to study organizational cultures, accounting for the effect of the sport itself. For example, in the same way that we might expect that accounting firms might share some cultural traits, so might we predict that judo clubs do also. Similarly, the tradition and discipline central to a judo club might be expected to encourage cultural characteristics different to the youthful and eclectic philosophy found in a BMX club. Furthermore, these cultural characteristics might seep into the executive officers and employees of the clubs. Since so many sporting organizations covet tradition and the accomplishments of the past, they also tend to be resistant to change. However, before any change can occur, an organization's culture needs to be accurately diagnosed.

Case 9.2   From the superficial to the deep

Saskatchewan is a province in Canada. Its official sport is curling, but like many Western societies, it is supportive of an eclectic variety of sports, including gymnastics. Conversely, the largest city in the US state of California is Los Angeles, which hosts several prominent professional sport clubs, including the National Basketball Association team, the Los Angeles Lakers. In this case study, some of the organizational culture differences between the Gymnastics Saskatchewan (GS) and the Los Angeles Lakers (LA Lakers) are considered. Specifically, readers are invited to visit the respective websites of the two organizations as we imagine what deeper values and cultural characteristics might reside behind the public profiles that are displayed on the internet.

Gymnastics Saskatchewan
http://www.gymsask.com/mission.html

Los Angeles Lakers
http://www.nba.com/lakers/

Organizational culture analysis can begin with the obvious. For example, what is the first impression given by each internet site? While sites change in content and composition over time, it is likely that the GS site will remain relatively simple with the intention of providing some basic information. Although a modestly sized sport organization, GS still presents a professional image, through the use of a logo and appropriately coloured web pages. The photos in the 'About Us' section reveal the chief 'business' of the organization in the form of gymnasts performing and practising. The content of the site further reinforces a strong orientation toward athletic development and participation. This is clearly articulated in the 'Mission' page in a brief set of strategic statements. The values listed include the following:

Respect: We respect each other as individuals, our organization and its properties.
Quality: We strive to achieve personal bests in everything that we do.
Discipline/Ethical: We behave according to high moral standards in accordance with the organization's rules of conduct and ethics.
Commitment: We are committed to the goals of the organization.
Teamwork: We work together to achieve the goals of the organization.
Honesty: We are truthful with ourselves and others in everything we do.
Fairness/Impartial: We do not show favour in making judgments and we put all individuals on an equal footing.

Contrast the GS website to that of the LA Lakers. Neither a governing body nor a non-profit entity, the LA Lakers site is demonstrably commercial in orientation. The homepage is packed with game and player information and the cursor is even automatically converted to a sponsor's logo (at the time of writing this was the McDonald's arches). In addition to news, schedules and player statistics, visitors can purchase a vast range of merchandise. The site is cluttered with information and permeated by the LA Lakers colours and logo.

From these websites it is already clear that the organizational cultures of GS and the LA Lakers are likely to be quite different. GS seems to value participation in their sport, while the Lakers are unashamedly concerned with on-court and financial (they go hand in hand) success to the exclusion of most else.

Do the above brief observations constitute an organizational culture analysis? Absolutely not. It would be dangerous to assume that we now have anything more than the most superficial understanding of the two cultures, but an exercise like this is nevertheless instructive. Organizational culture presents itself through both superficial and covert communication and both are reflective of an underlying set of values that drive the organization. Sometimes, however, the overt and covert do not match. Obvious symbols can be masks covering deeper realities. For example, we are naturally suspicious when fast food restaurants claim to be interested in promoting health. Similarly in sport, we need to be cautious before making assumptions about organizational culture from the superficial.

Diagnosing and managing organizational culture

The central problem is that in order to grasp the concept of culture and its relationship to the individual, the group, and the organization, an in-depth approach is required. Sport organizations create intentions and atmospheres that influence behaviour, routines, practices and the very thought systems of people. These systems and processes subsequently form patterns that are acquired primarily through socialization, or learning over time from the reactions and behaviours of others. In essence, individuals within an organization are exposed to what researchers call 'culture revealing' situations, which might include the observable behaviour of other members, their organizational methods, 'artefacts' – the photos, honour boards and other memorabilia on show – and interactive communication, or the way in which individuals talk to each other. Some of these common superficial and observable representations of organizational culture are reproduced in Table 9.1. These are important to recognize because the driving values and belief systems behind them can never been seen as anything more than observable 'symptoms'.

Table 9.1 Observable symptoms of sport organizational culture

Symptom	Explanation
Environment	The general surroundings of an organization, like the building it is housed in and the geographical location, like the city or in a grandstand.
Artefacts	Physical objects located in the organization from its furnishings to its coffee machine.
Language	The common words and phrases used by most organizational members, including gestures and body language.
Documents	Any literature including reports, statements, promotional material, memos and emails produced for the purpose of communication.
Logos	Any symbolic visual imagery including colours and fonts that convey meaning about the organization.
Heroes	Current or former organizational members who are considered exemplars.
Stories	Narratives shared by organizational members based at least partly on true events.
Legends	An event with some historical basis but has been embellished with fictional details.
Rituals	Standardized and repeated behaviours.
Rites	Elaborate, dramatic, planned set of activities.

Although the superficial aspects of culture can be observed, the difficulty comes in their interpretation because they are merely surface representations of deeper values. Thus, a useful cultural diagnosis will always seek to understand what drives the observable behaviour. For example, what does it mean if an employee makes a mistake and is severely reprimanded by his or her boss? What does common jargon imply? Why are certain rituals typical, like the celebration of employee's birthdays?

The question remains as to how observations made translate into deeper values. Most researchers recommend some form of classification system that describes organizational culture in the form of 'dimensions', each one a deeper, core value. These dimensions reflect on particular organizational characteristics as an aid to categorizing cultures. The summation of these characteristics is used to describe an organization's culture, which can then allow for comparisons to be undertaken between varying organizations. For example, observable evidence in the form of an end of season awards night in a sporting club might be suggestive of the nature of the organization's reward/motivation values. Enough observable evidence can lead a sport manager to make some tentative conclusions about each dimension. Table 9.2 lists some common dimensions used to describe organizational culture. They can be seen as continua, an organization's position somewhere between the two extremes.

Any analysis that captures the complexity of organizational culture may have great difficulty in separating the interwoven strands of organizational history and personal relationships. As a result, concrete conclusions may be difficult to establish. It is therefore important to take advantage of the symbolism created by myth, ritual and ceremony that is abundant in sport organizations in order to gain a complete understanding of the full range of human behaviour within a complex organization. The traditions, folklore, mythologies, dramas, and successes and traumas of the past, are the threads that weave together the fabric of organizational culture.

A psychological approach is helpful in identifying and interpreting human behaviour in organizations as cultural phenomena. Psychologists, originally stimulated by the work of Carl Jung, suggest that there are different levels of behavioural awareness, from the conscious to unconscious. Organizational psychologists have appropriated this kind of thinking and transposed it to culture. The key analogy is that an organization is like a mind.

From the psychological viewpoint, the readily apparent and observable qualities of a sporting organization are the same as the conscious part of an individual mind. These include the physical environment, the public statements of officials, the way individuals interactively communicate, the form of language used, what clothes are worn, and the memorabilia that fills the rooms and offices. Another of the most important observable qualities involves the place of sporting heroes. They are culturally rich and are highly visible indicators of the culture that is sought. Heroes give an insight into the culture of an organization, since they are selected by the rank and file as well as the power brokers. In addition, they indicate those qualities in individuals which are respected and admired by a wider audience. The hero is a powerful figure in a sporting organization, and may be simultaneously an

Table 9.2 Cultural dimensions

Dimension	Authors	Characteristics
Stability/changeability	Cooke & Szumal, 1993; Quinn & Rohrbaugh, 1983	Disposition toward change: Degree to which organization encourages alternative 'ways of doing things' or existing ways.
Cooperation/conflict	Denison & Mishra, 1995; Hofstede, 2001; Schein, 1997	Disposition toward problem resolution: Degree to which organization encourages cooperation or conflict.
Goal focus/orientation	Sashkin, 1996; Van der Post & de Coning, 1997	Clarity and nature of objectives and performance expectations.
Reward/motivation	Bettinger, 1989; Robbins, 1990	Nature of reward orientation of organizational members: Degree to which organization encourages seniority or performance.
Control/authority	Sashkin, 1996; Schein, 1997	Nature and degree of responsibility, freedom and independence of organizational members.
Time/planning	Hofstede, Neuijen, Ohayv & Sanders, 1990; Van der Post & de Coning, 1997	Disposition toward long-term planning: Degree to which organization encourages short-term or long-term thinking.

Reproduced from: Smith, A. & Shilbury, D. (2004). Mapping Cultural Dimensions in Australian Sporting Organizations, *Sport Management Review*, 7(2): 133–165.

employee and ex-player. The hero may also be charismatic, entrepreneurial, or just plain administrative, which often characterizes business enterprises. By understanding the orientation of hero figures, both past and present, it is possible to map the trends in cultural change. Heroes can be both reactionary and progressive. Heroes that reinforce the dominant culture will not change the values and attitudes that the culture emphasizes. On the other hand, a hero that transcends and transforms the dominant culture will be a catalyst for change in the behaviours and values of a club. Often a hero is the most powerful medium for change management to be successful.

Tradition is another window into the culture of an organization. Like heroes, traditions are readily observable through memorabilia, but it is important to note that the underlying values and assumptions that give meaning to heroes and tradition reside in the deeper levels of a culture. Tradition may on one hand be preserved by the present cultural identity, while on the other hand the sporting organization may have developed a contemporary cultural personality. Thus, it is useful to acknowledge the importance of tradition and history to a sporting organization because it may be a cultural linch-pin, or a stepping stone from which their cultural character has launched itself.

In order to bypass the obstacles (in the form of stereotypical views and superficial signs) that can block an assessment of culture, it is essential to analyse and explore natural, observable outcroppings of culture; places where the cultural understandings can be exposed. By analysing these sites, it is possible to gain a practical insight into the underlying culture of the organization. Thus, this level deals with organizational rites because, firstly, their performance is readily apparent, and secondly, in performing these rites, employees generally use other cultural forms of expression, such as certain customary language or jargon, gestures, and artefacts. These rites, which are shared understandings, are additionally conveyed through myths, sagas, legends, or other stories associated with the occasion, and in practical terms may take the form of barbecues or presentations. In order to actively assess this level of culture, not only must observational techniques be employed, but meanings must be attached to them. This requires more than a superficial level of analysis.

There are also 'unconscious' parts of organizations as well. In effect, it is the unconscious that controls the individual. This incorporates the beliefs, habits, values, behaviours and attitudes prevalent in a sporting organization. An accurate assessment of this level of culture is difficult and fraught with danger. For example, how employees say they behave and what they state they believe, has to be compared to their actual behaviour.

As a cautionary note, it is relevant to be aware of the fact that there are different interpretations possible of the same evidence. For example, one way of looking at culture is to focus attention on consistency and congruence of policies and practices within an organization as members are confronted with problems to solve. In contrast, it is also valid to consider ambiguities and inconsistencies in behaviour. These anomalies often represent the difference between espoused values and actual values. Cultural manifestations can be interpreted in multiple ways, and change over time and location. As Schein counselled, it is important to look for both patterns and exceptions.

Changing organizational culture with mapping

Cultural understanding stems from successfully translating information into meaning. Every aspect of a sporting organization is symbolically representative in some way of its culture. All information is not equal, however, yet all possible data must be analysed in order to establish the most holistic representation possible of the existing culture. In order for a culture to be created and bolstered, shared values and beliefs must in some way be reinforced and transferred to organizational members through tangible means. Case Study 9.3 describes the types of information that communicate culture, and is a useful tool for mapping a sporting club's organizational culture, in this case illustrating the features of the Ferrari Formula One Team. A cultural map summarizes the predominant features of a sporting organization's culture, and provides a means in which raw data can be interpreted into measurable criteria. It works by providing sets of categories in which information can be collected and summarized with the intention of identifying the main themes that continually emerge. Some researchers believe that this approach can also be used in a more statistical form, the numbers attached to responses from questions derived from the dimensions and answered by organizational members (e.g. Howard, 1998).

Case 9.3   A Cultural map of Ferrari Formula One

Ferrari Formula One motor racing team has enjoyed remarkable success, including six constructor's and five consecutive driver's championships up to and including season 2004. The team may well be a contender for the greatest ever sporting team. Led by Ferrari President and CEO Luca di Montezemolo, Team Manager Jean Todt, chief driver, Michael Schumacher, and design and engineering managers, Ross Brawn and Rory Byrne, the team brought about a massive cultural change beginning in the mid-1990s after a prolonged period of poor performance.

While a genuinely insightful cultural diagnosis requires long-term access to an organization, the following hypothetical map for the Ferrari Formula One Team creates an initial picture of the organization's culture. Keep in mind that in a thorough map, each of the variables under the heading 'Evidence Suggests' would include detailed data. Collectively, the information in the map paints a picture of the organization's cultural characteristics. The kinds of cultural traits that are suggested in this brief summary map might be considered against those that might be imagined for the Japan Sumo Association described in Case 9.1.

Cultural Dimensions and Variables		Evidence Suggests
Dimension 1: Change		
1	Preparedness to change	High
2	History of change	Low
3	Method of change	Rapid
4	Types of change	Transformational
5	CEO attitude to change	Strong focus
6	Staff attitude to change	Generally positive
7	Board attitude to change	n/a

Cultural Dimensions and Variables	Evidence Suggests
8 Process of change	Strategic re-focus followed by structural change
9 Supporter/member reaction to change	Very positive
10 Organization's financial position	Excellent
11 Organizational budget	Largest in class (US$300m)
12 Human resources	Yes – department
13 Staff age	Youthful, but experienced
14 Staff turnover	Medium (high pressure)

Dimension 2: Competitors

1	Organizational perception of competition	Respectful
2	Organizational competitors readily identified	Yes

Dimension 3: Customers

1	Organizational supporters/members considered customers?	Yes
2	Principal revenue sources	Indirectly from fans
3	Supporter base location	Global, mainly Europe
4	Organizational focus	Commercial

Dimension 4: Decisions

1	Decision-making process	Fast and de-centralized
2	Involvement of Board members in operations	No
3	Organizational perception of Board involvement	n/a
4	Involvement of controlling body	Subservient to strict rules of the FIA
5	Staff background as competitors	Some, but mainly professionally-trained
6	Board background as competitors	No
7	Professional Board members	Yes

Dimension 5: Goals

1	Service focus	Yes
2	Goal focus – financial? Memberships? On field success? Participation?	Winning

Dimension 6: Heroes

1	On-field heroes	Yes (Schumacher)
2	Off-field heroes	Yes (Todt)
3	Heroes' traits	Dynamic, successful
4	Organizational recognition of past heroes	Strong
5	Organizational use of heroes for promotion	Moderate
6	Public perception of heroes as role models	Strong

Dimension 7: History and Tradition

1	Internal formal recognition of history and tradition	Very strong, particularly of Enzo Ferrari
2	Maintenance of sport/athlete archives	Yes
3	Perception of sport/club success	High
4	Financial impact of success on organization	Vast impact
5	Age of organization	Moderate (approaching a century)
6	Organizational attachment to traditions	Flexible

Dimension 8: Risk

1	Organizational approach to risk	High risk

Dimension 9: Rituals

1	Organizational celebration of success	Regular and strong
2	Office atmosphere after victory/defeat	Subdued, but not depressed

Dimension 10: Symbols

1	Positioning of memorabilia	Prominent
2	Organizational value attached to memorabilia	High
3	Staff wearing uniforms	Yes
4	Staff dress requirement	Yes
5	Staff appearance	Immaculate

Dimension 11: Values

1	Employees work in excess of 40 hours per week	Far in excess

Cultural Dimensions and Variables	Evidence Suggests
2 Employee motivations	Money is relevant, but staff are motivated by passion for the sport and company
3 Organizational gender bias	Strong toward males
4 Organizational use of performance reviews	Strong
5 Employees provided with specific job descriptions	Yes
6 Average current employment length	Uncertain, but due to the stress and travel, relatively short for junior and middle-level positions
7 Employee sporting participation background	Yes, in some form of motor sport
8 Specific employee performance measures in place	Yes, thorough measures in all facets of performance
9 Office atmosphere	Reported to be strong morale, and strong pressure for work ethic
10 Employee duties	Fixed
11 Employee supervision	Line reporting
12 Organizational use of volunteers	No
13 Organizational recognition of volunteers	n/a
14 Employees working outside business hours	Constantly
15 Employee handbook provided	Yes, induction system
16 Females hold senior management positions	No
17 Employee association with the organization	Strong

Dimension 12: Size

1	Number of staff	800+
2	Number of members	Fan groups estimated in the millions globally

Dimensions adapted from: Smith, A. & Shilbury, D. (2004). Mapping Cultural Dimensions in Australian Sporting Organizations, *Sport Management Review*, 7(2): 133–165.

While the range and diversity of information available for cultural analysis is profound, many cultural studies ignore all but the most apparent and accessible data. A holistic cultural analysis will utilize every available piece of information, with the more obvious elements becoming vehicles for the transmission of less tangible, more subjective facets of culture. However, the culture of any one sporting organization cannot be classified into one of just a few categories, even though there are many models (e.g. Goffee & Jones, 1996) which offer four quadrants or divisions. There are as many organizational cultures as there are sporting organizations, and they cannot be generically categorized into one of a fixed number of groups. Sporting clubs are immersed in tradition, history, values, and myths, and these should figure prominently in any diagnosis. From an accurate diagnosis change is possible.

The main lesson for cultural change is that it cannot be tackled without a clear prior understanding of an organization's chief cultural traits and how they are manifested. Once an accurate diagnosis has been undertaken, through some form of formal or informal cultural map, elements of culture can be managed. Since a sport manager cannot literally change peoples' minds, they instead have to change peoples' actions. To some extent this can be imposed or encouraged, but it is a slow process. For example, new rituals can be introduced to replace older, less desirable ones, like a club dinner instead of a drinking binge. Entrenched values and beliefs can be extremely difficult to change, and even with the right introduction of new symbols, language, heroes, stories, employees etcetera, genuine cultural change in an organization can take a generation of members to take hold.

Summary

In the world of sport management, organizational culture has gained prominence as a concept useful in assessing and managing performance. Sport organizational culture can be defined as the collection of fundamental values and attitudes that are common to members of a sport organization, and which subsequently set the behavioural standards or norms for all members. The difficultly is, however, that the deep values common to organizational members are not easy to access. As a way of getting around this inaccessibility problem, sport managers can use cultural dimensions which suggest some of the possible values that are present. A step further, cultural maps show the variables and observable manifestations of culture that need to be investigated. These maps use the tip of the cultural iceberg (the accessible aspects of culture like symbols and artefacts) to estimate the iceberg's underwater composition (the deep values and beliefs of organizational members). Once a thorough diagnosis has been completed, sport managers can work toward adapting and replacing undesirable cultural characteristics.

Review questions

1. What is the difference between organizational culture and national culture?
2. Why is organization culture important to sport managers?
3. Explain how organizational culture can be manifested at different levels.
4. Describe the difference between superficial elements of culture and deeper elements of culture.
5. What is a cultural dimension?
6. How can organizational culture be measured in a sport organization?
7. How does measuring organizational culture help in changing it?
8. Select a sport organization you belong to or have belonged to. Create a list of attributes or values that you believe embodies its organizational culture. Which are the characteristics that distinguish it from other similar sport organizations?
9. Select a sport organization you belong to or have belonged to. Describe 10 artefacts that are on show in its premises and explain how each illuminates organizational culture.
10. With a colleague or group, select a website of a sport organization no one has heard of before. Based on what is on the website, create a list of organizational cultural characteristics, in order from the superficial to the deep.

Further reading

Colyer, S. (2000). Organizational culture in selected Western Australian sport organizations. *Journal of Sport Management*, 14, 321–341.

Hofstede, G. (2001). *Culture's Consequences: Comparing Values, Behaviors, Institutions and Organizations across Nations*. Thousand Oaks, CA: Sage.

Schein, E. (1997). *Organizational Culture and Leadership* (3rd edn). San Francisco: Jossey-Bass.

Van der Post, W. & de Coning, T. (1997). An instrument to measure organizational culture. *South African Journal of Business Management*, 28(4), 147–169.

Relevant websites

The following websites are useful starting points for further information on sport organizational culture:

* 'Measures of Organizational Culture' at
  http://www.uwec.edu/Sampsow/Measures/Culture.htm
* 'Organizational Culture Links' at
  http://www.new-paradigm.co.uk/Culture.htm
* 'Organizational Culture & Leadership – Edgar Schein' at
  http://www.tnellen.com/ted/tc/schein.html

Chapter 10
Sport governance

Overview

This chapter reviews the core concepts of organizational governance, provides examples of the unique features of how sport organizations are governed, and summarizes the key research findings on the governance of sport organizations. The chapter also provides a summary of principles for governance within community, state, national and professional sport organizations.

After completing this chapter the reader should be able to:

- Identify the unique characteristics of organizational governance for corporate and non-profit sport organizations;
- Differentiate the various models and theories of governance relevant to sport organizations;
- Understand the role of boards, staff, volunteers, members and stakeholder groups in governing sport organizations;
- Understand some of the challenges facing managers and volunteers involved in the governance of sport organizations; and
- Identify and understand the drivers of change in governance systems within sport organizations.

What is governance?

Organizational governance is concerned with the exercise of power within organizations and provides the system by which the elements of organizations are controlled and directed. Governance is necessary for all groups – nation states, corporate entities, societies, associations, and sport organizations – to function properly and effectively.

An organizational governance system not only provides a framework in which the business of organizations are directed and controlled but also 'helps to provide a degree of confidence that is necessary for the proper functioning of a market economy' (OECD, 2004, p. 11). Governance deals with issues of policy and direction for the enhancement of organizational performance rather than day-to-day operational management decision-making.

The importance of governance and its implied influence on organizational performance was highlighted by Tricker (1984) when he noted 'if management is about running business, governance is about seeing that it is run properly' (p. 7). The Australian Sports Commission (ASC) defines governance as 'the structures and processes used by an organization to develop its strategic goals and direction, monitor its performance against these goals and ensure that its board acts in the best interests of the members' (ASC, 2004). Good organizational governance should ensure that the board and management seek to deliver outcomes for the benefit of the organization and its members and that the means used to attain these outcomes are effectively monitored.

A 1997 report to the Australian Standing Committee on Recreation and Sport (SCORS) identified as a major concern amongst the sporting community, the 'perceived lack of effectiveness at board and council level in national and state sporting organizations' (SCORS Working Party on Management Improvement, 1997, p. 10). Major sport agencies in the UK, New Zealand and Canada have also identified improving governance of sport organizations as a strategic priority. Failures in the governance of national sport organizations such as the Australian Soccer Association and Athletics Australia in 2003 and 2004 respectively, together with reviews of professional sport governance such as those conducted by the Football Governance Research Centre at the University of London, continue to highlight the importance of developing and implementing sound governance practices in both amateur and professional sport organizations.

Corporate and nonprofit governance

The literature on organizational governance can be divided into two broad areas: (1) corporate governance that deals with the governance of profit seeking companies and corporations that focus on protecting and enhancing shareholder value, and (2) nonprofit governance that is concerned with the governance of voluntary based organizations that seek to provide a community service or facilitate the involvement of individuals in social, artistic or sporting activities.

Studies of corporate governance have covered 'concepts, theories and practices of boards and their directors, and the relationships between boards and shareholders, top management, regulators and auditors, and other stakeholders' (Tricker, 1993, p. 2). The literature in this field focuses on the two primary roles of the board in first, ensuring conformance by management, and second, enhancing organizational performance. Conformance deals with the processes of supervision and monitoring of the work of managers by the board and ensuring that adequate accountability measures are in place to protect the interests of shareholders. Enhancing organizational performance focuses on the development of strategy and policy to create the direction and context within which managers will work.

The unique characteristics of nonprofit organizations demand a governance framework different to that of the corporate firm. Nonprofit organizations exist for different reasons than do profit seeking entities, and generally involve a greater number of stakeholders in their decision-making structures and processes. The relationships between decision-makers – the governance framework – will therefore be different to that found in the corporate world. The management processes employed to carry out the tasks of the organizations might well be similar, but a fundamental difference between nonprofit and corporate organizations is found in their governance frameworks.

While many sports organizations such as major sporting goods manufacturers, athlete management companies, retail companies and venues can be classed as profit seeking, the majority of sport organizations that provide participation and competition opportunities are non-profit. These organizations include large clubs, regional associations or leagues, state or provincial governing bodies and national sport organizations.

Is there a theory of sport governance?

Clarke (2004) provides a unique overview of the development of theories of corporate governance. Some of the important theories applied to the study of organizational governance include agency theory, stewardship theory, institutional theory, resource dependence theory, network theory, and stakeholder theory. In this section we shall examine each of them in turn and review how relevant they are to understanding the governance of sport organizations.

Agency theory proposes that shareholders' interests should prevail in decisions concerning the operation of an organization. Managers (agents) who have been appointed to run the organization should be subject to extensive checks and balances to reduce the potential for mismanagement or misconduct that threatens shareholders' interests. This has been the predominant theoretical approach to the study of corporate governance and has focused on exploring the best ways to maximize corporate control of managerial actions, information for shareholders and labour in order to provide some assurance that managers will seek outcomes that maximize shareholder wealth and reduce risk. In relation to corporations operating in the sport industry that have individual, institutional and government shareholders, this theory helps explain how governance systems work. For the majority of nonprofit sport organizations, which have diverse stakeholders who do not have a financial share in the organization (aside from annual membership fees), agency theory has limited application.

Stewardship theory takes the opposite view to agency theory and proposes that rather than assume managers seek to act as individual agents to maximize their own interests over those of shareholders, managers are motivated by other concepts such as a need for achievement, responsibility, recognition and respect for authority. Thus, stewardship theory argues that managers' and shareholders' interests are actually aligned and that managers (agents) will act in the best interests of shareholders. This theoretical view can also be applied to sport corporations such as Nike, FoxSports or a listed professional football club franchise. The application of either agency or stewardship theory is dependent on the actions of the managers (who choose to act as agents or stewards) and the view of shareholders (who create either an agent or stewardship relationship through their conscious choice of governance framework). Stewardship theory is arguably more applicable than agency theory to the study of nonprofit sport organizations where managers may have a connection to the sport as an ex player, coach or club official and therefore have a deeper sense of commitment to the organization and are more likely to act as stewards.

Agency and stewardship theories focus on the internal monitoring issues of governance. Three theories that seek to explain how organizations relate to external organizations and acquire scarce resources are institutional theory, resource dependence theory and network theory. Institutional theory argues that the governance frameworks adopted by organizations are the result of adhering to external pressures of what is deemed acceptable business practice, including legal requirements for incorporation. Such pressures reflect wider societal concerns for proper governance systems to be employed. Further, if all organizations of a similar type and size seek to conform to these pressures they are likely to adopt very similar governance frameworks, a situation known as institutional isomorphism. Evidence of this is apparent throughout club-based sporting systems such as in Canada, Australia, New Zealand and the UK where most national and state or provincial sporting organizations operate under remarkably similar governance frameworks.

Resource dependence theory proposes that in order to understand the behaviour of organizations, we must understand how organizations relate to their environment. Organizations paradoxically seek stability and certainty in their resource exchanges by entering into interorganizational arrangements which require some loss of flexibility and autonomy in exchange for gaining control over other organizations. These interorganizational arrangements take the form of mergers, joint ventures, co-optation (the inclusion of outsiders in the leadership and decision-making processes of an organization), growth, political involvement, or restricting the distribution of information (Pfeffer & Salancik, 1978). Such arrangements have an impact on the governance structure adopted, the degree to which stakeholders are involved in decision-making, and the transparency of decision-making.

A final theory that attempts to explain elements of governance based on how organizations relate to external organizations is network theory.

Network theory posits that organizations enter into socially binding contracts to deliver services in addition to purely legal contracts. Such arrangements create a degree of interdependency between organizations, and facilitate the development of informal communication and the flow of resources between organizations. This is particularly true of sport organizations that, for example, rely on personal contacts to facilitate the success of major events by securing support of high profile athletes, using volunteers in large numbers from other sports organizations, and depend on government support for stadia development of event bidding. Network theory can help explain how governance structures and processes, particularly concerning the board of sports organizations, evolve to facilitate such informal arrangements.

These three theories emphasize the need to examine governance in terms of the external pressures that organizations face, and the strategies, structures and processes they put in place to manage them. Such an approach offers a more realistic view of how and why organizations have a particular governance framework more so than agency and stewardship theories.

Stakeholder theory provides another perspective for examining the relationship between organizations and their stakeholders. It argues for conceptualizing a corporation as a series of relationships and responsibilities which the governance framework must account for. This has important implications for corporations acting as good corporate citizens and particularly for sport organizations who need to manage a myriad of relationships with sponsors, funding agencies, members, affiliated organizations, staff, board members, venues, government agencies and suppliers.

Much of the writing and research on organizational governance has been based on corporations rather than nonprofit entities. Applying a particular theory to the study of sport organizations must be done with regard to the type and industry context of the sport organization being studied. Sport organizations and their governance frameworks have diverse elements that prevent the development of an overarching theory of sport governance. The value of the theories presented here is that each of them can be used to illuminate something of the governance assumptions, processes, structures and outcomes for sport organizations.

Governance structural elements

The governance elements of a corporate or profit seeking sport organization are the same for any general business operation. These elements can include paid staff, including a CEO who may or may not have voting rights on a board, a board of directors representing the interests of many shareholders (in the case of a publicly listed company), or directors who are direct partners in the business. The real differences in governance elements can be found in volunteer sport organizations.

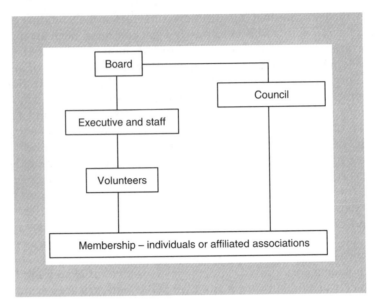

Figure 10.1 Typical governance structure of a VSO

A simple governance structure of VSOs is depicted in Figure 10.1 and comprises five elements: members, volunteers, salaried staff, a council and a board. Normally, members meet as a council (usually once per year at an annual general meeting) to elect or appoint individuals to a board. If the organization is large enough, the board may choose to employ an executive and other paid staff to carry out the tasks of the organization. Together with a pool of volunteers, these employees deliver services to organizational members. The board acts as the main decision-making body for the organization and therefore the quality of its activities is vital to the success of the organization.

Members of a VSO can be individual players or athletes, or in some cases, members are classified as other affiliated organizations such as a club that competes in a league provided by a regional sports association. Members can also be commercial facility providers such as basketball, squash or indoor soccer stadiums. The membership council comprises those people or organizations that are registered members and may be allocated voting rights according to membership status. The board comprises individuals who have been elected, appointed or invited to represent the interests of various membership categories, geographic regions or sporting disciplines in decision-making. The senior paid staff member, often designated the CEO, is employed by and reports directly to the board. Other paid staff is appointed by the CEO to assist in performing various organizational tasks. These staff must work with a variety of volunteers in sport to deliver essential services such as coaching, player and official development, marketing, sport development and event delivery. Finally, a wide range of stakeholders such as sponsors, funding agencies, members, affiliated organizations, staff, board members, venues, government agencies and suppliers must be consulted with and managed in order for the organization to operate optimally.

The majority of national and state or provincial sport organizations that provide participation and competition opportunities in club-based sporting systems are governed voluntarily by elected office bearers, who fill positions on either committees or boards. Most of these VSOs operate under a federated delegate system with club representatives forming regional boards, regional representatives forming state or provincial boards and state or provincial representatives forming national boards.

This traditional governance structure has been criticized for being unwieldy and cumbersome, slow to react to changes in market conditions, subject to potentially damaging politics or power plays between delegates, and imposing significant constraints on organizations wishing to change. On the other hand, the majority of sports organizations still use this model today and value its ability to ensure members have a say in decision-making, the transparency of decisions and the autonomy granted to organizations at every level of the system. Case 10.1 explains a typical governance structure of a VSO.

Case 10.1   Hockey Canada

Hockey Canada is the sole governing body for amateur hockey in Canada. More than 4.5 million Canadians are associated with Hockey Canada as players, coaches, officials, trainers, administrators or volunteers. Hockey Canada employs 75 staff and has offices in most Canadian provinces. The organizations that affiliate with Hockey Canada include 13 Branch associations, the Canadian Hockey League and Canadian Inter-University Sport. In conjunction with these member organizations, Hockey Canada facilitates participation in amateur hockey leagues, teams and games through player, coach and referee development, grading of competitions and establishing appropriate rules and regulations for amateur hockey across Canada. The governance structure of Hockey Canada reflects the nature of these activities and incorporates a range of decision-making groups to ensure the interests of all stakeholders are considered in relation to strategic planning and resource allocation by the national organization. The articles, by-laws and regulations for Hockey Canada are encapsulated in an 185-page document that sets out in detail the rights and responsibilities of the members of Hockey Canada and the processes to be used to govern its activities. The governance structure can be viewed at http://www.hockeycanada.ca/e/about/structure.html.

An important element of the structure to note is the large size of the Board of Directors which comprises Officers (eight), Branch Presidents (13), Council Representatives and Directors (eight) and Special Advisory Council Members (five). Each of these positions represents a specific constituent group within Hockey Canada. In addition, the Board of Directors receives reports from a Hockey Development Council of 24 members, again made up of individuals representing the specific interests of regional affiliates, or membership types (i.e. coaches, officials). The Board of Directors has a number of policy subcommittees (five) that deal with areas such as elite competitions, women's programmes, policy development, programmes of excellence and junior development. Finally, there are 10 standing subcommittees that report to the Board on issues such as insurance, marketing, finance, management and other areas of activity. This appears to be a very cumbersome way to manage the affairs of a relatively simple activity like facilitating games of ice hockey, but the sheer scale and geographic spread of its constituents requires Hockey Canada to maintain a comprehensive governance structure that facilitates decision-making and communication amongst its 4.5 million participants.

Sources: Hockey Canada (website www.hockeycanada.ca) and Hockey Canada (2004). *Annual Report 2004.* Calgary, CA.

Governance models

There are three generic governance models that can be applied to nonprofit sport organizations: the traditional model outlined by Houle (1960, 1997); the Carver policy governance model (1997); and the Executive led model (after Block, 1998; Drucker, 1990; Herman & Heimovics, 1990, 1994). A governance model can be defined as a set of policies and practices that outline the responsibilities of the various governance elements, and the processes used to carry out the governance function. All of the following models relate to organizations that are governed by boards that employ a paid executive and staff as opposed to more informal organizations that maintain a collective and informal structure. The models are more relevant to these organizations because boards that carry out the 'hands on' work of the organization, such as a small community club, are 'usually so strongly influenced by personalities and special circumstances that few generalizations can be made about their general nature or how they may be improved' (Houle, 1997, p. 3).

Traditional model

Houle (1960, 1997) outlined a 'traditional model' for governance of nonprofit organizations that is based on five elements. The first of these is the human potential of the board where the board ensures a systematic recruitment process is in place accompanied with on-going board member development. Second, the work of the board is structured according to a set of by-laws, policies are clearly defined and minutes of the board and committee meetings are consistently reported. Third, the roles of and relationships between the board, executive and staff should be well defined and developed enabling clear decision-making to occur. Fourth, the operation of the board should be undertaken in a positive group culture and based on an annual work plan, regular meetings with well-managed agendas and on-going evaluation of the board and its work. Finally, the board has a focus on maintaining external relationships through formal and informal representation of the organization to the community. The model advocates that 'the work is done by the staff, the administration by management and the policy making by the board; in this traditional model, the board is truly in charge of the organization' (Fletcher, 1999, p. 435).

This model has been widely used amongst nonprofit organizations and is probably the most widely used by nonprofit sport organizations. It clearly separates the tasks of staff and volunteers and highlights volunteer board members as being accountable for the organization. The model has been criticized for the idealistic view that the board alone has ultimate responsibility for the organization (Heimovics & Herman, 1990), and the rather simplistic notion of the board making policy while the staff do the work (Herman & Heimovics, 1990) which does not reflect the reality of the working relationships that occur in most nonprofit organizations.

Policy governance model

Carver (1997) outlines five elements of a 'policy governance' model for the effective governing board. The first of these is determining the mission and strategic direction of the organization, with a focus on the desired outcomes, rather than becoming immersed in the detail of the means to achieve them. Secondly, setting executive limitations or constraints for the work practices and the means that staff employ to achieve the mission set by the board. Thirdly, establish clear board and executive roles and relationships. Fourthly, ensuring governance processes are clearly defined in areas such as board member selection and succession, the reporting of activities of the board and staff, and ensuring the board focuses on the policies of the organization rather than cases or specific issues. Finally, the board's role should be more than simply ensuring conformance to financial procedures and ethical management practice; it should also develop clear performance measures related to strategic outcomes.

Like the Traditional model, Carver's model has been criticized for its 'idealized view of the board, operating above the messiness of the board–executive relationship as it really exists in nonprofit organizations' (Fletcher, 1999, p. 436). The model also does not address the important role of the board in managing external relationships and it 'clearly subordinates the CEO to the board and expects the board alone to set the parameters of the relationship' (Fletcher, 1999, p. 436).

Executive led model

The Executive led model, in contrast to the previous models, advocates the executive as central to the success of nonprofit organizations. Drucker (1990) argued that the ultimate responsibility for the performance of a nonprofit organization, including its governance, should rest with the executive. His views were supported by Herman and Heimovics' (1990) research that found that the reality of most boards was that they depended on their executive for information almost exclusively and looked to them to provide leadership. Hoye and Cuskelly (2003) also found this was the case in VSOs. Block (1998) argued that because the executive is working in an organization much more than the average board member, they have better access to information and therefore they must also 'be at the core of leadership and decision-making activities' (p. 107).

Board–staff relationships

The gradual introduction of professional staff into VSOs over the last 20 years has created the need for volunteers and paid staff to work together at all levels, including the board table. This has led to some degree of uncertainty about what roles should be performed by each group and the extent to which staff and volunteers should be involved in strategic planning, policy development, performance evaluation and resource acquisition. The potential for tension between these groups as they negotiate their respective roles has been well established, as has the ongoing desire of volunteers to maintain a degree of involvement in decision-making while at the same time utilizing the expertise of paid staff to assist them in running their organizations. This then is the crux of board–staff relationships: What areas do volunteers maintain control over and which does paid staff control?

Hoye and Cuskelly (2003) found that VSO boards perform better if a degree of trust exists between the board and staff and that board leadership was shared amongst a dominant coalition of the board chair, executive and a small group of senior board members. As mentioned earlier, the executive controls the flow of information to board members and so the quality, frequency and accuracy of this information are vital to their ability to make decisions. Ensuring the board and executive work together effectively would enhance this information flow and therefore the performance of the board.

Principles of good organizational governance

The idea of what constitutes good organizational governance extends beyond the ideas of monitoring to ensure conformance and developing to improve performance discussed earlier in this chapter. Henry and Lee (2004) provide a list of seven key principles for good organizational governance in sport organizations:

1. Transparency – ensuring the organization has clear procedures for resource allocation, reporting and decision-making;
2. Accountability – sports organizations need to be accountable to all their stakeholders;
3. Democracy – all stakeholder groups should be able to be represented in the governance structure;

4. Responsibility – the board has to be responsible for the organization and demonstrate ethical stewardship in carrying out that responsibility;
5. Equity – all stakeholder groups should be treated equitably;
6. Efficiency – process improvements should be undertaken to ensure the organization is making the best use of its resources; and
7. Effectiveness – the board should establish and monitor measures of performance in a strategic manner.

This list of principles is not exhaustive but it does give us a clear indication of the philosophical approach organizations should adopt in designing and implementing an appropriate governance framework. Case 10.2 provides a snapshot of a review of the governance performance of professional football clubs in England.

Case 10.2   Corporate governance of English Premier League football clubs

Corporate governance of English Premier League football clubs has come under increasing scrutiny in recent years, due in part to the annual reviews of corporate governance undertaken by the Football Governance Research Centre (FGRC) based at Birkbeck in the University of London. The Premier League (PL) is the flagship of the game's governing body in England – the Football Association (FA). The FA is in turn under the control of the European governing body – the Union of European Football Associations (UEFA), which in turn is a member of the world's governing body – the Federation of International Football Associations (FIFA).

The regulatory system for Premier league clubs comprises four elements: (1) regulation by the Football Authorities, (2) regulation through the legal system in terms of company law, consumer law, labour law and competition law; (3) regulation by a code of corporate governance developed by the Premier League; and (4) shareholder activism and stakeholder participation. The Football Authorities (namely FA and UEFA) have developed criteria such as a 'fit and proper person' test aimed at improving the quality of individuals appointed or elected to govern Premier League clubs, and the development of a code of corporate governance that provides guidelines for good governance. These actions are largely designed to ameliorate the effects of poor financial management within the Premier League clubs (since 1992 50% of PL clubs have been in hands of administrators or insolvent) and to improve the sustainability of clubs that are promoted or relegated between the FA leagues. The FGRC noted that the PL clubs that regularly compete in the UEFA Champions' League hold a distinct financial advantage over other PL clubs. As a consequence the governing body for the PL must be cognizant of the more powerful clubs and their potential to influence decision-making at the board table.

The English legal system requires PL clubs to fulfil a number of obligations for communicating with shareholders, consultation with fans, the use of customer charters, and dialogue with Supporters' Trusts. The FGRC noted that while the majority of PL clubs do an adequate job in this area, there was room for improvement. In addition PL clubs that are listed public companies must follow a Combined Code that sets out principles for the activities of directors, director's remuneration, accountability and audit requirements, relations with shareholders, and institutional shareholders. The FGRC found that while PL clubs are moving towards having more independent directors, they fall short compared to other listed companies.

There are now more than 70 Supporters' Trusts for clubs in the FA, and about 60% of PL clubs have a Supporter's Trust. The trusts fulfil an important governance role, with 25% of PL clubs having a trust representative on their board. This representation means that committed fans have the chance to participate in decision-making at the highest level in regard to the future of their club, and in return support the club in sport development, marketing and fundraising activities.

While there are signs that PL clubs have generally accepted good governance practices and abide with the majority of codes of conduct and principles for good governance, they do fall down in certain areas of governance practice. These include the lack of performance evaluation of individual directors or the overall board in a small number of clubs, and a significant portion of clubs failing to adopt standard strategic planning practices. While the English PL enjoys enormous global profile as a leading football competition, the governance of the member clubs does not reach such exalted heights. More information is at http://www.football-research.bbk.ac.uk.

Source: Football Governance Research Centre (2004). *The state of the game: The corporate governance of football clubs 2004*, Research paper 2004 No. 3, Football Governance Research Centre, Birkbeck, University of London.

Board performance

Board performance has been found to be related to the use of appropriate structures, processes and strategic planning, the role of the paid executive, whether the board undertakes training or development work, personal motivations of board members and the influence of a cyclical pattern in the life cycle of boards. How to measure board performance, however, is a subject of ongoing debate. Herman and Renz (1997, 1998, 2000) support the use of a social constructionist approach to measure board performance based on the work of Berger and Luckmann (1967). Their view is that the collective judgements of those individuals directly involved with the board can provide the best idea of its performance. A widely used scale, the Self Assessment for Nonprofit Governing Boards Scale (Slesinger, 1991), uses this approach and provides sporting and other nonprofit organizations with an effective way to gauge board performance.

Aspects of board activity that are evaluated using a scale of this type include: the working relationship between board and CEO, working relationships between board and staff, CEO selection and review processes, financial management, conduct of board and committee meetings, board mission statement and review of the mission, strategic planning, matching operational programmes to the mission and monitoring programme performance, risk management, new board member selection and training, and marketing and public relations. The performance of the board in undertaking these activities is then rated by board members, executives and the chair of the board. While this approach is open to criticism of self-reporting bias, the fact that the whole group makes judgements on performance and then compares perceptions is an aid to board development and improvement.

The evaluation of individual board member performance is more problematic. Research into the human resource management practices related to board members shows that smaller sports organizations may struggle to find board members, while larger sports have an element of prestige attached to them so the problem is the opposite – how to engage in succession planning within a democratic electoral process. Very few board members are inducted, trained, provided with professional development opportunities, and evaluated at all in regards to their role and the role of the board, a potentially serious problem for nonprofit sport organizations given the significant responsibilities with which board members and board chairs are charged.

Drivers of change in governance

VSOs are increasingly under pressure from funding agencies to improve the delivery of their core programmes and services. Funding agencies recognize that sports' capacity for this delivery depends to a large extent on sport organizations being appropriately governed and as a result have implemented a range of measures to improve the governance of VSOs. For example, the Australian Sports Commission has a dedicated programme of management improvement for NSOs that provides advice on governance issues, funding to undertake reviews of governance structures, and provides information on governance principles and processes. Sport England has negotiated detailed strategic plans with NSOs to improve the delivery and coordination between regional sport organizations.

The threat of litigation against sport organizations, their members or board members has forced sport organizations to address issues such as risk management, fiduciary compliance, incorporation, directors' liability insurance, and board training and evaluation. The heightened awareness of the implications of governance failure due to several much publicized corporate cases of impropriety worldwide has also forced sport organizations to improve their governance systems. Legislative changes to address issues of equity and diversity are additional pressures sports organizations must face and their governance systems, particularly membership criteria, voting rights, and provision of information must change accordingly.

The threat of competition in the marketplace has also forced sports organizations to become more commercial and business focused, primarily through employing paid staff. Large clubs and regional sports associations that in the mid-1990s were exclusively run by volunteers are increasingly investing in paid staff to manage the increased compliance demands from government and their members and customers. As discussed earlier, the employment of paid staff changes the governance structures, the decision-making processes and the level of control exerted by volunteers. Maintaining governance structures devised decades ago creates many problems for sports organizations. Case 10.3 highlights some of the problems that result from poor governance and how one organization has been forced to change.

Case 10.3   Soccer Australia

In August 2002, the Australian Federal Minister for the Arts and Sport, Senator Rod Kemp, announced that Soccer Australia (SA) had agreed to a major structural review of soccer in Australia to be managed by the Australian Sports Commission. The review was undertaken after almost two decades of crises in the sport with the result that in mid-2002, SA was $AUD2.6M in debt, had reduced staffing levels at the national office, was racked by political infighting, had a lack of strategic direction and had enjoyed mixed results in the international arena. The review examined the structure, governance and management of soccer at all levels across Australia.

During the course of the review it was found that many of the constituent bodies at state and regional levels suffered from similar financial difficulties, political infighting and inappropriate governance systems. These created problems of mistrust and disharmony, a lack of strategic direction, inappropriate behaviour, and factionalism that hampered national decision-making. While the sport enjoyed a large grass-roots participation base, a good talent pool for national teams, good training programmes, strong growth in female participation, and passionate public support, its governance system was preventing it capitalizing on these strengths.

The review found that the governance system needed to change in four key areas:

1. Ensuring independence of the governing bodies;
2. Separating governance from day-to-day management;
3. Change the membership and voting structures for the national and state organizations; and
4. The relationship between SA and the National Soccer League.

In all, the review made 53 recommendations aimed at improving the structure, governance and management of SA. The first three recommendations in the report illustrate the parlous state of affairs that existed in the organization in 2002. The review recommended that (1) the membership of SA be changed to recognize key interest groups and reduce the power of larger states and the NSL, (2) the need to develop a new constitution, and (3) that each state affiliate adopt a model constitution and membership agreements. These recommendations alone represent wholesale change in the governance system, but the review went on to recommend a further 50 changes to governance processes and structures throughout the sport.

The sweeping changes made to the governance systems of Soccer Australia as a result of the review, and the subsequent appointment as Chief Executive Officer of John O'Neil (ex-CEO of the Australian Rugby Union) ushered in a new era for the sport. On the 1st January 2005, Soccer Australia changed its name to Football Federation Australia as part of the ongoing process of repositioning the sport.

Source: Australian Sports Commission, (2003). *Independent soccer review: Report of the independent soccer review committee into the structure, governance and management of soccer in Australia*, Canberra: Australian Sports Commission.

Summary

Organizational governance has been described as the exercise of power within organizations and provides the system by which the elements of organizations are controlled and directed. Good organizational governance should ensure that the board and management seek to deliver outcomes for the benefit of the organization and its members and that the means used to attain these outcomes are effectively monitored.

A distinction is made between corporate governance that deals with the governance of profit seeking companies and corporations that focus on protecting and enhancing shareholder value, and non-profit governance that is concerned with the governance of voluntary based organizations that seek to provide a community service or facilitate the involvement of individuals in social, artistic or sporting activities.

Sport organizations and their governance frameworks have diverse elements that prevent the development of an overarching theory of sport governance. A number of theoretical perspectives, namely agency theory, stewardship theory, institutional theory, resource dependence theory, network theory, and stakeholder theory can be used to illuminate parts of the governance assumptions, processes, structures and outcomes for sport organizations.

The traditional governance structure for VSOs outlined earlier has been criticized for being unwieldy and cumbersome, slow to react to changes in market conditions, subject to potentially damaging politics or power plays between delegates, and imposing significant constraints on organizations wishing to change. On the other hand, the majority of sports organizations still use this model today and value its ability to ensure members have a say in decision-making, the transparency of decisions and the autonomy granted to organizations at every level of the system.

A number of models for sport governance exist, each emphasizing different levels of responsibility for the chair of the board and paid executive. VSO boards perform better if a degree of trust exists between the board and staff and that board leadership is shared amongst a dominant coalition of the board chair, executive and a small group of senior board members. While evaluation systems for board performance are still relatively simplistic, they do cover a wide range of board activities. Evaluation of individual board member performance is more problematic and is the subject of ongoing research.

Finally, VSOs are increasingly under pressure from funding agencies to improve the delivery of their core programmes and services. The threat of litigation against sport organizations, their members or board members, has forced sport organizations to address issues such as risk management, fiduciary compliance, incorporation, directors' liability insurance, and board training and evaluation. The heightened awareness of the implications of governance failure due to high profile corporate cases worldwide has also forced sport organizations to improve their governance systems.

Review questions

1. Explain the difference between corporate and non-profit governance.
2. What theory would you apply to the study of negligence on the part of a board of directors of a sport organization?
3. Explain the role played by boards, staff, volunteers, members and stakeholder groups in governing sport organizations.
4. What criteria would you apply to gauge the performance of a nonprofit VSO? How would these criteria differ for a professional sport club?
5. What are the important elements in developing good relationships between boards and paid staff in VSOs?
6. Compare the governance structures of a multi-disciplinary sport (e.g. gymnastics, canoeing, athletics) with a single discipline sport (e.g. field hockey, netball, rugby league). How do they differ? What impact does this have on volunteers involved in governance roles?
7. Review the governance performance of a VSO of your choice using Henry and Lee's (2004) seven principles of governance presented in this chapter.
8. What issues does a potential amalgamation present for a VSO?
9. How are board performance and organizational performance linked?
10. Interview the CEO and the Board Chair of a small VSO. Who do they perceive to be the leader of the organization?

Further reading

Carver, J. (1997). *Boards that make a difference: A new design for leadership in non-profit and public organizations* (2nd edn). San Francisco: Jossey-Bass.

Clarke, T. (Ed.) (2004). *Theories of corporate governance.* Oxon, UK: Routledge.

Henry, I. & Lee, P.C. (2004). Governance and ethics in sport, in J. Beech & S. Chadwick (Eds), *The business of sport management*, England: Prentice Hall.

Hindley, D. (2003). *Resource guide in governance and sport*, Learning and teaching support network in Hospitality, Leisure, Sport and Tourism at http://www.hlst.ltsn.ac.uk/resources/governance.html.

Houle, C.O. (1997). *Governing boards: Their nature and nurture.* San Francisco: Jossey-Bass.

Hoye, R. & Inglis, S. (2003). Governance of nonprofit leisure organizations, *Society and Leisure*, 26(2), 369–387.

Organization for Economic Co-operation and Development (2004). *Principles of Corporate Governance*, Paris: OECD.

Relevant websites

The following websites are useful starting points for further information on the governance of sport organizations:

* Australian Sports Commission at http://www.ausport.gov.au
* Football governance research centre in the UK at http://www.football-research.bbk.ac.uk/index.htm
* Sport and Recreation New Zealand at http://www.sparc.org.nz/
* Sport Canada at http://www.pch.gc.ca/progs/sc/index_e.cfm
* Sport England at http://www.sportengland.org
* Sport Scotland at http://www.sportscotland.org.uk

Chapter 11

Performance management

Overview

This chapter examines the ways in which sport organizations can manage their operations and evaluate their performance. Particular attention will be given to the special features of sport organizations, and how these features create the need for a customized performance management model. The imperative of using a multi-dimensional model of performance management will be highlighted, together with the need to accommodate the conflicting demands that arise from the claims of multiple stakeholders. Throughout the chapter cases and incidents will be used to illustrate the concepts and principles that underpin effective performance in sport organizations.

After completing this chapter the reader should be able to:

- Explain the concept of performance management;
- Describe how the special features of sport necessitate the formulation of a customized performance management model;
- Identify the stakeholders that need to be taken into account when building a performance management model for sport organizations;
- Construct a multi-dimensional model of performance management that accommodates sport's special features, and gives appropriate weight to financial factors, internal processes, market awareness and penetration, and social responsibility; and
- Apply the model to a variety of sport situations and contexts.

Sport and performance

From a management perspective sport is a very interesting institution to study since it is both similar to and different from traditional business organizations (Smith & Stewart, 1999). Its similarities have arisen out of its relentless drive over the last 30 years to become more professionally structured and managed. Large segments of sport have consequently copied the values and practices of the business world, and as a result players and administrators are paid employees, and strategic plans are designed. In addition, games and activities become branded sport products, fans become customers to be satisfied and surveyed, and alliances with corporate supporters are developed (Slack, 1997).

At the same time, sport is also different from business (Smith & Stewart, 1999). First, it has a symbolic significance and emotional intensity that is rarely found in an insurance company, bank or even a betting shop. While businesses seek employee compliance and attachment, their primary concern is efficiency, productivity and responding to changing market conditions. Sport, on the other hand, is consumed by strong emotional attachments that are linked to the past through nostalgia and tradition. Romantic visions, emotion and passion can override commercial logic and economic rationality (Stewart & Smith, 1999). Second, predictability and certainty, which are goals to be aimed for in the commercial world, particularly with respect to product quality, are not always valued in the sporting world. Sport fans are attracted to games where the outcome is uncertain and chaos is just around the corner (Sandy et al., 2004). Third, sport is not driven by the need to optimize profit in the ways that large commercial businesses are. In practice, sport organizations face two conflicting models of organizational behaviour when deciding upon their underlying mission and goals. The first is the profit maximization model, which assumes that a club is simply a firm in a perfectly competitive product market and that profit is the single driving motivational force. The second is the utility maximization model, which emphasizes the rivalry between clubs, and their desire to win as many matches as possible (Downward & Dawson, 2000). The utility view assumes that sporting organizations are by nature highly competitive and that the single most important performance yardstick is competitive success. These differences therefore beg the question of where to begin when setting up a performance management system for sport organizations.

Where to begin?

In many respects sport is always subject to intense scrutiny. For example, in elite competitive sport, players and teams are rated and ranked continuously. In cricket, for example, an ever-expanding array of statistics are used to calculate not only batter scoring rates and bowling strike rates, but also patterns of scoring and fielding efficiency. Moreover, everyone has an opinion on the performance of coaches in various professional sport leagues which range from win-loss ratios to how the game strategies impact on scoring efficiency and player movements. At the same time, many sporting clubs do not take the time to undertake a comprehensive evaluation of their off-field performance. And, if they do, they limit their analysis to just a couple of issues like operating profits and membership levels. We argue here that it is better to use an evaluation model that embraces a variety of measures.

A systematic approach to performance management is an essential tool for identifying strengths and weaknesses, and revealing the ways in which overall organizational performance can be improved. It is also important for deciding where scarce resources should be allocated in order to achieve the best possible outcome. It can also give a picture of how one organization, club or league is doing in relation to other organizations, clubs or leagues. In short, the use of some sort of performance management model is crucial to the long-term success of sport organizations. However, the question remains as how to best to go about implementing an appropriate model of performance management, and where to begin?

A good starting point is to look at performance management from a strategic perspective. That is, we should initially focus our attention on what the organization wants to achieve. In other words, as we noted in Chapter 5, a performance management system should be linked to an organization's vision, goals and objectives (Robbins & Barnwell, 2002). These objectives can be used to identify what it needs to do well to improve its performance. It is at this point that the primary goals of sport organizations become quite different from those of business organizations. While commercial leisure centres and most American professional sport teams seem to be focused on maximizing profits, most other sports clubs, even with a large revenue base, are more concerned with priorities like winning more games than their rivals, and servicing the needs of members. However it is not always clear just what the primary goal of a sport organization is, or what is the best measure for deciding how well the organization has performed. In commercial terms the most successful association football (or soccer) club is Manchester United, closely followed by Real Madrid. However, neither Manchester United or Real Madrid got to the Champions' League final in 2003, which was won by Porto, a relative pauper. In the USA National Football League, the Cincinnati Bengals rarely get to the end of season play-offs, but because of its frugal spending and League's income equalization strategy, makes a greater profit than some of the better known teams. However, despite these anomalies, it is clear that any performance management system must take into account, and indeed, reflect, the primary goal of the relevant club, team, facility, event or league.

Case 11.1 Financial measures of sport organization performance

As indicated above, sport organizations are faced with the dilemma of deciding which of profit maximizing or win maximizing will drive their operations. In practice sport organizations, no matter how strongly they want to achieve on-ground success, must operate within clearly defined financial parameters. There are, of course, examples of extreme behaviours where associations and clubs can on one hand decide to win a premiership or pennant at any cost, or on the other, be so frugal and cost-efficient that any chance of achieving on-field success is completely negated. One of the best examples of the former is Leeds United Football Club. Leeds had been in the top half of the English Premier League throughout the 1990s, and in 2001 reached the semi-finals of the UEFA Champions' League. However in wanting to succeed in the big-league it generated enormous levels of debt by spending extravagant amounts of money on the purchase of players. A modest net profit of just over 600 000 pounds in 1999 exploded into an overwhelming net loss of nearly 34 million pounds in 2002. The loss represented 35% of total club turnover for the year. Quite the opposite state-of-affairs exists with the Cincinnati Bengals, a member of the USA National Football League. The Bengals had the worst playing record in the league from 1990–1999, but was also one of the most profitable clubs. This counter-intuitive, and in some ways bizarre result, arose from the club's decision to operate at the lowest possible cost to ensure its long-term financial viability. Its capacity to do this was assisted greatly by the league's revenue-sharing policy which involves around 70–80% of its total revenue being shared equally amongst the competing teams (Sandy et al., 2004). This policy gives every club a guaranteed minimum income regardless of their on-field performance. As a result, the Bengal's lack of competitiveness was offset by its ability to remain the league's fifth most profitable team. This begs the question as to which of Leeds or Cincinnati was the better performing team. It also begs the question as to precisely what measures can be used to clearly identify the financial strengths and weaknesses of sport organizations.

As we indicated in the earlier part of this chapter, sport is both similar to and different from business. As a result, the sort of financial analysis that gets done on commercial businesses may not always be the most appropriate for sport organizations. Many sport organizations, for instance, are non-profit entities, and therefore a return-on-equity ratio would not be all that useful. However, other ratios that measure levels of liquidity and indebtedness would be essential for the analysis of sport organizations. Table 11.1 provides a selection of financial measures that can be employed in assessing the financial performance of sport organizations.

Building a performance management model from a stakeholder perspective

Performance management should also be linked to an organization's key stakeholders (Atkinson et al., 1997). If stakeholders are satisfied with the organization's performance, then clearly it is doing well. In a publicly owned

Table 11.1 Financial performance indicators for a sport organization

Ratio name	Definition	What it measures
Operating profit	Operating income (revenue) profit less operating expenses (costs)	Indicator of ability to be sustainable in medium term.
Profit ratio	Profit as a proportion of income	Indicator of capacity to cover total expenses
Wage-turnover	Wages as a proportion of turnover or income	Indicator of ability to manage wages and related costs
Working capital	Difference between current assets (cash, short-term deposits and creditors) and current liabilities (debtors)	Indicator of ability to pay short-term debts when they fall due
Debt/equity	Long-term debt as a proportion of shareholders funds or accumulate profits	Indicator of degree of dependency on debt to fund operations/activities
Net assets	Difference between total assets and total liabilities	Indicator of the net worth or real wealth of the organization

sports retail business for example, a large profit and dividend will be good for management and shareholders alike. However in a member-based sport club, success will be more about on-field performance and member services than massive profits. On the other hand, for a sport's governing body the interests of its registered players may take the highest priority. In other words, different types of sport organizations will have their own unique goals and priorities, which will in turn reflect the ways in which they rank their stakeholders (Friedman et al., 2004).

Stakeholders may also have conflicting needs. Sponsors may want maximum media exposure and access to players, but the clubs have a primary interest in improving player performance, which may mean less, not more player involvement in sponsor activities. In the case of a national sporting body, the national government may want international success to justify its investment in elite training and coaching programmes, whereas the rank-and-file players who make up the bulk of the membership may want more local facilities. Sport organizations are therefore required to balance the often-conflicting needs and 'contradictory interests' of the various stakeholders (Chappelet & Bayle, 2005). The major sport organization stakeholders and their expectations are summarized in Table 11.2.

The key point to note here is that a sport organization will have multiple stakeholders, and their interests will have to be integrated into its evaluation processes.

Table 11.2 Stakeholder expectations of sport organizations

Stakeholder type	Expectations of sport organization
Players	• On-field success • Appropriate pay and benefits • Low injury rates
Employees	• Appropriate pay and benefits • Job security • Professional development
Equipment suppliers	• Reliability of demand • Player endorsement • Brand awareness
Members	• Services and benefits • Overall satisfaction
Owners/Shareholders	• Return on investment • Public recognition of club or association
Sponsors	• Positive reputation of club or association • Brand awareness and recognition
Player agents	• High player morale • Payment of market rates
Fans	• Game quality and excitement • High win-loss ratio
Community/Society	• Civic pride • Provides role models for young adults
Media	• Mass market • High level of public interest

An input–output approach to performance management

In developing a model for evaluating a sport organization's performance, a number of additional principles should be utilized. A second approach is to focus on inputs and outputs. This involves looking at things like quality, quantity, efficiency, cost–benefit ratios, and employee productivity (Bouckaert, 1995). This approach provides a checklist of essential performance dimensions that need to be addressed. It ensures that no one measure is dominant, and also provides for measures that not only focus on internal processes, but also look at the organization's relationships with key suppliers and customers. A summary of the ways in which input–output analysis can be applied to sport organizations is illustrated in Table 11.3.

Table 11.3 An input–output approach to performance management in sport

Dimension	Measure
Output: Quantity	• Premierships • Attendance • Membership • Participation
Output: Quality	• Standard of play • Features of venue/facility • Standard of service • Overall customer experience
Output: Cost–benefit	• Operating profit • Costs of operation • Net economic benefit • Social benefit
Input: Efficiency	• Cost of providing service • Administrative support cost • Waiting time
Input: Staff performance	• Customer/member/fan satisfaction ratings • Staff skills and experience • Staff achievements

A balanced and multi-dimensional approach to performance management

A third approach is to avoid the often obsessive emphasis that shareholders place on financial measures by balancing it against the benefits that might accrue to customers, suppliers, and employees (Harvard Business Review, 1998). This approach is exemplified in the Balanced Scorecard (BSC) model designed by Kaplan and Norton (Kaplan & Norton, 1992, 1996). The BSC has four dimensions which are reviewed below.

One of the first things Kaplan and Norton note is that a good performance measurement tool should not be a 'controlling system' obsessed with keeping 'individuals, and organizational units in compliance with a pre-established plan' (p. 25). Rather it should be primarily a 'learning system' concerned with 'communication and informing' (p. 25). To this end Kaplan and Norton aimed to design a performance measurement system that balanced external and easily quantifiable measures like market share and return on investment against internal and more ephemeral factors like administrative processes and staff development.

Kaplan and Norton's first dimension is 'Financial Perspective'. Although they argue that too much emphasis has traditionally been given to the so called bottom-line result, financial measures are nevertheless a fundamental starting point for evaluating the economic sustainability of an organization. They can range from total sales, operating income and net cash flow, to return on assets, debt to equity ratio and net profit. This dimension answers the question 'how do we look to shareholders'?

The second dimension is 'Customer Perspective'. In this instance the emphasis is on identifying the 'customer and market segments in which the business will compete', and to develop measures that will indicate how well the organization competes in these segments (p. 26). These measures will include total sales in each segment, market share, customer acquisition, customer retention, and customer satisfaction. Kaplan and Norton also suggest that for this performance dimension attention should be given to the factors like short lead times and on-time delivery that actually underpin the levels of customer satisfaction and retention. This dimension addresses the question 'how do customers see us'?

The third dimension is the 'Internal-Business-Process Perspective'. This perspective requires management to identify the 'critical internal processes in which the organization must excel' in order to secure a competitive advantage (p. 26). Kaplan and Norton note that it is not just a matter of ensuring that current value-adding processes are efficient and streamlined, but that there are also systems in place to improve and re-engineer existing processes and products. This dimension addresses the question 'what must we excel at'?

The fourth dimension is the 'Learning and Growth Perspective'. Kaplan and Norton see this perspective as crucial to the long-term success of organizations. In a turbulent business environment there is an ever-increasing likelihood that the technologies and processes required to sustain a market advantage and competitive edge may race ahead of the technical and managerial skills of the staff who are responsible for managing those technologies and processes. In order to close this gap organizations will 'have to invest in re-skilling employees, enhancing information technology and systems, and aligning organizational procedures and routines' (p. 27). This dimension addresses the question 'can we continue to improve and create value'?

Finally, Kaplan and Norton suggest that each of the above perspectives should be linked to a common overarching objective that ensures consistency and mutually reinforcing conduct. In other words, the BSC is more than a 'dashboard' of 'critical indicators or key success factors' (p. 29). In order to be effective it must reflect the organization's mission and goals.

Costs and benefits of a performance management system

Planning and implementing a performance management system can be costly, since it involves a lot of time-intensive analysis of an organization's processes and activities. It can also become a bureaucratic nightmare since it can produce hundreds of microscopic statements about the way things should be done, and how they must be measured. It should be remembered that the concept of performance management arose out of the mechanistic time-and-motion studies of Frederick Winslow Taylor in the early part of the twentieth century. According to Taylor the key to increasing productivity was to systematically analyse work practices in order to identify the most efficient process, which could then become a best-practice template (Stewart, 1989). Taylorism also underpinned the development of Management by Objectives (MBO) and Total Quality Management (TQM) which were later refined into a broader model of performance management (Bouckaert & van Doren, 2003). As a result, a rigidly structured performance management system can stifle initiative and creativity by setting narrowly defined work standards and strict standards of workplace behaviour.

At the same time, a well thought out performance management system can provide a number of long-term benefits (Williams, 1998). First, it makes sure that the core activities of an organization are directly linked to its primary aims and goals. Second, it can motivate employees by setting targets which are rewarded when they are attained. Third, it ensures greater accountability by clearly identifying not only what is to be achieved, but also who is responsible for making it happen. Fourth, it completes the management cycle by making sure processes are monitored, and outcomes are measured against some sort of minimum performance standard. Finally it forces management to come up with a quantifiable measure of its key outputs, and eliminate ambiguous aims and nebulous objectives.

Case 11.2 Measuring the performance of Australian Football Leagues

The Australian Football League is the showcase competition for Australia's only indigenous game of any significance, Australian Rules football. Australian Rules football was invented in Melbourne in 1858, and went on to become one of the nation's most popular sports (Hess & Stewart, 1998). However unlike cricket and tennis, it really ever only embraced the southern states of Australia. Whereas it captured the hearts and minds of people living in Victoria, South Australia, Western Australia and Tasmania, its presence in New South Wales and Queensland was for the most part marginal. In these two states, rugby league was the most popular football code, with rugby union being the second most popular code. Association football, or soccer as it is more commonly identified in Australia, was very much a minor code in every state. During the 1950s and 1960s in particular, European migrants, who had been immersed in the soccer culture at home, were amazed that the world-game had been relegated to the periphery of Australia's sporting landscape.

However, at the beginning of the 21st century, things had changed quite dramatically. The rapid commercialization of sport during the 1980s and 1990s had produced a number of national sport leagues, the most powerful being the football codes. The National Soccer league had the earliest beginnings, having been established in 1978. However, it went through many traumatic changes, and clubs were rarely able to trade profitably. In 2003 the league was abandoned while the national governing body was reformed, and a new eight-team league was set up. It was completely re-badged, and clubs were stripped of their ethnic origins. The A-League, as it is now called, will commence in 2006. The National Rugby League competition (NRL) is far more robust. Although the competition was fractured with the establishment of a rival Super League in 1995, it is now solidly entrenched in New South Wales and Queensland, and to a lesser extent Victoria. However, the competition no longer has teams in either South Australia or Western Australia, although this structural problem is slightly compensated for by having a team playing out of Auckland in New Zealand. Rugby Union is an interesting case because like League, it has only moderate support in Australia's southern states, but is a major code in New South Wales and Queensland. Union's Super-12 competition comprised five New Zealand teams, three Australian teams, and four South African teams. However, in 2006 another two teams will be added to the competition, namely Perth in Western Australia, and a fifth South African team, thereby making it a Super-14 competition. Finally, there is the Australian Football League (AFL), which arose out of the Victorian Football League in 1986. The AFL has teams in every state, and over the last ten years has made significant inroads in the hostile rugby territory of New South Wales and Queensland.

Each of the above football codes have their own unique history and culture, but it is also the case that they are serious rivals in a highly competitive sporting marketplace. There are many arguments about the relative strengths of each code, and which national competition is the most successful (Stensholt & Thomson, 2005). In performance management terms, this is an interesting issue to address. Neither is it immediately clear as to how one should best go about doing a comparative evaluation of the performance of the leagues. This is because there are many different ways of undertaking the performance management task.

The management team of each national competition is very sensitive to developments in the rival leagues. They are also eager to trumpet and promote their successes, particularly if it means they have secured some strategic advantage over their competitors. At the same time, there are a number of critical success factors that commonly used to rank the performance of the national leagues. These factors are first, total season attendance, second, total club membership, third, aggregate league revenue, fourth income from television broadcast rights, and finally weekly television audiences. The five somewhat crude measures give a very good indication of just how well each league performs. However, over recent times some additional measures have been incorporated into their performance management models. First there is the issue of the viability of teams, and the ability to balance their budgets. Second, there is the competitive balance of the league, and the extent to which it can guarantee fans a close and exciting contest. Third, there is the reputation of the league and the extent to which it is seen as a responsible sporting citizen. To this end the leagues are eager to promote equal opportunity for players and administrators, put in place anti-harassment rules, and have a strong anti-doping policy. In general the leagues are very sensitive to criticism about player misconduct, particularly when it involves some sort of sexual assault. A sample of key indicators for measuring the performance of Australian national football leagues is listed in Table 11.4.

Table 11.4 Performance measures for Australian national sport leagues

Item	Descriptor/measure	Examples
Financial stability	• League turnover • Net assets	Australian Football League (AFL) turnover is more than $170 million. National Rugby League (NRL) turnover is around $90 million
Corporate support	• Sponsorship income • Stadium suites	AFL supported by more national brands (e.g. Vodafone, Air Emirates, Toyota), than NRL
Broadcasting rights' fees	• Fees from TV stations • Fees from radio stations	AFL TV rights fee currently $100 million pa; NRL TV rights fee currently around $50 million
Media exposure	• Television rating • Print media coverage	AFL grand final draws 2.8 million TV audience; NRL grand final draws 2.1 million TV audience.
Public interest	• Brand awareness • Match attendance	AFL average match attendance 33,000; NRL average match attendance 16,000.
Spread/coverage	• Media coverage • Spread of teams and venues	AFL teams spread around five of six states; NRL teams spread around three of six states plus New Zealand.
Competitive balance	• Win-loss ratios for each team • Premierships won by each team	NRL teams have slightly more closely aligned win-loss ratios (i.e. smaller standard deviation).
Game development	• Junior development programmes • Regional development programmes	AFL spends $22 million a year on community development; NRL spends $11 million on community development

Designing a performance management model appropriate for sport

The BSC has many strengths, but it requires significant adjustment to make it better fit the special requirements of sport organizations. One approach is to maintain the four basis dimensions that underpin the BSC, and use it to design a customized performance model that reflects the special features of sport organizations. To this end the following '9 point' model of performance management has been designed.

The first performance dimension focuses on wins, awards, and successes. This dimension recognizes the fact that most sport associations and clubs want be seen to be doing well and producing winning players and teams. In other words, faced with the choice of winning a championship, or increasing profits, most clubs would prefer the winner's pennant or medal.

However, like all organizations, sport leagues, associations and clubs need ongoing funding to ensure their long-term viability, to pay their debts when they fall due, and cover their operating costs from year to year. Therefore the second dimension is concerned with financial sustainability. In this respect, measures of revenue growth will not be enough, and more specific measures of profit, liquidity, long-term indebtedness, return on investment, and net asset growth are all useful indicators.

The third dimension is market distribution, or the extent to which a sport league, association or club is able to facilitate the consumption of its particular sporting practice. If its major concern is with participation, then it needs to be aware of how many facilities it provides, their location and spread, and the experiential quality they offer. If the major concern is the potential audience that can be attracted, then it needs to be aware of the number of spectator seats it can provide, the radio exposure it will receive, and the scale and breadth of any television broadcast.

The fourth dimension is market size and share. It is one thing to have a broad range and spread of facilities and venues, and a large number of television-broadcast hours, but it is another thing to attract a consistently large number of participants, spectators and viewers. It is also important to compare the numbers for these indicators with the numbers for other related sports that are seen to be competitors.

The fifth dimension is customer satisfaction, which is really a measure of how strongly participants, fans, and members approve of the performance of the league, association or club. Sport organizations usually engender very passionate connections with their customer and member base, but there are also many instances when they attend games or activities less frequently, or more seriously downgrade their involvement. Surveys of participants, members and fans can reveal early signs of dissatisfaction, or alternatively indicate what is sustaining the relationship.

The sixth dimension is internal procedures and processes. Like Kaplan and Norton's similarly labelled dimension, it aims to highlight the key links in the value-chain and how each stage is performing relative to the others. For sporting organizations it often begins with how well players are recruited, their numbers, and overall quality. The recruitment and retention of members is also an important consideration, and the question often arises as to the capacity of members to contribute time, expertise, and money to the association and club's activities. The ability of players to improve their skill and overall performance is also a function of the support system, and in particular the skill and abilities of the coaching staff. This leads to the capacity of the organization to ensure a safe environment where the management of risk is taken seriously, and the incidence of litigation is slight. All the above processes are of course linked to administrative functions that can either enhance the player and member experience as poor training or sloppy systems can make the experience both unpleasant and costly. Many of the above factors can be difficult to quantify, but they nevertheless need serious consideration.

The seventh dimension is product improvement. In this respect sport is no different from business in that it operates in a very competitive marketplace, and constant innovation and product improvement is essential to attract new customers and retain the old. Some sports have been very successful in modifying their games to suit the needs of special groups, while others have been unable to move beyond their traditional practices. In some spectator sports there have been very slow improvements in venue quality, while in others there has been a virtual revolution in terms of stadium design and spectator comfort. Progressive changes in the design of sporting equipment have also improved product quality. In tennis, for example, the use of carbon fibre racket frames and the creation of larger 'sweet-spots' have enabled average club-players to improve their standard of play and overall skill levels.

The eighth dimension is staff development and learning. Sport is a very person-centred, time-absorbing activity, and therefore requires staff who have highly refined social skills, and the capacity to create an organizational culture that retains players and members. The growing technical sophistication of sport also means that traditional administrative, officiating and coaching skills are no longer adequate, and therefore large-scale re-training and education are necessary to ensure a proper fit between the staff competencies and the new technologies and infrastructure that underpin contemporary sport.

The ninth dimension covers the economic, social and environmental impact that a sport league, association or club has on its surrounding community. Increasingly the level of support a government will provide a sport organization is contingent upon the organization's ability to produce a positive economic, social or environmental impact. This trend has been exaggerated by the growing popularity of the triple-bottom-line accounting concept, which highlights the importance of going beyond profitability and wealth creation as the sole measure of an organization's contribution to society to include environmental and social impacts (Norman & MacDonald, 2004). In this case sport organizations also have a responsibility to carefully manage and sustain its environment, and establish an organizational culture that values things like diversity, equal opportunity, and the fair treatment of gays, lesbians, and religious minorities.

This nine-dimensional model has the advantage of being broad and inclusive, and geared to the needs of sport in general. But, it needs to be customized to fit different sporting organizations. As we indicated before, an organization's strategic intent, and stakeholder interests, will shape the design of a performance evaluation model (Atkinson et al., 1997; Robbins & Barnwell, 2002; Williams, 1998). For example the evaluation model for a national sporting body should be different from the model used to evaluate a professional sport club. The national sporting body will be more interested in participation rates, club development, and the provision of quality local facilities. On the other hand, a professional sport club will be more concerned with its win-loss ratio, sponsor income, television ratings, and membership levels.

Performance measures

Once a model is in place, it is then crucial to design performance measures. These measures should be able to precisely identify and quantify specific indicators of success or failure. Sometimes it is difficult to 'put a number' on a measure. Customer and fan 'satisfaction' readily comes to mind in this respect, but there are often ways of converting a subjective opinion into a measurable indicator.

It is one thing to identify some key performance indicators, and to collect some data under each heading. However it is another thing to make sense of the data. It is therefore important to develop some sort of benchmark or standard by which to measure the performance of a sport organization. There are two ways of doing this. The first is to undertake a longitudinal study that examines the progress of a sport organization over time. Take for example the performance of Athletics Australia (AA), the national governing body for athletics in Australia. A ten year analysis of its financial performance would show it has been increasingly unable to balance its books over the last few years. By 2003 it had accumulated a seriously worrying level of debt which brought on an organizational crisis. By any financial measure, AA's performance had fallen dramatically over this period. The same sort of longitudinal analysis could be applied to its participation levels and elite international performance. In each the data indicated very little improvement over the last ten years.

Another way of looking at AA's performance would be to compare it with other national sport bodies to see how it ranks. That is, it will also be important to undertake a comparative study by which the performance of AA is stacked up against a number of other national sport organizations. There are two ways of doing this. The first way would be to compare it with similarly funded Australian national sport bodies like Swimming Australia or Rowing Australia. In this case, AA has not performed well, since both swimming and rowing have achieved regular gold medal winning performances at both World Championships and Olympic Games over the last ten years. The second way is to compare AA's performance with an equivalent national athletic association from another country. An appropriate point of comparison here might be the Canadian Athletics Federation, since both countries have similar populations, and the national athletic associations have a similar resource base. In this case the comparison would yield an elite performance outcome substantially better than the one with Swimming Australia.

The lesson to be learnt here is that the performance of a sport organization cannot be measured in a vacuum, or without some yardstick and point of comparison. At the minimum, either some form of longitudinal or comparative analysis should be undertaken. Ideally, a mixture of both methods would provide the best set of results.

Case 11.3   Measuring performance in a community leisure centre

As we indicated in the early part of this chapter, performance management systems have infiltrated their way into every nook and cranny of the business environment and public sector (Bouckaert & van Doren, 2003; Robbins & Barnwell, 2002). Moreover, they are not only applied to corporate performance, but also to many of the so-called micro activities that comprise the day-to-day operations of business enterprises. Community leisure centres in particular lend themselves to micro measurement. In the first place, they provide an array of person-centred activities that are subject to strong user responses and perceptions. Second, their services are not only rated on the scale, range and quality of its tangible facilities, but also on the quality of the service provided by the staff. Third, many community leisure centres are funded and subsidised through local government rates and taxes, and therefore need to ensure that scarce community resources are utilized as efficiently as possible.

It is useful to examine the performance of community leisure centres from two perspectives. The first perspective focuses on the efficient use of funds, staff and space. To get some idea of how funds are being used it is always good to start with some idea of the relationship between operating costs and income. This will generate an operating profit indicator, and an expense recovery rate. And where more detail is needed, something like fees (admission charges) per visit or fees per unit of space can be calculated. It is also very important to identify not only the gross subsidy that may apply, but also the subsidy per visit. There are also a number of sales and marketing related measures that can be used to indicate how well funds are being used in attracting visitors. They include things like total visits per space used, and promotion cost per visitor. It is also important to measure facility usage. In this instance measures include visit per metre of space, maintenance cost per unit of centre expenditure, and energy cost per metre of space. Finally, there are a number of measures that provide an indication of how well staff are being utilized. They include

Table 11.5 Sample of efficiency indicators for a community leisure centre

Indicator	Description	Examples
Expense recovery rate	Ratio of total centre income to total centre expenses	Income of $5 million, expenses of 4.5 million, expense recovery rate is 111
Admission fees per visit	Total fees divided by number of visits	1000 visits per week, $6000 in fees, admission fee per visit is $6.
Visits per space available	Visits divided by amount of space	1000 visits per week, 50 square metres of space, visit per metre-space is 200.
Promotion costs per visitor	Promotion costs divided by number of visitors	1000 visits per week, $1000 of promotion per week, promotion cost per visit is $1.
Maintenance costs rate	Ratio of total centre maintenance costs to total centre income to	Maintenance costs are 1.5 million, centre income is $5 million, maintenance cost rate is 0.30 or 30%.
Staff costs per unit of space	Staff costs divided by space	Staff costs are $3 million, space is 50 square metres, staff cost per unit of space is $6000.

staff cost as a percentage of total income, staff costs as a percentage of total centre expenditure, and the ratio of desk staff to programming staff. A sample of performance indicators for community leisure centres is listed in Table 11.5.

The second perspective focuses on the level of service quality. In this instance it is a matter of finding out what visitors think of their experiences in the centre (Beech & Chadwick, 2004). Their experiences are usually divided into five categories. They are first, the quality of the tangible product or service itself, second, the reliability and dependability of the service, third, the responsiveness of staff and their willingness to assist, fourth, an assurance that staff will be trustworthy and courteous, and finally, the degree to which staff are empathetic and provide individual attention. There are many models to choose from, and many rating tools. Some of the more sophisticated tools aim to calculate a service delivery gap, which is nothing more than the difference between what customers expected, and what they experienced (Graaff, 1996). In the end, all they are doing is providing a customer rating of the facilities and personal service provided. Typically this will be done by a survey or questionnaire that asks visitors to score the specific services on a rating scale of 1–5. Ratings of 1 usually indicate low levels of satisfaction, while ratings of 5 will indicate high levels of satisfaction.

Summary

The above discussion suggests that while the introduction of performance management systems into sport organizations can be costly, and sometimes create an administrative straightjacket for its staff, officials, volunteers and members, it can also bring substantial benefits. In fact a sport organization that does not provide a systematic evaluation of its performance would be derelict in its duty to stakeholders. The question is really one of what form and shape the performance management system should take. At this point it is important to say that there is no one best performance management system. It all depends on the particular sport organization being studied, its primary strategic goals, and the environment in which it operates. A good starting point is to use Kaplan and Norton's BSC as the foundation, and customize it to fit the sport organization's specific needs. The 9-point model described above gives a number of possibilities, but at all times the measures should be quantifiable, linked to the sport organization's primary goals, and consistent with stakeholder expectations.

Review questions

1. What does a performance management system aim to do?
2. What are the origins of performance management, and what do these origins tell us about its possible strengths and weaknesses?
3. What might prevent a sport organization from implementing a system of performance management?
4. What are the benefits that will follow from the implementation of a performance management system?
5. What are the key components of Kaplan and Norton's BSC?
6. How might you go about modifying the BSC to make it better fit the special features of sport organizations?
7. What specific measures can best reveal the financial performance of a sport organization?
8. How can the intrinsically vague concept of customer satisfaction be 'hardened-up' to provide a quantitative, concrete measure of the service quality in a community leisure centre?

Further reading

To get a more detailed picture of the fundamentals of performance management, and how it has been used in both private and public sectors, see Williams (1978) and Bouckaert and van Dooren (2003). In order to obtain a fuller appreciation of the theoretical foundations of performance management, its relation to organizational effectiveness, and problems of implementation, refer to Chapter 3 of Robbins and Barnwell (2002), and Bouckaert (1995).

Relevant web sites

* For an update on the balanced scorecard approach to performance management, go to http://www.balancedscorecard.org

* Japan's professional soccer (i.e. association football) league, the J.League is one of Japan's most popular sport competitions. To obtain a general picture of its overall level of performance, go to http://www.j-league.or.jp

* In Australia, the Australian Football League is highly profitable, but paradoxically some of its member clubs have had to fight severe financial turbulence over many years. The Institute of Chartered Accountants undertakes an annual survey of club finances. For further details go to http://www.icaa.org.au/news/index

Part Three
Future Challenges

Chapter 12
Future sport management challenges

Overview

Globalization, defined by the International Monetary Fund (IMF) as an increase in the integration of economies around the world (IMF, 2005), is the major force impacting on the future of the sport industry. It has been widely acknowledged that the most recent wave of globalization is a result of the dramatic increase in opportunities for people to travel, combined with the widespread integration and application of communication technology that puts 'everyone in touch with everyone' in a split second. In turn, these facilitating factors of globalization have led to increases in trade, more intense and entangled financial interaction, more frequent movement of labour, and intensified transmission of knowledge, technology, culture and ideologies.

Three themes are common in literature concerning the nature and impact of globalization. First, the world has entered an irreversible global age, and the consequence of this 'new world order' is that traditional power (economic, financial, political) of the State is starting to shift to multinational corporations. Second, it seems that the economic progress paradigm is dominant, which transcends national boundaries, turning the world into the ultimate (for the time being) marketplace. Finally, as a result of globalization there are not only winners, but also many marginalized fringes and masses.

This final chapter will briefly examine what the future may have in store for sport, and as such, what the future may hold for those that have to (and want to) manage sport. The chapter will also analyse the principal factors that drive change in the world of sport. This will lead to an overview of how globalization is likely to impact sport management and indeed, how sport managers need to be prepared. A brief introduction to the production and consumption of sport in the future will be outlined through the discussion of the DreamSport Society. The DreamSport Society presents six market segments comprising different types of sport consumers. These segments provide the context for sport consumption in which sport managers need to prepare for the main challenges that the future holds. These challenges will be summarized relative to the specific foci of Chapters 5 to 11: strategic management, organizational structure, human resource management, leadership, organizational culture, governance and performance management. Cases are not presented in this chapter as the cases about the future are still to be written (and acted out) by the readers of this book.

By the end of this chapter readers should be able to:

- Speculate about the future of sport management based on some trend extrapolation;
- Identify a number of scenarios that can be used to plan for the future of sport (business and management);
- Outline and argue what the potential impact of different scenarios may be on the future of sport management;
- Integrate an element of 'futures thinking' into their strategic planning activities; and
- Summarize the contents of this book by way of discussing future challenges that sport managers face.

Globalization and its impact on sport management

In a report published by the United States Intelligence Council (2000), a range of factors that could influence the 'ways of the world' were identified. Westerbeek and Smith (2003) selected three of these factors as the most influential drivers of change in regard to the business of sport in a globalized marketplace: economy, technology and culture.

Economy

As a result of disappearing economic borders (the nations are still there, but trade does not recognize national borders anymore) there will be increasing opportunities to gain popularity in previously untapped and unexplored markets. There will also be more financial (investment) capital available through the global money markets, for sport ventures that show mass market potential, for example, the markets of Asia and South America. Many Western countries are likely to follow the lead of the American sport system, where business people have already taken over from the national sporting bodies and federations that have been too slow to react to market forces. As a result of increasing Gross Domestic Product (GDP) in developing countries, more money and time will become available to spend on sport and related leisure activities.

It is likely that some of the stronger sporting clubs around the world will pool their mass market potential (for example, the G14 of strongest European football clubs) and threaten the established governing bodies by organizing their own competitions. Although technology will assist in 'bringing the world closer' to those who are connected, unequal access to economic resources is likely to widen the gap between the sporting 'haves' and 'have nots', both from a consumer and producer point of view. In summary, the economy as a driving factor of change in the global world of sport is likely to keep pushing the industry towards an increasingly business-like approach to sport service production and delivery. Mass market opportunities to sell sport will continue to gain prominence over the smaller niche sports.

Technology

The integration of super-fast means of communication will not necessarily lead to equal opportunities for sport organizations in different countries. One would think that with the availability of digital television and broadband internet, any sport can now beam its pictures and excitement around the world to anyone who wants to see it. However, increased (cheap) distribution opportunities do not necessarily lead to increased popularity! 'Old' technology, such as television, will remain 'the first contact with sport' for those people living in parts of the world that are yet to see television. Television will be a battering ram for many of the bigger sport organizations and their media partners to open up new markets, before they can move in and introduce newer technology.

New technology will allow smaller sport organizations to gain more control over the production and distribution of their products, rather than always be dependent on the rich and powerful media organizations alone. Next to the opportunities and limitations presented by the 'new' communication technology, the developments in the field of biotechnology need to be watched closely as well. Sport organizations have long been familiar with the issue of performance enhancing drugs, but in comparison to what can (and probably will) happen over the next ten years in relation to biomedical applications of knowledge to sport, many sport governors will long for the days when monitoring athletes for doping was a simple task. The prospect of using genetic information and manipulating it to create self-sustaining injury repair protein structures and energy-generating micro-engines, to be implanted into our bodies, may sound alien to us now, but if the current rate of technological development is sustained, this science fiction may become reality within a decade. Humans may literally be in a position to 'build' super athletes, or worse, parents may be able to design their children into the athletes they never could be in the 'old days'.

Culture

Sport has played a long and important role at the local, regional, national and international level. Local and regional sport has often functioned as the glue that brings communities together to play, and forget about differences between people for a short time. Sport, at the level of the community club, has not only provided people with a 'neutral' forum to get together, but has also facilitated the welcoming, integration and acceptance of outsiders into those communities. For example, football (soccer) in Australia played a vital role throughout the immigration waves of the 1950s and 1960s for millions of European migrants in building new communities on the other side of the world, a safe haven away from their home countries. It is likely that in the future, sport at the local level will continue to be used as 'cultural glue' for community cohesion and integration.

At the national and international level, sport has played an important role (for some nations more than others) in creating a sense of national identity. Relatively 'young' migrant countries in particular, such as the United States of America (USA) and Australia, have used sport to demonstrate their national prowess on a world stage. Sport has also often been used as a vehicle for propaganda. Hitler's Nazi Germany, Mussolini in Fascist Italy and more recently the Communist regimes of former East Germany and the USSR have all used sport to illustrate the physical, mental and moral superiority of their nations and political systems.

The global sport marketplace is currently dominated by the American way of doing business. Even the more traditional football clubs and competitions of Europe seem to have forgotten the fans in favour of shareholders and media barons. This may well lead to cultural alienation of everything that is 'American' in countries that are yet to be introduced to the American and European sports. According to Dejonghe (2001) the global sport system is based on cultural affinity of peripheral countries with the sports' country of origin (the centre country). He argues that when a peripheral country is passive in its acceptance of imported sport, it either embraces the external culture, or is not in a position to fight it. This can be called 'cultural imperialism' and in countries located in sub-Saharan Africa, Latin America and the Caribbean, countries like Britain and the USA have introduced their sports in that way.

Imported sport can also be critically assessed and considered in the context of a host culture, and deemed as beneficial, neutral or threatening. This is when the peripheral country's attitude can be termed 'participative'. Former British colonies like South Africa, Canada, New Zealand and Australia have embraced sports that they in turn used to define themselves as independent nations. It has to be noted though, that they have rejected sports that did not fit their newly found national identity. A peripheral country's 'conflict evoking' response to imported sport, is the result of significant cultural difference and incompatibility with the centre country's orientation. The current global political climate is such that most sports are introduced and 'implanted' in an Americanized way, which in many cases will lead to a conflict evoking response by the host country.

The main challenge for the sport manager of the future, from this perspective, is to be culturally sensitive, and not only seek the ways in which sport *can* be introduced in new markets, but also ensure that a particular sport can be linked to the (cultural) sporting *needs* of that market. Leading up to the development of the Cold War, the former Soviet Union and its satellite states initially rejected all forms of sport that were direct expressions of Western capitalism. However, when they realized that the truly international sports could be used as tools of cultural and economic warfare, mainly to express moral superiority, they embraced most 'capitalistic' sports, and further refocused on developing minor sports that were represented at international competitions such as the Olympic Games in order to boost their medal tally.

Having outlined the three principal drivers of the globalization of sport, in the next section the concept of the DreamSport Society is introduced. Six key market segments for sport consumption will be presented through the Dream-Sport Society, in order to present an overview of the type of products that will be consumed in the sport marketplace of the future. These products will have major implications for sport managers in regard to what they manage, and how they manage it.

The DreamSport Society and the implications for sport managers

Given the impact of a globalizing economy on sport, the exponential development of communication and scientific technologies, and the mediating and potentially conflicting effects of cultural difference, what can we expect will be the response of the sport consumer in the next 15 years or so? Based on the work of futurist Rolf Jensen (1999), who painted a picture about life in the future in his book *The Dream Society*, Westerbeek and Smith (2003) developed a framework to discuss the future of sport which they called the *DreamSport Society*.

According to Jensen (1999), people living in the Dream Society will strive towards achieving the emotional wealth that typified early human civilization because it combines material wealth (which means we no longer struggle to survive) with emotional wealth and fulfilment. Westerbeek and Smith proposed six new markets for sport in the DreamSport Society: sport entertainment, sport fantasy, sport quality, sport identity, sport tradition and sport conscience.

Sport entertainment

Sport consumers have an increasing emotional need for adventure, as evidenced by the escalation of activities such as bungee jumping and extreme sports. People do not attend sporting contests merely to watch the game anymore, they are also seeking pre-game, half-time and post-game entertainment. Sport consumers of the future can be better entertained by satisfying their need for adventure, which will ultimately lead to some form of participation *in* the game. In other words, in order to realize their emotional peak they must have some influence *on* the game.

If interactivity is the key to success, then new technology will be used and applied to facilitate a spectator's emotional connection to the sport product by engaging them in a variety of ways. In the future, supertechnology may well lead to a situation where people can artificially experience (through supercomputer mediation) what it means to perform at the highest level of sporting achievement. For example, a sport consumer may be able to run the 100 metre Olympic final against the stars of the past and present. They might simply 'log in' their brain and select from a range of programmes which are on offer at the right price for the sport organization. For sport managers, the implication is to be able to satisfy a person's emotional need through sport products that meet their need for adventure.

Sport fantasy

Sport fantasy products are all about the satisfaction of people's emotional need for togetherness, about the creation of consumption situations that can bring people together. At the heart of this emotional requirement is the desire for comradeship and direction and the role that sport has played in migrant communities in building new communities and facilitating friendship and social interaction through community sport. This is also true in the arena of professional sport. For more than 200 years the great clubs and teams of the world have played their games in order to please large crowds of onlookers, in the process of tying and bonding them together as fanatical and loyal followers. In the future people will continue to select local sporting clubs to get together and be drawn to winning teams because they provide a convenient opportunity to experience the pleasure of togetherness.

However, how sport managers will communicate with those club members and fans will dramatically change, as will the ways in which these people get together. It will not come as a surprise that the Internet will provide mass market opportunities for the bigger sport organizations. For the club members and fans it will provide a convenient way of communicating and participating in fan forums with people from all corners of the globe, meeting and greeting online.

Sport quality

The sport quality consumer segment of the DreamSport Society is focused on satisfying the need for people to 'care about others', combined with a sense of pure enjoyment of sport. As volunteers have been the backbone of club-based sport systems, sport has had a long standing history of providing opportunities to care. However, the sport consumer (in this case the sport volunteer) of the future will no longer be satisfied with their position as a semi-detached sports lover. Many people involved in sport at all levels will seek quality sport experiences that reach a deeper level, where they can fulfil their need to show they care intensely about their sport and the quality at which it is played.

For athletes to appeal to this group of sport consumers, they need to care as well. Athletes increasingly realize that they should be viewed and positioned as 'good corporate citizens' and this is of particular interest to the sport managers of the future. They are required to balance the need to maintain the sports' and athletes' integrity and purity with the pressure to make the sport as commercially attractive as possible in order to secure operating funds. As noted by Westerbeek and Smith (2003) 'where economic imperatives drive the amount of money associated with sport and force the evolution of new "elite of elite" leagues, and foster the development of super-athletes to perform in these competitions, the sport quality segment will happily consume sport. [Superathletes, by the way, will not simply be "the best" in the way that today we look up to Ian Thorpe, David Beckham and Annika Sorenstam. The athletes of the future will be genetically modified and surgically adjusted "freak" athletes, and increasingly, overambitious parents will be in a position to medically "select" their preferred "child athlete".] However, where these pressures erode the quality of the game, or manipulate it to an extent that the pure element of the game is lost, then the segment will react unfavourably' (p. 211). Sport managers, beware!

Sport identity

Sport identity is about satisfying the emotional need to answer the question 'who am I?' Jensen (1999) refers to this as the 'who-am-I' need, and sport fans have a history of eliciting a sense of identity and meaning from their association with sport teams and clubs. For the sport manager of the future to successfully operate in the market for sport identity, he or she has to look beyond the focused sport watchers who closely follow the state of the game and their team, and who are obsessed by the most trivial team-related information. What they really are looking for is self-definition. The team or club needs to offer opportunities for a personal identity to be merged and moulded with a club or a supporter group. But in a world of hypercommercialism these sport consumers can also be easily alienated. If sport managers interfere with the identification process in ways that are harmful to the sport consumer, for example, when fans are locked out of venues in favour of corporate ticket holders and hospitality services, there will be a distancing of the fan from their beloved club, and a consequent weakening of their identity.

Sport tradition

Sport organizations have always placed great importance on their heritage and history and in the DreamSport Society there is a particular segment of consumer who wants to satisfy the emotional need relating to 'peace of mind', or in other words, reminiscing about the good old days. In a way they are the sporting traditionalists, usually older spectators who are sophisticated in the way they assess the value of sport participation and sport watching. They will become interested when sport can offer them a chance to re-ignite past values. This is why commercialism and corporatization can disenfranchise them.

On the other hand, commercial exploitation of sport in the form of corporate hospitality, for example, can offer some of the special treatment that the traditionalist needs to satisfy their sense of personal service and value. The sport managers of Major League Baseball in the USA, for example, are using the rich history of the game to their commercial advantage. Many of the MLB clubs are, or have been involved in stadium renovation or re-building in the style that was prominent at the height of baseball's community success during the early 1900s, providing physical evidence of the value that the League places on tradition and history.

Sport conscience

The market segment of sport conscience is a reflection of the emotional requirements of consumers who are more interested in the big picture, rather than only looking at sport or clubs themselves. Sport conscience consumers have a sincere desire to accomplish something worthwhile that affects people in more ways than merely enjoying playing or watching sport. Sport conscience consumers are on a mission to serve their communities and in this context, are concerned with the needs of others in their association with sport. They participate in sport at all levels of involvement (play, manage, govern, watch, etc.) to please others and to contribute to the community interest.

The sport conscience segment includes the mothers and fathers who bring the half-time tea or oranges, provide the taxis and coach the team, to the individuals who turn up to the local game because the team 'needs the support', or because they view it as a manifestation of their community pride. The 'morally righteous' needs of sport conscience consumers often are fulfilled by being able to create and deliver benefits to the community, or at least to people other than themselves. Sport is their 'charity', and to express their conscious mind they will only purchase the shoes that were manufactured in 'appropriate' circumstances, consume healthy, organically grown foods and attend sporting contests and events that show themselves to be worthy community contributors. These consumers may well become the leaders of popular sport opinion and turn into the moral sport knights that guard the pure domain of sport, actively working against movements in which performance enhancing drugs are becoming the norm rather than the exception.

These six market segments that may eventuate in the future will provide sport managers of the future with a number of opportunities and challenges. Sport organizations will not be able to cater for small homogenous groups of consumers. The differences in consumer expectations that will prevail in these groups will force managers to develop and deliver sport products, services and experiences in new ways. The management tools they have at their disposal include the seven areas of management that have been outlined in the preceding chapters. The following section outlines the challenges to be faced in each of these areas.

Future challenges

Strategic management

Strategic management is all about achieving competitive advantage. In other words, how can a sport organization position itself so that it is better prepared to take advantage of opportunities in the marketplace than its direct and indirect competitors? In the context of the DreamSport Society, strategic management will require sport managers to examine their organization's internal strengths and weaknesses and the external opportunities and threats in the DreamSport marketplace, where (and how) can it best deliver its services in the future, and minimize exposure to risk and competition.

Many of the answers for the sport organizations of the future, be they public, for-profit or not-for-profit, can be found by following the same process of strategic decision-making, yet the outcomes of that process will most likely lead the organizations in different directions. All organizations need to start with identifying the impact of the economy, technology and culture on their business operations, followed by asking questions about their internal capabilities to better service one DreamSport segment over the other. Naturally, the for-profit organizations will be guided by the profit (economic) incentive and hence, select consumer segments that are willing and able to pay a good price for services delivered. Public sport organizations, on the other hand, will largely be guided by societal (cultural) issues that have, or will have, an impact on communities, and therefore (partly) be funded by government to play an active role in tackling societal issues through sport.

Professional sport organizations have to make up their mind about the size and scope of their marketplace, for example, as a result of the increasing influence of technology on professional sport delivery. The largely domestic Australian Football League, for example, is faced with the question of what their marketplace of the future constitutes of: are they an Australian or potentially global brand of football? By answering that question, they will also find direction in regard to which DreamSport segments of sport consumers are more suitable to target than others. If they want to be an Australian brand the sport tradition segment will be more important, yet if they want to be a global brand, sport entertainment and sport fantasy will be more important segments to target.

Organizational structure

The old adage that 'structure follows strategy' holds true in Chapter 6. As soon as you have decided on where you want to go and how you are going to do it (strategy), you need to create the structure that enables you to implement the strategy and make it happen. Once again, you need to consider the macro influences of economy, technology and culture before making 'delivery structure' decisions in regard to the market segments in the DreamSport Society that you want to service.

In Chapter 6 we noted the importance of the size of the organization in regard to the structure that needs to be adopted in order to achieve the best fit with the environment in which the organization exists. Most sport organizations in the Western world have moved towards the bureaucratic organizational form during the past decade. In other words, with increasing size (as a result of extra funding), higher levels of specialization and formalization and more decentralized decision-making were required.

In order to be ready to serve consumers in the DreamSport Society it can be argued that the combined factors of environmental uncertainty and technology will drive the structural changes that need to be adopted by (some) sport organizations. With rapidly increasing levels of competition between sport organizations, the delivery structures of sport organizations need to be geared towards market responsiveness, in order to command viable portions of market share. This not only requires even higher levels of specialization (university educated sport professionals) but the structure also needs to be geared towards technology-mediated and -facilitated communication with customers- and technology-driven delivery of products and services. Levels of centralization need to be pushed down further in order to allow those who service the customer to be responsive to the customer.

In response to increasing competitive pressures it is likely that professional sport organizations will follow the lead of the 'straight' for profit (non-sport) organizations in 'restructuring' themselves towards diversification. Diversification is the practice of either producing more products, servicing more markets or a combination of both. Diversification is used in order to capitalize on new opportunities or indeed, to spread the risk of being too dependent on just a few products or services that are delivered to the market. As outlined earlier in this chapter, a reconceptualized view of the market for sport products (the DreamSport Society) will allow many sport organizations to stick to their roots, yet offer a greater variety of products into the markets for sport entertainment, sport fantasy, sport quality, sport identity, sport tradition and sport conscience, marketplaces they may not have considered previously. Public and/or nonprofit organizations are less likely to significantly change their structure in the short term as they often are funded to fulfil a particular task that has been identified by the funding agency. Their structural changes will be reactive rather than proactive.

Human resource management

In Chapter 7 we argued that the performance of human resources in for-profit sport organizations is easier to measure than in nonprofit entities. It is much easier to link what people do on a day-to-day basis to the money that is made in the for-profit sport organization, rather than the variety of tasks and objectives that are to be achieved in nonprofit sport organizations. We will further elaborate on the future of sport performance management in the last part of this chapter. In specific regard to the challenges that HR managers in sport organizations are facing we have to return to some of the characteristics that distinguish the HR function in sport organizations from nonsport organizations.

Decisions made in regard to strategy and structure will have a significant impact on how the sport organization of the future will need to be staffed.

In professional sport the need to acquire the best (and most expensive) players will be important. This will also lead to potentially recruiting medical staff who can assist in making athletes perform best, or in the extreme scenario, contribute to building the best athletes. Nonprofit sport organizations will strive to attract the best quality volunteers and paid staff, but will need to provide incentives other than money. All sport organizations will need to recognize that fundamentally, better organizational performance will come from resource maximization, either to deliver a surplus to 'shareholders', or to reinvest in the purpose of the nonprofit sport organization. In that regard, will the for-profit organization carefully balance the opportunity to recruit 'free labour' (volunteers) with the need to professionally deliver a service? For both organizational types the real challenge is to find new and better ways to satisfy the needs of volunteer staff and at the same time, improve their ability to deliver better service. In that regard, do all sport organizations need to concentrate on servicing the sport quality and sport identity segments of the DreamSport Society, for the simple reason of survival? Neither profit nor nonprofit sport organizations can do without volunteers.

Leadership

In Chapter 8 we outlined a range of challenges for the leaders in the sport industry. We will not repeat those challenges here, but rather position leadership at the heart of all future challenges for sport managers. It is not a coincidence that our discussion of leadership challenges is preceded by strategic, structure and HR challenges, and followed by challenges in relation to organizational culture, governance and performance management. The leader is at the heart of all organizational and management challenges.

Management effectiveness rests in the ability to plan and budget; organize and staff; and control and solve problems, whereas leadership is principally founded upon the ability to establish direction, align people; and to motivate and inspire. In other words, leaders achieve change whilst managers succeed in maintaining the status quo. The greatest challenge for leaders in sport, therefore, can be summarized as choosing the *best* direction for the organization moving into the DreamSport Society, and to motivate and convince stakeholders of the organization to join the leader into that direction. A vision, translated into a solid strategy, implemented through an appropriate structure that is staffed with the right people, puts the leader in a perfect position to start working on the organizational culture that is best suited to maximize the governance and performance of the organization.

Organizational culture

As explained in Chapter 9, sport organizations often have a long tradition of fanatical and emotional followership and are rich in symbolism and rituals, elements that play an important role in the establishment of strong organizational cultures. Most people that are interested in sport and in one way or the other affiliate with a particular sport, team, club or athlete, also feel strongly about their sporting heroes and the values that underpin the often 'traditional' delivery and consumption of sport participation or spectatorship.

In the DreamSport Society many things will have changed in the conservative landscape of sport. We can already observe a strong move towards commercialization in sport, where just a decade ago most sporting organizations – elite or participation-based – were largely run and supported by volunteer labour without working towards a profit or revenue maximization incentive. Although the DreamSport Society marketplace will continue to offer a wide range of sport products, it is likely that most sport organizations will be forced to dramatically change their attitude towards producing and delivering their goods and services. For example, changes in attitude towards sport consumption in the competitive environment may well force sport leaders to change their organizational cultures accordingly. This can be summarized by the following overview of a change from traditional values to future values in sport (organizations).

- From community to commerce
- From play to play hard
- From winning on the field to winning off the field
- From happy ignorance to brutal accountability
- From naivety to responsibility
- From citizen to citizenship
- From the sidelines to active participation
- From the best athlete to the best genetics
- From volunteer to professional
- From nonprofit to profit

The major challenge for sport managers is to strike a balance between the demands and expectations that the new customers in the DreamSport Society place on the sport organization, and the ways that the organization can best deliver upon those expectations internally. It seems logical that with an increase in the number of professionally educated and paid employees comes a natural change in work attitudes and values. However, in the interest of what many people believe are core values of sport (access to all, healthy mind in a healthy body, brings people together, etc.), it is up to the sport managers of the future to develop and nurture organizational cultures that respect the traditional values of (the) sport, but at the same time, are well suited to serve the needs of increasingly demanding and diverse consumer groups in the DreamSport Society.

Governance

Irrespective of for-profit or non-profit principles, the DreamSport Society is certain to deliver some major governance headaches to sport organizations. As already stated in Chapter 10, sport organizations are increasingly under pressure from funding agencies to improve the delivery of their core programmes and services. The increasing threat of litigation has forced sport organizations to ensure they have better systems and policies for risk management, fiduciary compliance, incorporation, directors' liability insurance, and board training and evaluation. However, in the future of the DreamSport Society decision-making in regard to a range of privacy and 'humanity' issues need to be considered.

For example, how can sport organizations ensure that when they want to maximize the attractiveness of their sport, they do not cross ethical boundaries (e.g. the genetic manipulation of athletes or the structural use of performance enhancing drugs or devices) that will be held against the organization and its governors down the track? If the executive led model is to become the dominant sport governance model (we don't know, but it is possible), who is to say that sport executives will not fall into the same traps that corporate executives have? The main challenge of the managers of sport in the future will be to find exactly where their sport organization needs to be positioned to be considered a good corporate citizen. In other words, in order to find the 'right' governance model for any sport organization, it needs to be clear where the organization adds its value in society. A good and appropriate governance structure should be a derivative of 'where and how' the organization seeks to add value and this is ultimately an outcome of the strategic management process. For non-profit sport organizations, in that regard, it probably is easier to steer away from dangerous and tempting opportunities because it simply is not in their constitution or list of objectives to aggressively seek and pursue opportunities in search of profit. However, for the profit or revenue maximization seeking sport organizations, future (medical and information) technology will most likely offer great opportunities for economic advancement, opportunities that undoubtedly require strong, visionary and capable governance from a range of highly qualified people.

Performance management

In this final section we briefly look forward to how performance in the sport organization of the future will be or should be measured. As performance management is one of the most contentious issues in any organization, it may not come as a surprise that in sport organizations the challenges are varied and substantial. Identifying the range of 'special characteristics of sport' that we outlined in Chapter 11, and combining these with some of the projections that we extrapolated into the DreamSport Society, it seems that 'winning' in sport will be measured in a variety of ways in the future.

The 9-point performance management model proposed in Chapter 11 provides a useful framework for current performance evaluation. However, the tracking of service delivery performance in the DreamSport Society by looking at sport entertainment delivery outcomes, for example, will be measured in a different way compared to sport fantasy, sport quality, sport identity, sport tradition or sport conscience. In each of those marketplaces different stakeholders will keep a close and watchful eye on how stakeholder needs are satisfied. Where sport entertainment seekers will judge the quality and excitement levels of the adventure, the sport fantasy stakeholders will look towards the frequency and quality of interaction with other sports lovers. Sport quality organizations will be judged on the value they add to different parts of society, for example, by looking at how many people were motivated to take up healthier sporting lifestyles, whereas the sport identity performance will be measured on the ability of the sport organization to help individuals 'define' themselves, for example, by building very strong and exciting sport brands that people would like to associate with.

Sport organizations operating in the sport tradition marketplace will be judged on some of the issues that we talked about in regard to organizational culture, in this case, the preservation of traditional values that are held in high regard by long time customers as well as new and younger customers that are attracted to a sense of tradition. Such organizations will be judged on, amongst other things, their ability to present physical evidence of 'the good old days', for example, in architecture of building or traditional ways of servicing customers. Finally, performance in the sport conscience segment will be judged on the manner in which the organization maintains a high sense of morality. In the same way that people have a conscience, it is expected that the sport organization take a stand on how sport should be consumed and is best used to contribute back to society as a whole. Sport organizations will be judged on the position they take (or fail to take) on the payment of athletes, the off-field behaviour of athletes, genetic manipulation of athletic performance and so on. The main performance indicator in that regard is public opinion, which greatly impacts the ability of the sport organization to generate external funding.

In this last section we have chosen to focus on presenting some performance management challenges in particular relation to the six segments of the DreamSport Society. The reality is that very few sport organizations in the future will exclusively deliver to only one segment of the DreamSport Society. Sport organizations from all sectors (professional, non-profit, and government) will need to consider the needs of different sport consumers and will be constantly challenged to make decisions about which customers they want to service.

Performance management issues internal to the organization will be equally challenging compared to performance demands that external stakeholders place upon it, but suffice to say that winning in sport now and in the future has many faces. Gone are the days that a win on the weekend was the most important victory of them all. Sport has become an incredibly diverse and complex global industry whose performance is increasingly being judged at levels of corporate sophistication and scrutiny. It is hoped that this book has contributed to the better preparation of the sport managers of the present and future, to work in and contribute to an industry that deserves the best management possible, for the simple reason that sport is too important not to be managed professionally.

Summary

In this final chapter we discussed the future challenges for sport managers in regard to strategic management, organizational structure, human resource management, leadership, organizational culture, governance and performance management. This discussion was founded upon the principal factors that drive global change in the world of sport. The chapter also included a discussion about the production and consumption of sport in the future in the so-called DreamSport Society. Six market segments comprising different types of sport consumers including sport entertainment, sport fantasy, sport quality, sport identity, sport tradition and sport conscience were used to paint a picture of the sport business future.

Review questions

1. Looking at your own future, where do you see yourself in 10 years from now? What will you need to do to get there? What will be the main obstacles to get there?
2. How will technology shape the future of sport management? Justify your answer by using some of the trends you see today and extrapolate them into the future.
3. What will be most affected by change in future sport organizations: structure of the organization or the people (human resources) working in them? Justify your answer.
4. Brainstorm the top 5 list of issues that need to be considered by sport managers when considering to expand their sport business internationally.
5. Do you foreshadow a positive future for community sport? Why or why not?
6. Do you think professional sport in the future will be as popular as it is now? Justify your answer in terms of the concepts presented in this chapter.
7. Do you think governments will seek to intervene in the sport industry more or less so in the future? Why?

Further reading

International Monetary Fund. (2000–2005). *Globalization: Threat or opportunity?* Retrieved March 1, 2005 from: http://www.imf.org/external/np/exr/ib/2000/041200.htm.

Jensen, R. (1999). *The Dream Society*. New York: McGraw-Hill.

National Intelligence Council. (2000). *Global Trends 2015: A dialogue about the future with non government experts*, Washington DC: National Foreign Intelligence Board.

Smith, A. and Westerbeek, H. (2004). The Sport Business Future. London: Palgrave MacMillan.

Relevant websites

* The International Monetary Fund at http://www.imf.org/
* The World Fact Book at http://www.cia.gov/cia/publications/factbook/
* The United Nations University at http://www.unu.edu/
* The Millennium project at http://www.acunu.org/

References

Allison, M. (2002) *Sports Clubs in Scotland Summary: Research Digest no. 59.* Edinburgh: Sports Scotland.

Amis, J. & Slack, T. (1996) The size-structure relationship in voluntary sport organizations. *Journal of Sport Management*, **10**, 76–86.

Atkinson, A., Waterhouse, J.H. & Wells, R.B. (1997) A stakeholder approach to strategic performance measurement. *Sloan Management Review*, Spring, 25–37.

Australian Bureau of Statistics (2005) *Involvement in Organised Sport and Physical Activity, Australia, Cat. No. 6285.0.* Canberra.

Australian Sports Commission (2000) *Committee Management, Active Australia Club/Association Management Program.* Canberra: Australian Sports Commission.

Australian Sports Commission (2003) *Independent Soccer Review: Report of the independent soccer review committee into the structure, governance and management of soccer in Australia.* Canberra: Australian Sports Commission.

Australian Sports Commission (2004) *Sport Innovation and Best Practice – governance* at http://www.ausport.gov.au/ibp/governance.asp. Canberra: Australian Sports Commission.

Baldwin, R. & Cave, M. (1999) *Understanding Regulation: theory, strategy and practice.* Oxford: Oxford University Press.

Bass, B.M. (1985) *Leadership and Performance Beyond Expectations.* New York: The Free Press.

Bass, B. M. (1990) *Bass & Stogdill's Handbook of Leadership: Theory, research, and managerial applications*, 3rd edn. New York: Free Press.

Bass, B.M. & Avolio, B.J. (1994) *Improving Organisational Effectiveness Through Transformational Leadership.* London: Sage Publications.

Beech, J. & Chadwick, S. (eds) (2004) *The Business of Sport Management.* Harlow: Prentice Hall.

Berger, P. & Luckmann, T. (1967) *The Social Construction of Reality: A treatise on the sociology of knowledge.* London: Penguin.

Bettinger, C. (1989) Use corporate culture to trigger high performance. *Journal of Business Strategy*, **10** (2), 38–42.

Block, S.R. (1998) *Perfect Nonprofit Boards: Myths, paradoxes and paradigms.* Needham Heights: Simon Schuster.

Bloomfield, J. (2003) *Australia's Sporting Success: The inside story.* Sydney: University of New South Wales Press.

Bouckaert, G. (1995) Improving performance management. In *The Enduring Challenges in Public Management* (Halachmi, A. & Bouckaert, G., eds). San Francisco: Jossey-Bass.

Bouckaert, G. & van Doren, W. (2003) Performance measurement and management in public sector organisations. In *Public Management and Governance*, (Bovaird, T. & Lofler, E., eds). London: Routledge.

Boyle, R. & Haynes, R. (2000) *Power Play: sport, the media and popular culture*. Sydney: Longman.

Brohm, J. (1978) *Sport: A prison of measured time*. London: Ink Links.

Carver, J. (1997) *Boards That Make a Difference: A new design for leadership in non-profit and public organizations*, 2nd edn. San Francisco: Jossey-Bass.

Cashman, R. (1995) *Paradise of Sport*. Melbourne: Oxford University Press.

Chalip, L., Johnson, A. & Stachura, L. (eds) (1996) *National Sports Policies: An international handbook*. Westport: Greenwood Press.

Chappelet, J. & Bayle, E. (2005) *Strategic and Performance Management of Olympic Sport Organisations*. Champaign: Human Kinetics.

Chelladurai, P. (1999) *Human Resource Management in Sport and Recreation*. Champaign: Human Kinetics.

Clarke, T. (ed.) (2004) *Theories of Corporate Governance*. Oxford: Routledge.

Cook, R.A. & Szumal, J.L. (1993) Measuring normative beliefs and shared behavioral expectations in organizations: The reliability and validity of the organizational culture inventory. *Psychological Reports*, **72**, 1290–1330.

DaCosta, L. & Miragaya, A. (eds) (2002) Sport for all worldwide: a cross national and comparative research. In *Worldwide experiences and trends in sport for all*. Oxford: Meyer and Meyer.

Dejonghe, T. (2001) *Sport in de wereld: Ontstaan, evolutie en verspreiding*. Gent: Adacemia Press, p. 117.

Deming, W. (1993) *The New Economics for Industry, Government, Education*. Cambridge: MIT.

Denison, D. & Mishra, A. (1995) Toward a theory of organizational culture and effectiveness. *Organizational Science*, **6**, 204–224.

Dess, G. & Lumpkin, G. (2003) *Strategic Management: creating competitive advantages*. Boston: McGraw-Hill Irwin.

Downward, P. & Dawson, A. (2000) *The Economics of Professional Team Sports*. London: Routledge.

Dressler, G. (2003) *Human Resource Management*. New Jersey: Prentice Hall.

Drucker, P.F. (1990) Lessons for successful nonprofit governance. *Nonprofit Management and Leadership*, **1**, 7–14.

Fan Hong (1997) Commercialism and sport in China. *Journal of Sport Management*, **11**, 343–354.

Fiedler, F.E. (1967) *A Theory of Leadership Effectiveness*. New York: McGraw-Hill.

Fletcher, K. (1999) Four books on nonprofit boards and governance. *Nonprofit Management and Leadership*, **9**, 435–441.

Football Governance Research Centre (2004) *The State of the Game: The corporate governance of football clubs 2004*, Research paper 2004 No. 3. Birkbeck, University of London: Football Governance Research Centre.

Friedman, M., Parent, M. & Mason, D. (2004) Building a framework for issues management in sport through stakeholder theory. *European Sport Management Quarterly*, **3**, 170–190.

Frisby, W. (1986) The organizational structure and effectiveness of voluntary organizations: The case of Canadian national sport governing bodies. *Journal of Park and Recreation Administration*, **4**, 61–74.

Frosdick, S. & Walley, L. (eds) (1997) *Sport and Safety Management*. Oxford: Butterworth-Heinemann.

Goffee, R. & Jones, G. (1996) What holds the modern company together? *Harvard Business Review*, **74** (6), 133–149.

Graaff, A. (1996) Service quality and sport centres. *European Journal for Sport Management, xx/2.*

Gratton, C. & Taylor, P. (1991) *Government and the Economics of Sport*. London: Longman.

Greenfield, S. & Osborn, G. (2001) *Regulating Football; commodification, consumption and the law*. London: Pluto Press.

Harvard Business Review (1998) *On Measuring Corporate Performance*. Boston: Harvard Business Review Press.

Heimovics, R.D. & Herman, R.D. (1990) Responsibility for critical events in nonprofit organizations. *Nonprofit and Voluntary Sector Quarterly*, **19**, 59–72.

Henry, I. & Uchium, K. (2001) Political ideology, modernity, and sport policy: a comparative analysis of sport policy in Britain and Japan. *Hitotsubashi Journal of Social Studies*, **33** (2), 161–185.

Henry, I. & Lee, P.C. (2004) Governance and ethics in sport. In *The business of sport management* (Beech, J. & Chadwick, S., eds). London: Prentice Hall.

Herman, R.D. & Heimovics, R. (1990) The effective nonprofit executive: Leader of the board. *Nonprofit Management and Leadership* **1**, 167–180.

Herman, R.D. & Heimovics, R. (1994) Executive leadership. In *The Jossey-Bass handbook of nonprofit leadership and management* (Herman, R.D., ed.). San Fransisco: Jossey-Bass, pp. 137–153.

Herman, R.D. & Renz, D.O. (1997) Multiple constituencies and the social construction of nonprofit organizational effectiveness. *Nonprofit and Voluntary Sector Quarterly*, **26**, 185–206.

Herman, R.D. & Renz, D.O. (1998) Nonprofit organizational effectiveness: Contrasts between especially effective and less effective organizations. *Nonprofit Management and Leadership*, **9**, 23–38.

Herman, R.D. & Renz, D.O. (2000) Board practices of especially effective and less effective local nonprofit organizations. *American Review of Public Administration*, **30**, 146–160.

Hersey, P. & Blanchard, K. (1977) *Management of Organizational Behaviour: Utilizing human resources*. Englewood Cliffs: Prentice-Hall.

Hess, R. & Stewart, R. (eds) (1998) *More Than a Game: an unauthorised history of Australian football*. Melbourne: Melbourne University Press.

Hillary Commission (2000) *The Growing Business of Sport and Leisure: The impact of the physical leisure industry in New Zealand*. Wellington: Hillary Commission.

Hindley, D. (2003) *Resource guide in governance and sport*. Learning and teaching support network in Hospitality, Leisure, Sport and Tourism at http://www.hlst.ltsn.ac.uk/resources/governance.html.

Hofstede, G. (1991) *Cultures and Organizations: software of the mind*. London: McGraw Hill.

Hofstede, G. (2001) *Culture's Consequences: comparing values, behaviors, institutions and organizations across nations.* Thousand Oaks: Sage.

Hofstede, G., Neuijen, B., Ohayv, D. & Sanders, G. (1990) Measuring organizational cultures: A qualitative and quantitative study across twenty cases. *Administrative Science Quarterly*, **35**, 286–316.

Houle, C.O. (1960) *The Effective Board.* New York: Association Press.

Houle, C.O. (1997) *Governing Boards: Their nature and nurture.* San Francisco: Jossey-Bass.

Houlihan, B. (1997) *Sport Policy and Politics: a comparative analysis.* London: Routledge.

Houlihan, B. & White, A. (2002) *The Politics of Sport Development: Development of sport or development through sport?* London: Routledge.

House, R.J. (1971) A path-goal theory of leader effectiveness. *Administrative Science Quarterly*, **16**, 321–338

House, R.J. & Mitchell, T.R. (1974) Path-goal theory of leadership. *Contemporary Business*, **3** (Fall), 81–91.

Howard, L. (1998) Validating the competing values model as a representation of organizational cultures. *International Journal of Organizational Analysis*, **6** (3), 231–251.

Hoye, R. & Cuskelly, G. (2003) Board-executive relationships within voluntary sport organisations. *Sport Management Review*, **6** (1), 53–73.

Hoye, R. & Inglis, S. (2003) Governance of nonprofit leisure organizations. *Society and Leisure*, **26** (2), 369–387.

Hughes, H. (1981) *News and the Human Interest Story.* London: Transaction Books (reprint of the 1940 University of Chicago Press edition).

Hylton, K., Bramham, P., Jackson, D. & Nesti, M. (eds) (2001) *Sport Development.* London: Routledge.

Ibsen, B. & Jorgensen, P. (2002) Denmark: The cultural and voluntary development of sport for all. In *Worldwide experiences and trends in sport for all* (DaCosta, L. & Miragaya, A., eds). Oxford: Meyer and Meyer.

International Monetary Fund (2000–2005) *Globalization: threat or opportunity?* Retrieved March 1, 2005 from: http://www.imf.org/external/np/exr/ib/2000/041200.htm

Jensen, R. (1999) *The Dream Society.* New York: McGraw-Hill.

John, G. & Sheard, R. (1997) *Stadia: a design and development guide.* Oxford: Architectural Press.

Johnson, G. & Scholes, K. (2002) *Exploring corporate strategy*, 6th edn. London: Prentice-Hall, pp. 4–11.

Kaplan, R. & Norton, D. (1992) The balanced scorecard: measures that drive performance. *Harvard Business Review* (January–February), 71–79.

Kaplan, R. & Norton, D. (1996) *The balanced scorecard.* Boston: Harvard University Press.

Kikulis, L.M., Slack, T., Hinings, B. & Zimmermann, A. (1989) A structural taxonomy of amateur sport organizations. *Journal of Sport Management*, **3**, 129–150.

Kikulis, L.M., Slack, T. & Hinings, B. (1992) Institutionally specific design archetypes: A framework for understanding change in national sport organizations. *International Review for the Sociology of Sport*, **27**, 343–367.

Kikulis, L.M., Slack, T. & Hinings, B. (1995b) Toward an understanding of the role of agency and choice in the changing structure of Canada's national sport organizations. *Journal of Sport Management*, **9**, 135–152.

Kotter, J.P. (1990) *A Force for Change: How leadership differs from management.* New York: The Free Press.

Leisure Industries Research Centre (2003) *Sports volunteering in England 2002: A report for Sport England.* Sheffield: Leisure Industries Research Centre.

Lewis, G. (1993) Concepts in strategic management. In *Australian Strategic Management: concepts, context and cases* (Lewis, G., Morkel, A. & Hubbard, G., eds). Sydney: Prentice-Hall, pp. 5–38.

Li, M., Hofacre, S. & Mahony, D. (2001) *Economics of Sport.* Morgantown: Fitness Information Technology.

Locke, E.A. (1991) *The Essence of Leadership: The four keys to leading successfully.* New York: Lexington Books.

Lyons, M. (2001) *Third Sector: The contribution of nonprofit and cooperative enterprises in Australia.* Crows Nest: Allen & Unwin.

Mechikoff, R. & Estes, S. (1993) *A History and Philosophy of Sport and Physical Education.* Madison: Brown and Benchmark.

Miles, R.E. (1975) *Theories of Management: implications for organizational behaviour and development.* New York: McGraw-Hill.

Miller, T., Lawrence, G., McKay, J. & Rowe, D. (2001) *Globalisation and Sport.* London: Sage.

National Intelligence Council (2000) *Global Trends 2015: A dialogue about the future with non government experts.* Washington DC: National Foreign Intelligence Board.

Norman, W. & MacDonald, C. (2004) Getting to the bottom of 'triple bottom-line accounting'. *Business Ethics Quarterly*, **14** (2), 243–262.

Ogbonna, E. & Harris, L.C. (2002) Organizational culture: A ten year, two-phase study of change in the UK food retailing sector. *Journal of Management Studies*, **39**, 673–706.

Organisation for Economic Co-operation and Development (2004) *Principles of Corporate Governance.* Paris: OECD.

Oriard, M. (1993) *Reading Football.* Chapel Hill: University of North Carolina Press.

Perryman, M. (ed.) (2001) *Hooligan Wars: causes and effects of football violence.* Edinburgh: Mainstream Publishing.

Pettigrew, A.M. (1979) On studying organizational cultures. *Administrative Science Quarterly*, **24**, 570–581.

Pfeffer, J. & Salancik, G. (1978) *The external control of organizations: A resource dependence perspective.* New York: Harper & Row.

Porter, M. (1980) *Competitive Strategy*, The Free Press, New York.

Porter, M. (1985) *Competitive Strategy: creating and sustaining superior performance.* New York: Simon & Schuster.

Porter, M. (1996) What is strategy? *Harvard Business Review*, November–December, pp. 61–78.

Productivity Commission (2003) *Social Capital: reviewing the concept and its policy implications.* Canberra: Commonwealth of Australia.

Putnam, R. (2000) *Bowling Alone: the collapse and revival of American community.* New York: Simon and Schuster.

Quinn, R. & Rohrbaugh, J. (1983) A spatial model of effectiveness criteria: Towards a competing values approach to organizational analysis. *Management Science*, **29**, 363–377.

Quirk, J. & Fort, R. (1992) *Pay Dirt: the business of professional team sports*. Princeton: Princeton University Press.

Riordan, J. (1977) *Sport in Soviet Society*. Cambridge: Cambridge University Press.

Riordan, J. (ed.) (1978) *Sport under Communism: The USSR, Czechoslovakia, The GDR, China, Cuba*. Canberra: Australian National University Press.

Robbins, S. (1990) *Organization Theory: structure design and applications*. New Jersey: Prentice Hall.

Robbins, S. & Barnwell, N. (2002) *Organisation theory*. Frenchs Forest: Pearson Education Australia.

Robbins, S.P., Bergman, R., Stagg, I. & Coulter, M. (2004) *Management*, 3rd edn. Sydney: Pearson Education.

Robbins, S.P., Millett, B. & Waters-March, T. (2004) *Organizational behaviour*, 4th edn. Sydney: Pearson Education.

Rowe, D. (1999) *Sport, Culture and the Media: the unruly trinity*. Buckingham: Open University Press.

Sandy, R., Sloane, P.J. & Rosentraub, M. (2004) *The Economics of Sport: an international perspective*. Basingstoke: Palgrave Macmillan.

Sashkin, M. (1996) *Organizational Beliefs Questionnaire: pillars of excellence*. Amherst: Human Resource Development Press.

Schein, E. (1984) *Coming to a New Awareness of Organizational Culture*. San Francisco: Jossey-Bass.

Schein, E. (1985) How culture forms, develops and changes. In *Gaining Control of the Corporate Culture* (Kilman, R.H., Saxton, M.J. & Serpa, R. et al., eds). San Francisco: Jossey-Bass, pp. 17–43.

Schein, E. (1997) *Organizational Culture and Leadership*, 3rd edn. San Francisco: Jossey-Bass.

Schermerhorn, J.R., Hunt, J.G. & Osborne, R.N. (1994) *Managing Organizational Behaviour*, 5th edn. Brisbane: John Wiley & Sons, Inc.

Schudson, M. (1978) *Discovering the News: a social history of American newspapers*. New York: Basic Books.

Senge, P. (1990) *The Fifth Discipline*. New York: Currency Doubleday.

Slack, T. (1997) *Understanding Sport Organizations: The application of organization theory*. Champaign: Human Kinetics.

Slesinger, L.H. (1991) *Self-assessment for Nonprofit Governing Boards*. Washington, DC: National Centre for Nonprofit Boards.

Smith, A. & Stewart, B. (1999) *Sports management: a guide to professional practice*. Sydney: Allen & Unwin.

Smith, A. & Shilbury, D. (2004) Mapping cultural dimensions in Australian sporting organizations. *Sport Management Review*, **7** (2), 133–165.

Standing Committee on Recreation and Sport Working Party on Management Improvement (1997) *Report to the standing committee on recreation and sport July 1997*. Canberra: Standing Committee on Recreation and Sport Working Party on Management Improvement.

Statistics Canada (2004) *Cornerstones of community: Highlights of the national survey of nonprofit and voluntary organizations*. Ottawa: Statistics Canada.

Stensholt, J. & Thomson, J. (2005) Kicking goals. *Business Review Weekly*, March 10–16, 38–42.

Stewart, R. (1989) The nature of sport under capitalism and its relationship to the capitalist labour process. *Sporting Traditions*, **6** (1), 43–61.

Stewart, R., Nicholson, M., Smith, A. & Westerbeek, H. (2004) *Australian Sport: better by design? The evolution of Australian sport policy*. London: Routledge.

Stewart, R. & Smith, A. (1999) The special features of sport. *Annals of Leisure Research*, **2**, 87–99.

Theodoraki, E.I. & Henry, I.P. (1994) Organizational structures and contexts in British national governing bodies of sport. *International Review for the Sociology of Sport*, **29**, 243–263.

Thibault, L., Slack, T. & Hinings, B. (1991) Professionalism, structures and systems: The impact of professional staff on voluntary sport organizations. *International Review for the Sociology of Sport*, **26**, 83–97.

Tribe, J. (2005). *The Economics of Recreation, Leisure and Tourism*. 3rd edn. London: Elsevier.

Tricker, R.I. (1984) *Corporate Governance*. London: Gower.

Tricker, R.I. (1993) Corporate governance – the new focus of interest. *Corporate Governance*, **1** (1), 1–3.

Van der Post, W. & de Coning, T. (1997) An instrument to measure organizational culture. *South African Journal of Business Management*, **28** (4), 147–169.

Viljoen, J. & Dann, S. (2003) *Strategic Management*, 4th edn. Frenchs Forest: Prentice Hall.

Volunteering Australia (2004) *Snapshot 2004: volunteering report card*. Melbourne: Volunteering Australia.

Westerbeek, H.M. & Smith, A.C.T. (2003) *Sport Business in the Global Marketplace*. London: Palgrave Macmillan.

Westerbeek, H. & Smith, A. (2005) *Business Leadership and the Lessons from Sport*. London: Palgrave Macmillan.

Wexley, K.N. & Yukl, G.A. (1984) *Organizational Behaviour and Personnel Psychology* (revised edn.) Homewood: Richard D. Irwin, Inc.

Whitson, D. (1998) Circuits of promotion: media, marketing and the globalization of sport. In (Wenner L, ed.). *MediaSport*. London: Routledge, pp. 57–72.

Williams, R. (1998) *Performance Management: perspectives on employee performance*. London: Thomson Business Press.

Index